The CHORDETTES
of SHEBOYGAN

MR. SANDMAN, SEND ME A DREAM

By Scott W. Lewandoske

PRINTED IN THE UNITED STATES OF AMERICA

ISBN: 9781076011732

INTRODUCTION

The Chordettes were formed in Sheboygan, Wisconsin in 1946 as a barbershop quartet and by 1947 had bookings to sing all across the United States. In 1949, they appeared in a contest on the popular Arthur Godfrey Show and were regulars on Arthur Godfrey's various shows for almost four years. In 1953, they tried a different kind of music and the following year, they recorded, "Mr. Sandman" a song that would reach number one on the pop charts and sell over two million copies. From 1956 to 1959, the Chordettes had a song on the top 100 chart nearly every week.

This book tells the story of the Chordettes from their high school days in Sheboygan through 2004 when the Chordettes were honored in their hometown of Sheboygan, Wisconsin, before a crowd of more than 500 people.

This book also includes information on Cadence Records and its owner, Archie Bleyer. Bleyer married one of the Chordettes and lived his final years in Sheboygan.

The information was gathered from newspaper articles, scrapbooks, record albums, and interviews with the Chordettes themselves. Much of the information on the Chordettes in books and the Internet is not accurate. This book seeks to correct that misinformation.

ACKNOWLEDGEMENTS

There are many people who helped make this book possible.

First, a big thanks the Chordettes themselves. Carol and Robert Buschmann and Dorothy and Bill Schwartz kindly allowed me to visit them at their homes and borrow photos, scrapbooks, newspaper articles, and magazine articles to copy. They also let me ask many, many questions.

Via correspondence questions were asked of Chordettes, Lynn Evans Mand, Marjorie Latzko, Joyce Creatore, and Nancy Overton. Each of these ladies responded within a few days of receiving my letters. Nancy sent an email saying that she had received my letter and would answer my questions, but it would take a while. Surprisingly, the very next day, I received a five-page email from her answering every question. When Marjorie and Lynn came to Sheboygan, they brought along photos for me to copy and use in the book. I thank them for their kindness and enthusiasm.

Another person who went out of her way to help was Kaye Hunt, Jinny's daughter. She supplied me with some information about her mother and also her grandfather, King Cole. She invited me to visit her in Palm Springs, California and go through her mother's Chordettes items. Unfortunately, I couldn't take her up on her generous offer. Jackie Everly, daughter of Janet Bleyer also gave me a call and answered some of my questions.

Bob Harker, Kathleen Smith, Nancy Koeppen, Bob Spatt and other staff members of the Sheboygan County Historical Society and Museum shared information and photos and allowed me to make copies and take photos of Chordettes' items in the museum collection. Also, Beth Dippel of the Sheboygan County Historical Research Center and Bill Wangemann, City of Sheboygan historian shared collection items for the publication. I thank them all.

Peter Fetterer searched through the Kohler Company archives for articles on the Chordettes in the 1949 Kohler Company newspapers when the Chordettes appeared at a Kohler Company picnic. Jim Daniels scanned around 100 photos of the Chordettes and made them available for use. Thank you Peter and Jim.

Also, thanks to:

Mary Daniels who told me about a web site that has newspaper pages archived on it and when I did a search for Chordettes, over 800 articles on the Chordettes came up.

Elmer Koppelmann for his encouragement and sharing newspaper articles.

The Sheboygan Press and Sheboygan Beacon newspapers for running short notes saying that I was looking for information on the Chordettes.

Mike Callahan for letting me use parts of an interview that he did with three of the Chordettes, for "Both Sides Now" magazine.

The Vocal Group Hall of Fame for sending information. Chuck Miller sent photos of the induction of the Chordettes into the Vocal Group Hall of Fame and permission to use them in this book.

Dorothy Reuter, archivist of the Heritage Hall Museum of Barbershop Harmony, which is part of the Society for the Preservation and Encouragement of Barber Shop Quartet Singing in America (S.P.E.B.S.Q.S.A.) for sending information on the Chordettes and King Cole.

Michael and Janet Faulhaber, son and widow of Charles Faulhaber, for information on Charles, who was the music teacher at Sheboygan Central High School. He had three of the Chordettes as students and suggested to Jinny, girls who had the best voices for the group she was putting together.

There were also other people, some of whose names I never learned. I received anonymous packages in the mail filled with Chordettes information. I also, posted messages in various Yahoo Clubs on the Internet. The first time I posted a message asking for information, I received responses from people in Canada and New Zealand, who sent scans of Chordettes' albums from their countries.

Last, but certainly not least, is Theresa Dees, formerly of Mead Public Library in Sheboygan. Theresa pulled out information from the library files for me, and helped me get books through interlibrary loan on Arthur Godfrey and barbershop singing. She also filled out form after form after form, for days in a row in order for me to get newspaper microfilm through interlibrary loan. Mead Library has a policy where you can only make five requests for newspaper microfilm per day and each month is a different request, even if it is the same newspaper. At one time, I was waiting for 56 months of newspaper microfilm. This was in addition to what I had already looked at. Theresa always had a smile and would say, "I'm just doing my job." But, Theresa was also kind enough to be a proofreader for this book. That was not part of her job and it is greatly appreciated.

DEDICATION

Virginia (Jinny) Cole Janis

This book on the Chordettes is dedicated to Virginia (Jinny) Cole Janis, founder of the "Chordettes." If not for her vision and love of Barber Shop singing and the use of her father's sheet music, the Chordettes may never have been formed.

Millions of people would never have had the enjoyment of listening to the Chordettes' music, and perhaps this book would never have been written.

SCOTT LEWANDOSKE

1957-2018

Scott has a great love for local history. He wrote articles about Sheboygan Falls for the Falls News and local history bits about Plymouth history for the Plymouth Review during the 1990s. He was president of the Oostburg Historical Society for eight years and was a volunteer at the Sheboygan County Historical Research Center and Sheboygan County Historical Museum.

Proud of his German Russian heritage, Scott did extensive research for the American Historical Society of Germans from Russian, Sheboygan Chapter.

As an author, he had two books published on Sheboygan history, "Born's Park, Sheboygan's Garden of Eden" and "Mayors of Sheboygan." He also wrote an unpublished book, titled, "The Chordettes From Sheboygan, Mr. Sandman, Send Me A Dream."

At the time of his death, he was working on a book about all of Sheboygan's taverns post-Prohibition.

He was passionate about his community and educating people about the history of Sheboygan, a city he dearly loved. Scott is missed.

Scott's book about the Chordettes, written about 2010, is being published in an altered form. Some photos had copyright issues and could not be used, but the rest of the book compiled by Scott still tells a great story; it conveys his encyclopedic knowledge of his favorite musical group.

Thanks to the *Sheboygan Press* for the ability to freely use information and photos.

TABLE OF CONTENTS

CHAPTER 1

SHEBOYGAN - 1946

Above is a postcard view showing North Eighth Street in Sheboygan,
looking north from New York Avenue. (From the Author's Collection)

The Chordettes were formed in Sheboygan, Wisconsin in 1946, a time of great change in both the United States and Sheboygan. The Second World War had ended the year before, and there were still many left over effects of the war that people had to endure. Men and women were still returning home from the war. Shortages of sugar and meat plagued shoppers.

During the war, many people of Sheboygan worked overtime to produce material needed to fight the war. Even though the people were working and had extra cash, they had very few items to buy, due to these lingering wartime shortages. The most noticeable item in short supply was the car. Shortly after the United States was attacked on December 7, 1941, the government ordered new car production to stop. As of February 1, 1942, no new cars were built. That lasted for more than 3 ½ years, until August 1945.

By 1946, even used cars were in short supply. As an example, in the August 16, 1946, *Sheboygan Press*, there were only two used cars for sale, an 11-year-old Chevrolet (1935) for $369 and a 14-year-old (1932) Dodge for $295. The original price for the 1935 Chevrolet was $580, which meant that an 11-year-old car was selling for over 60% of its original price. Before the war, you could have purchased an 11-year-old car for about $50.

A more urgent shortage in that summer of 1946 may have been a Sheboygan favorite, beer. The August 7, 1946, *Sheboygan Press*, published a large ad which read as follows, "NOTICE! To all Tavern Owners, Operators and all Customers of CESAR'S SHEBOYGAN MALT PRODUCTS CO. WE WILL BE CLOSED UNTIL THURSDAY, AUG. 15. Due to the shortage of beer the company is withholding shipment. We will resume deliveries of beer Thursday, August 15."

According to the Sheboygan City Directory, Sheboygan had a population of about 40,000 people in 1946 and comprised an area of 5.67 square miles. The city limits on the north, were in line with (in 2012) Mayflower Avenue and on the west, north of the Sheboygan River, about where North 26th Street is today. South of the Sheboygan River, the western city limit was about where South 23rd Street is today. The southern limit was where Mead Avenue is today to about South 12th Street, where the city limits went south to Wilson Avenue. The area where Shooting Park and the Sewage Treatment plant are, also were in the city limits, along with Evergreen Park.

In 1946, Sheboygan had 11,795 telephones in service. There were 19 parks and 45 churches. Total street mileage was 107.82 miles with 83.5 miles paved. Nearly 100% of the city was served with sewers. The fire department had 52 men with three fire stations and eight pieces of fire fighting equipment. The police department had 37 men, four squad cars, one detective car, three motorcycles, one ambulance, one patrol wagon, and one armored car. The armored car was actually left over from the 1930s when it was feared that gangsters from Chicago would come to Sheboygan. It was not the type of car used to carry money.

There were 15 public schools, which included two high schools (Sheboygan Central and Sheboygan North), and 15 parochial schools. Also, there was a public library with one main building and three branches, with a total of 72,000 books.

Major business in Sheboygan included American Chair Company, American Hydraulics, Armour Leather Company, Bank of Sheboygan, Citizens Bank, Dillingham Manufacturing Company, Garton Toy Company, Hand Knit Hosiery, Jung Shoe Company, Leverenz Shoe Company, Northern Furniture Company, Plastics Engineering Company, Polar Ware Company, C. Reiss Coal Company, Schreier Malting Company, Van Der Vaart Brick and Building Supply Company, Verifine Dairy, Wisconsin Oil Refining Company, Sheboygan Chair Company, Phoenix Chair Company, Wisconsin Power and Light, and Vollrath. Most of these businesses could trace their start back to the 1800s, yet few remain today. The largest employer was, and still is, Kohler Company located a short distance west of Sheboygan. Another major business in Sheboygan at this time was the Kingsbury Breweries Company. Kingsbury would be very important to the creation of the Chordettes.

All of the major stores were located on Eighth Street between Ontario and Center Avenues. These stores included H.C. Prange, J.C. Penney, Sears, Frank Geele Hardware, F.W. Woolworth, Sheboygan Dry Goods, Kresge, W.T. Grant, Montgomery Ward, and the People's Clothing Store. Today, all are gone.

For amusement, there were six motion-picture (movie) theaters with seating for 6,000 people. Additional entertainment included two golf courses and eight bowling alleys and an auditorium (Sheboygan Armory) with seating for 3,000 people.

Sheboygan also had a professional baseball team named the Sheboygan Indians. The team was a minor league farm club of the Brooklyn (now Los Angeles) Dodgers. The Indians' manager was Joe "Unser Joe" Hauser. Hauser was a former major leaguer who owned a sporting goods store in Sheboygan and was known in 1946, as the only professional baseball player to hit 60 or more home runs in a season, more than once. In 1930, he hit 63 home runs with the minor league Baltimore Orioles, and in 1933, he hit 69 home runs for Minneapolis. Hauser played in the major leagues for the Philadelphia (now Oakland) A's and the Cleveland Indians. In 1924, while with the A's, Hauser hit 27 home runs, second in the majors behind Babe Ruth.

Every weekend, the local newspaper, the *Sheboygan Press*, would be filled with ads for dances in Sheboygan and the surrounding area. There were a variety of singing groups that people could join. One of these groups was organized on August 1, 1945 and was for men interested in barbershop singing. The name of the group was the Sheboygan Chapter of the Society for the Preservation and Encouragement of Barber Shop Quartet Singing in America, Inc. The abbreviation was S.P.E.B.S.Q.S.A. The *Sheboygan Press*, in their Tuesday, August 2, 1945, issue, just referred to this group in the headline as, "Sheboygan Chapter Of Lots Of Initials Formed Here On Monday Night." The person who organized the group was O.H. "King" Cole, who was vice president of Kingsbury Breweries. Cole would later be the president of Kingsbury and National President of the S.P.E.B.S.Q.S.A. Over 75 men attended this meeting.

The weekend of Friday through Sunday, August 16 to 18, 1946, seemed like any other summer weekend in Sheboygan. There were the usual dances and picnics. The stores advertised their weekend specials. These specials included at the Superior Food Market on 13th and Superior, Hills Bros. Coffee for 33 cents a pound, a 25 pound bag of Pillsbury Flour for $1.69 and all brands of cigarettes were $1.59 a carton. These prices also included free delivery. The Michigan Avenue Cash Grocery at 927 Michigan Avenue also had 25-pound bags of Pillsbury Flour for $1.69. Some of their other specials included bananas for 11 cents a pound, Sunkist Oranges were 29 cents a dozen, and for 29 cents, you could get two pounds of "Sweet, Eating Plums." Luedke's Food Market featured chopped meat at 35 cents a pound, pork sausage for 45 cents a pound, and home-made bologna at 38 cents a pound. Luedke's was located at 2533 North 15th Street. Another store, H.J. Rammer Sons, at South 15th Street and Indiana Avenue, advertised a one-pound package of bacon for 41 cents, slicing cucumbers at five cents a pound, cantaloupe at 19 cents each, and a 17-pound crate of peaches for $1.49. To put these prices in perspective, earlier in the month of August, Vollrath Company was advertising for "Male Help Wanted" to

H. J. Rammer and Sons Meat Market, located at Indiana and 15th Streets in Sheboygan. This image is dated 1953.

The Foeste Hotel was once described as the most popular and plush place for travelers and businessmen. Built in 1893, it is seen here in the 1950s. The hotel had three major renovations over the course of its life before it was torn down at the end of 1960. At its peak it had two hundred rooms and was well-known for its business lunches (two martini).

work as press operators and other jobs. Starting wage was 60 cents an hour.

As stated earlier, there were six movie theaters in Sheboygan in 1946. The weekend of August 16 to 18, 1946, these theaters featured the following movies. The Majestic (located at 523 North 8th Street) was showing "One More Tomorrow" staring Ann Sheridan, Dennis Morgan, and Jane Wyman. Also included in the price of admission was a second movie, "Whistle Stop" staring George Raft and Ava Gardner. At the Wisconsin, (located at 701 New York Avenue) you could also see two movies for one admission. Its two movies were "Along the Navajo Trail" staring Roy Rogers and Trigger, "The Smartest Horse in the Movies" and "Cowboy Blues" staring Ken Curtis. Curtis would later star in the long running TV western, Gunsmoke.

At the Sheboygan, (located at 824 North 8th Street) a person could see Cary Grant starring in "Night and Day." The Rex (located at 931 North 8th Street) featured Myrna Loy and Don Ameche in "So Goes My Love." Their second feature was "Inside Job." The Strand (located at 1020 Michigan Avenue) featured "Tars and Spars" and "White Pongo." The State (located at 1511 South 12th Street) was featuring "Spellbound" with Ingrid Bergman and Gregory Peck. Their second feature was "Senorita From The West" starring Bonita Granville. Also at the State, you could see the fifth chapter of the serial, "Royal Mounted Rides Again" and a cartoon. The cost for all of this at the State was 29 cents plus tax (1 cent).

4

On August 18th, the Hotel Foeste, featured for their Sunday Dinner, the following menu:

Broiled Filet of Lake Michigan Trout, Drawn Butter, $1.35

Roast Prime Ribs of Beef, au Jus, $1.60

Roast Loin of Pork, with Green Apple Sauce, $1.35

½ Fried Chicken, Country Style, $1.50

Roast Young Vermont Turkey, with Cranberry Sauce, $1.50

Broiled Tenderloin Steak, $1.75

Shrimp Plate, au Garni, $1.25.

These prices included entrees, and a beverage. The bottom of the Hotel Foeste's ad noted, "Our Ceiling Prices are in conformance with provisions of the Emergency Control Act of 1946."

––––––––––––––––––––

On this same Sunday afternoon, while some people were at the Foeste for dinner, or at the movies, or at a picnic, four young Sheboygan women were gathering around a piano for the first time to sing some barbershop songs.

––––––––––––––––––––

Above: A postcard scene looking south on North 8th Street from Ontario Avenue around 1946. On the left is the Rex Theater and the Hotel Foeste is on the right.

Below: Postcard view from about 1930. This building still looks the same today. The *Sheboygan Press* was the daily newspaper for the city of Sheboygan and the surrounding area in 1946. Both are from the author's collection).

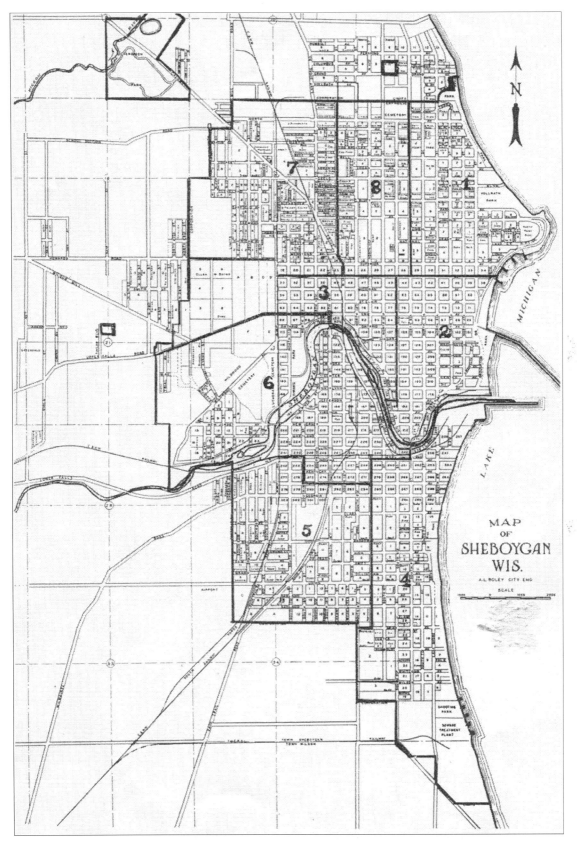

This map shows the city limits of Sheboygan in 1946. (Leberman)

CHAPTER 2

THE CHORDETTES ARE FORMED

On Sunday, August 18, 1946, four young women gathered around a piano to sing barbershop music at the home of Arthur and Emma Hummitzsch, 1435 Superior Avenue.

The women were Miss Dorothy (Dottie) Hummitzsch, Mrs. Virginia (Jinny) Osborn, Mrs. Janet Ertel, and Mrs. Alice Mae Phelps. The music was supplied by Virginia Osborn, who had borrowed the music from her father, H.O. (King) Cole, who was vice president of the local Kingsbury Brewery and president of the Sheboygan chapter of the Society for the Preservation and Encouragement of Barber Shop Quartet Singing in America, Inc. (S.P.E.B.S.Q.S.A.).

The original name SPEBSQSA was intended as a lampoon on Roosevelt's New Deal alphabet agencies.

Because of the name's length and the difficult-to-pronounce acronym, if was referred to as The Society.

The name Barbershop Harmony Society was an officially recognized and sanctioned alternate.

O. H. "King" Cole

O. H. King Cole At Barber Shop Singing Festival

O. H. King Cole, president of the Sheboygan chapter of the Society for the Preservation and Encouragement of Barber Shop Quartet Singing in America, Inc., was in Cleveland, Ohio, today bending a critical ear to some mellow old bits of musical Americana.

Fifteen of the best quartets that ever rendered an old favorite were warbling in the finals of the eighth international championship contest of the SPEBSQSA, and King Cole hoped to profit from the experience. An officer of the

CENTRAL HIGH SCHOOL SHEBOYGAN WIS.

Janet Hope Buschman's 1930 high school graduation photo. (From the author's collection)

Janet Hope Buschman Ertel, was the oldest at the age of 33, having been born in Sheboygan on January 21, 1913. Her parents were Albert and Alice Buschmann. She attended Jefferson Elementary School and graduated from the Sheboygan High School (Central) in 1930. In high school, she was involved in the Lake Breeze Weekly (school newspaper), Inter-Nos, G.A.A., and gym exhibition. The Inter-Nos was a club to promote the speaking and writing of Latin and G.A.A. was a letter club. If a member earned a certain number of points, they received a medal and for additional points, an "S" for use on a letter sweater. On July 18, 1936, she married John Ertel Jr. at Sheboygan's Ebenezer Reformed Church. She was also the mother of daughter, Jacqueline.

Alice Mae Buschman's 1943 high school graduation photo. (From the author's collection)

Janet's younger sister, 21-year-old Alice Mae Phelps was also one of the group that Sunday afternoon. Alice May was born July 30, 1925, in Sheboygan, Wisconsin and graduated in 1943, from Sheboygan North High School. (In 1930, when Janet graduated, there was only one high school in Sheboygan. In 1938, there was a second high school named North opened, and the old Sheboygan High School was renamed Central.)

She was very involved in high school activities. During her junior and senior years, she was active in cheerleading, Tri-Hi-Y, intramurals, school trio, auditorium committee, and dramatics production. Tri-Hi-Y was a club working to raise money for the war effort.

On May 2, 1945, she married Robert Phelps, but they were divorced just over a year later on May 22, 1946. Alice Mae worked in the office for the American Red Cross and lived at 1413 Mehrtens Avenue, with her father, Albert Buschmann, and sister Janet. Her mother, Alice had died one year earlier in May 1945.

Most of the rehearsals were held at this home, because it was the most centrally located for the four women. Alice Mae would only be with the group for a short time.

The 1945 high school graduation photo of Dorothy (Dottie) Margaret Hummitzsch. (From the author's collection)

Nineteen-year-old Dorothy Margaret Hummitzsch was also one of the women who got to-gether to sing that Sunday afternoon. Born in Sheboygan, Dorothy was a 1945 graduate of Central High School. She was the only single lady in the group.

At the time, Dorothy was working for the phone company in the business office. In the Central High School yearbook, from her senior year in 1945, the book said about her, "Dorothy Hummitzsch likes music. She was active for High School Night, and her ambition is to become a singer." At Central High, Dorothy was involved in the choir, student council, TRI-H-Y, and in the school production of "Royal Rumpus" in March 1945. The money from the production went to purchase war bonds, as World War II was still being fought. Dorothy formed and sang with two trios in high school, sang in her church choir, and sang with her brother's Minstrel Show.

In addition, Dorothy played third base for a woman's softball team. One of Dorothy's games was mentioned in the May 31, 1946, *Sheboygan Press*. Two days earlier, on the 29th, Dorothy's team, *Willie's Barrettes* won by the score of 64 to 0 in a five-inning game. The *Press* stated, "Dorothy Hummitzsch scored the incredible total of 10 runs in 10 trips to the plate."

cast of "letters to lucerne"

The cast's all here—except the "letters" — Virginia Cole, Harriet Van Der Puy, Eileen Raffelson, Phyllis Alexander, Walter Kraatz, Eugene Jaberg, Joan Patrie, Leroy Franz, Elizabeth Morss, Patsy Smith, Marge Schmidt, Andrew Burkart and Ruth Sonnenburg.

Shown here is the cast of the 1944 Sheboygan North High School play. Virginia "Ginny" Cole is the first person on the left side of the photo. (From the author's collection)

Virginia (Ginny) Cole Osborn was the fourth woman to join in singing. Ginny was also 19-years-old and was the only one of the four women not born in Sheboygan. She was born in Seattle, Washington on April 25, 1927. She moved to Sheboygan with her parents, O.H. (King) and Kay Cole in the early 1930s. King Cole came to Sheboygan to work at Kingsbury Brewery.

Ginny attended Downer Seminary in Milwaukee and Frances Shimer College in Illinois. Prior to attending those two schools, she attended Grant Elementary School and Sheboygan North High School. During her junior year at North, she took part in the school play, "Letters to Lucerne." Ginny was married to Otis B. Osborn and was living at 1925 North Sixth Street, along with their young son.

The four women decided that Sunday afternoon to form a female barbershop quartet and call themselves, "The Chordettes." Chord was a musical term, which the dictionary defined as, "a combination of three or more concordant tones sounded simultaneously." The "ettes" part of the name meant female.

In December 1999, Mike Callahan interviewed Ginny for the June 2002 issue of "Both Sides Now." Ginny said in that interview, "My father was a barbershopper. I was sitting at home doing nothing, and Dad was all excited, running around the state of Wisconsin starting up barbershop chapters. On Saturday nights, he'd drag me along. He'd emcee a show, and I'd hear the quartets sing and think, "That's what I want to do!" I had sung in high school with a trio. I came back from one of these shows in the summer of 1946, and my mother said, "Call. You'll never accomplish anything if you don't get on the phone." So I called a girl I sang with in high school, Alice Mae Buschmann. She was a good harmonizer, and I told her I'd probably be the top voice, but we needed two others. We needed someone to sing really low, a "bass," and she said, 'I'll bring my sister, Janet.' We started out looking at men's arrangements, which we had to transpose. When my father heard us, he said we sounded so good that if we could get a really good lead singer, he'd put us on the Sheboygan Barbershop Show, which was coming up in a couple of weeks. So, I called the high school music coach (Charles Faulhaber) in Sheboygan, and asked, "Who do you have who has a really strong lead voice, no vibrato if possible? The best girl you've got?" and he said, "Dorothy Hummitzsch, without a doubt!" We called Dottie,

Shown above is a postcard view of Sheboygan North High School in the 1940's. It was in the auditorium of this building that the Chordettes made their first public appearance on September 7, 1946. The doors to the auditorium are on both sides of the center tree. (From the author's collection)

and she agreed to sing with us. When we sang on the Sheboygan Show we sang two songs, "Beautiful Isle of Make Believe" and "Tell Me Why.

Less than three weeks later, on September 7, 1946, the Sheboygan Barbershoppers, Wisconsin Chapter No. 8, S.P.E.B.S.Q.S.A. (Society for the Preservation and Encouragement of Barbershop Quartet Singing in America) held their first annual parade of quartets in Sheboygan in the auditorium of Sheboygan North High School.

The auditorium was jammed with enthusiasts waiting to hear more than 100 barbershop singers from Sheboygan, Manitowoc, Appleton, Milwaukee, Beaver Dam, Chicago, St. Louis, and Grand Rapids, Michigan.

The *Sheboygan Press*, in their September 9, 1946 issue, described barbershop singing as follows, "Barbershop harmony for those who haven't studied the finer points, is defined by the S.P.E.B.S.Q.S.A. as a form of American music produced by four voices unaccompanied, when the lead sings the melody consistently below the tenor, with the baritone and bass rounding out the four parts, when rules of time, expression and word theme are frequently sacrificed to obtain more blending harmony satisfaction. With Barbershoppers, harmony comes first, last, and always."

The Press continued, "Having its origin in the early day barbershop where patrons gathered to swap news, tall stories, sing, and otherwise enjoy the clubby atmosphere, it is not surprising that such establishments lent their name to this distinct type of music."

"O.H. King Cole, (Father of Virginia Cole Osborn), president of both the Sheboygan and Manitowoc chapters, presided at the program as master of ceremonies, gave a brief history of

This photo was originally found in the *Sheboygan Press* of Monday, September 9, 1946.

It shows the Chordettes on stage during their first public appearance at North High School, two days earlier.

The original newspaper caption said, "The Sheboygan Chordettes invaded the male domain of the barbershop to take their share of applause from the audience.

They are from left to right, Virginia Osborn, Dorothy Hummitzsch, Alice Phelps and Janet Ertel."

(*Sheboygan Press* photo)

the rebirth of barbershop singing, and kept the program moving between numbers with humorous stories about the Barbershoppers."

The Press later added, "The parade of quartets began with the *Sheboygan Four* singing, "Sweet Rose" and "Sailing Away on the Henry Clay". Sheboygan's other contribution to the program was a quartet of girls, the *Chordettes*, who do not belong to the society, but work with it on such programs as that of Saturday evening. They sang, "Tell Me Why" and "Beautiful Isle of Make Believe" in the full male quartet range of tenor, lead, baritone and bass."

This was the first public appearance for the Chordettes and was on the same stage where Virginia Cole Osborn had performed in the North High School play, two years earlier. A photo of the Chordettes singing on stage was also included with the article. That photo is shown above.

Less than a month later, on October 1, King Cole was in Wisconsin Rapids organizing a local chapter of the S.P.E.B.S.Q.S.A. in that city. The local newspaper reported in their October 2, 1946 edition, "Old time Barber Shop harmony rang through the dining rooms of the Elks Club last night as more than 100 Elks attended the regular Tuesday Night Supper club meeting which was highlighted by the appearance of two of the state's top Barber Shop quartets.

"The Chordettes, a girls' quartet from Sheboygan, and the Cordials, a men's quartet from Manitowoc, together with Gordon Barner, a baritone soloist, and Milton Detjen, pianist and men's chorus director, both of Manitowoc, presented the well-received program." The interesting item in this article was that the Chordettes had only made one public appearance previous to this one, and they were already reported as one of the state's top quartettes.

The article continued, "Acting as master of ceremonies for the evening was O.H. "King" Cole, a director on the executive board of the Society for the Preservation and Encouragement of Barber Shop Quartet Singing in America. He was accompanied to Wisconsin Rapids, by Mrs. Cole, whose birthday was saluted in song during the supper meeting."

Katherine Cole was born in Sisterville, West Virginia, on October 1, 1896, daughter of Ernest and Adele Flack, both of whom were born in Sheboygan County. When she was a young girl, her family moved to Seattle, Washington, where she would later marry Mr. Cole on June 29, 1918.

Mrs. Cole would also be instrumental in the future success of the Chordettes. She would drive the Chordettes to various bookings, when they were unable to go by train, or later airplane. While she drove, the ladies practiced.

On October 12, the Manitowoc chapter of the S.P.E.B.S.Q.S.A. held their second annual parade of quartettes show at the Manitowoc Lincoln High School. The emcee was King Cole with help from "Milton (The Great) Detjen" according to the Manitowoc Herald-Times of October 14, 1946.

One of the quartettes in this male dominated show, were the Chordettes from Sheboygan. The Chordettes received only a one-sentence mention in the article, which was found on page two. But, their picture made the front page of the paper.

Under the photo, the *Herald-Times* stated, "Something new has been added-A pleasant surprise at the Parade of Quartets Saturday night at Lincoln High School auditorium was the Chordettes, four winsome girl singers of Sheboygan. Recently organized to sing ballads the barbershop way, Virginia Osborn, tenor; Dorothy Hummitzsch, lead; Alice Phelps, baritone; and Janet Ertel, bass, presented "Tell Me Why" and "The World is Waiting for the Sunrise" as their regular numbers and "Lullaby" in the finale with the chorus and combined quartets."

On November 2, the *Sheboygan Press* reported, "On Thursday, the Chordettes, girl members of the Barbershop singers, entertained at the Beer Wholesaler's convention in Milwaukee. The members are Dorothy Hummitzsch, Virginia Osborn, Alice Phelps, and Jeanette Ertel."

Ten days later, the Press again reported about the Chordettes success at the beer wholesaler's convention. Along with the usual listing of songs, the paper reports they met Don McNeill for the first time and were asked to sing for their breakfast, while making an appearance on his "Breakfast in Hollywood" show. This pivotal meeting got them on the radio for the first time and connected them to someone in the business with clout.

Don McNeill's "Breakfast Club" radio show started in 1933 and would be on air for 35 ½ years. When McNeill retired in 1968, he had the longest running show in radio history and would be known as one of the most popular figures ever in radio.

McNeill was always trying to promote Sheboygan on his radio shows, even though he was born in Galena, Illinois. At the age of three, he moved with his family to Sheboygan, Wisconsin, where he attended St. Clement's Catholic School and graduated from the Sheboygan High School in 1925.

At some point he became known as "Sheboygan's Gift To Radio." When the Chordette's appeared on his radio show, he was living in Chicago, but his parents, Mr. And Mrs. Harry McNeill were still living in Sheboygan.

November 20th saw the Chordettes in Fond du Lac, at a Lions Club luncheon. The next day, the *Fond du Lac Reporter* ran the headline, "Club Members Entertained By Ladies Quartet." In the article, the newspaper said, "The Chordettes included Virginia Osborne, tenor; Dorothy Hummitzsch, lead; Alice Phelps, baritone; and Janet Ertel, bass, all of Sheboygan. They were recalled several times by club members to sing such old favorites as "You Tell Me Your Dreams" and "That's Why I Love You."

In music, tenor is the highest natural adult voice; lead means the lead singer, baritone is a singer having a range higher than a bass and lower than a tenor, and bass is the lowest part in vocal singing.

Also, for entertainment, King Cole presented a discussion on the founding of the Society for the Preservation and Encouragement of Barber Shop Singing in America, Inc. Cole said "that the society had been organized by a Tulsa, Okla., businessman and 14 fellow-barber shop music lovers in 1938. Since then the society has become a national organization, boasting about 15,000 members at the present time. Lawyers, doctors, bricklayers, truck drivers, men from practically every walk of life, are members of the society, Cole declared. The Sheboygan chapter of the society was organized by the Kingsbury Breweries company executive about a year ago (in 1945), and now (1946) has about 90 members. Cole urged the appointment of a Lions Club committee to present the idea of organizing a Fond du Lac chapter of the society."

The Kingsbury Brewery was a prominent industry in Sheboygan in 1946. In 1847, two men, Leopold and Francis Gutsch, twin brothers, founded a brewery at New York Avenue and North Water Street in Sheboygan. The Gutsch Brewery quickly outstripped its competitors in Sheboygan, and became known as a fair-sized brewery. The demand for its products required brewing year round, instead of brewing in winter and selling their products in summer, like other breweries.

In 1878, Leopold Gutsch bought out his brother and was in charge until his son; Adolph F. Gutsch took over in 1885. In 1897, C.B. Henschel, Father-in-law of Adolph took over control of the company and ran the company until he died in 1917. After Henschel's death, his son-in-law, Robert G. Hayssen, took over and ran the company until 1926, when the plant was sold to the Manitowoc Products Company, which turned its production facilities to the brewing of Kingsbury Pale Cereal Beverage. In 1930 and 1933, the plant was enlarged. Also, in 1933, the name was changed to Kingsbury Breweries Company. The Sheboygan plant would also be enlarged again in 1948.

In 1946, the officers of Kingsbury were, William H. Pauly, Chairman of the board; Ernest C. Badger, President and Treasurer; Felix T. Pauly, Vice-President; O.H. "King" Cole, Vice-President in charge of sales; and A.M. Reinert, Secretary.

The Chordettes were again in Chicago on Sunday, December 15. This would be their last public performance for 1946. In Chicago, the Chordettes appeared on the Morris B. Sachs Amateur Hour radio show and were one of 12 contestants taking part. First prize was $75.00 and a wrist

Gutsch Brewery, the first brewery in town, was located at New York and Water Streets in Sheboygan.

watch, second prize was $40.00 and a wrist watch, and third prize was $20.00 and also a wrist watch. This may not seem like much money today, but remember a few months earlier in August; Vollrath was hiring machine operators for 60 cents an hour. This made the $75.00 first prize equal to about three weeks wages for the average person. The Chordettes were the first place winners and took the watch that they received and exchanged it for a man's watch and gave it to Milton Detjen. There will be more about Mr. Detjen later. As usual, they gave Ginny's mother money for gas and car expenses, since she was the one that drove them to Chicago for this event. After this, the remaining money was split among the four ladies.

The Chordettes started 1947 by appearing at the Hotel Hamilton in Two Rivers. The event was a dinner reunion party for the Carmen Chorus. In the following day's newspaper, there was a photo and a 13-paragraph article. Nine of the paragraphs were about the Chordettes.

Part of the article reported which songs the Chordettes sang and added, "The girls were attractively dressed in identical green and brown suits. Their apparent ease and grace, their excellent shading from a soft whisper to a resounding crescendo, and their catchy rhythms all were appreciated by the Carmen girls and the excellent enunciation of each member of the quartet was the envy of each and every member of the chorus. Especially pleasing was the fine quality of the voice of Janet Ertel, bass."

Later the article added, "They (Chordettes) have sung at the Hotel Schroeder in Milwaukee, the Stevens Hotel in Chicago and were present at the "Parade of Quartets" held in Manitowoc last September. Plans are being made to travel to Omaha, Nebraska in the near future."

The last paragraph that mentioned the Chordettes included, "It is no wonder that this quartet is barbershop inclined. Mrs. Osborn, the first tenor, is a daughter of Mr. and Mrs. O.H. King Cole, her father serving as president and organizer of both the Sheboygan and Manitowoc chap-

An old Gutsch Brewery /Kingsbury delivery truck, sometime between 1926 and 1933.

ters of the SPEBSQSA, and also a national director of the organization. The baritone, Alice Phelps, and the bass, Janet Ertel, are sisters, whose father is also an ardent barbershopper in Sheboygan."

Ten days later, on January 18, the Chordettes were far from home, as they performed for the first time west of the Mississippi River, appearing in Omaha, Nebraska. The event was a barbershop show by Omaha's Ak-Sar-Ben chapter of the SPEBSQSA. The following day, the Omaha newspaper reported on the show. All of the performers received a one-paragraph mention in the article, except for the Chordettes, who received a two-paragraph mention. The paper said about the Chordettes, "An enthusiastic audience brought nearly every group of harmonizers back for an encore. It saved its loudest cheers, however for four young women from Sheboygan, Wis., who called themselves the Chordettes. All are daughters of SPEBSQSA members."

". . . They wowed the crowd with "Beautiful Isle of Make Believe" and "Nothing Could Be Finer Than to Be in Carolina.""

Three days after this event, the Chordettes were back in Two Rivers, followed by a performance in Fond du Lac on January 25. After this, the Chordettes made their debut in New York, New York. On February 1, the Chordettes took part in the annual parade of quartets, sponsored by the Garden State Glee Club in Jersey City, New Jersey, which was the Jersey City chapter of the SPEBSQSA.

On Tuesday, February 4th, the *Sheboygan Press* ran a small article under the headline, "Chordettes On Radio Program." The article stated, "The Chordettes of Sheboygan, four young singers whose love of harmonization is bringing them nation-wide recognition will be appearing on the Fred Waring program over WMAQ (a Chicago radio station) from 10 to 10:30 a.m. Wednesday morning. They are Virginia Cole Osborn, Miss Dorothy Hummitzsch, Janet Buschmann Ertel and Alice Mae Buschmann. They with Mr. and Mrs. O.H. King Cole left the city Friday morning on their swing through the East, and have been on a number of programs and broadcasts. The group will be returning to Sheboygan Thursday."

The following day, the *Press* ran a photo of the Chordettes under the heading, "Sheboygan Chordettes Sing In New York." The caption under the photo reported, "The thrill of singing over a national network came to four from Sheboygan this morning, when the Chordettes were guests on the Fred Waring show, heard over WMAQ. "Loveland" was the number that the quartette harmonized so beautifully."

It was also announced on the show that they were being presented as a "Salute to Sheboygan" as an advance guard of the show's coming to Sheboygan on March 15. Also, at the end of the show, it was announced that the Chordettes had been invited to sing as part of the show in Sheboygan and had accepted. Another person who was mentioned on the radio show was Leonard Kranendonk who was a member of the shows chorus and was originally from Oostburg.

The article under the photo ended, "They (the Chordettes) have a long string of appearances booked, and will be singing at other barbershop singing programs in widely scattered cities, among them, Omaha, where they sang before 4,000 fans recently, Grand Rapids (Michigan), Oklahoma City, Topeka (Kansas), Louisville (Kentucky), and Evansville (Indiana) are among other cities that have invited them. Prior to going to New York, the Chordettes were on the Jersey City Barber Shop parade."

On February 8, 1947, the *Press* ran an editorial under the heading, "Girls Win Fame." The editorial read as follows, "O.H. King Cole received the thrill of his life when a quartette, organized by him, appeared on the Fred Waring program over NBC Wednesday morning. "

"Months ago these young ladies picked up some barbershop songs on the piano at the home of Mr. and Mrs. Cole, and this started their career. They have rendered numbers in public on several occasions, and have won acclaim wherever they appeared."

"In December, they appeared in Fond du Lac on the occasion of the visitation of the Grand Exalted Ruler of the Elks, a homecoming in his honor. On that occasion they were given a great ovation, and many were the predictions that they would go far in the musical world."

"In their appearance Wednesday, the announcer gave a salute to Sheboygan, and brought fame to the city. Perhaps it will be easier for the Bell Telephone girls (phone operators) to locate this city on the map in the future. Our difficulties have been most trying to spell and locate Sheboygan with a view of getting a call through. Just because we were all Indians at one time is no excuse for failing to recognize She-Boy-Again."

Upon their return to Sheboygan, the Chordettes spent the rest of February near Lake Michigan. The 7th, 19th and 22nd saw the Chordettes performing in Milwaukee, while they appeared in Chicago on February 20 and 21. They also performed in Sheboygan, on the 12th and 17th. Green Bay was another place where they performed on February 15th and 27th.

In Green Bay on the 12th, they appeared at Green Bay's Barbershop Society's second annual Harmony Jubilee with nine other barbershop quartets. All nine of these other quartets were male. This event was held in the auditorium of the Washington Junior High School and almost 1,000 people attended. The *Green Bay Press-Gazette* reported on this event in their February 17th issue. The paper reported, "Sheboygan's Chordettes, a feminine foursome, who looked alluring in full black skirts and white blouses proved they could compete on equal terms with the men. The Chordettes have been in demand ever since the daughter of a Sheboygan SPEBSQSA member found some of his music on the piano and got three of her friends to start singing with her. That's the way things happen in barber shop circles."

Also in February, there were ads almost daily about the Fred Waring show coming to Sheboygan on March 15 and that the Chordettes would also be taking part in the show. One of the ads included a map of the armory floor and what the prices would be for the various seats. Tickets on the main floor in front of the stage were the most expensive at $3.60, which included tax. The cheapest seats were $1.20, again including tax. These cheap seats were located in the upper section of the bleachers, where the stage could not be seen. Tickets could be purchased in advance by sending payment by mail order. But, for mail orders, you had to include a Self Addressed Stamp Envelope for the tickets to be mailed to you. Also appearing with Fred Waring and his Pennsylvanians would be Leonard Kranendonk, who joined the show in 1939. Kranendonk grew up in Oostburg, Wisconsin, (located in southern Sheboygan County) and later moved to Sheboygan. All together, there were over 70 performers with the Fred Waring show.

Following the show at the Armory on March 15th, the *Sheboygan Press* reported, in their Monday, March 17th issue, "Largest Crowd In History Of Armory Acclaims Fred Waring And Troupe As Tops In Shows." The article that followed stated, "The largest audience ever assembled there since the armory was built, on Saturday night, acclaimed Fred Waring and his Pennsylvanians, the finest entertainment treat ever seen or heard in these parts."

"Not only did Mr. Waring prove that he is a great leader of a great band and glee club, but he also showed the customers that he is a showman deluxe who can ad lib wisecracks with the best in the business. His musicians played their numbers with a combination of beauty and precision, which was nothing short of amazing in technique, his glee club clicked on every number, his soloists were also wonderful in their particular lines, and Mr. Waring clowned superbly throughout the evening. What more can one ask?"

The article continued, "There was special local pride in the appearance of Leonard Kranendonk, one of Mr. Waring's best soloists, because Leonard is originally from Oostburg and got his start singing over (Sheboygan Radio Station) WHBL. The pride shown by the community in him was well justified, Saturday night when he received tremendous ovations before and after his performance. He is a veteran member of the troupe of nine years standing."

"The second local contribution to the program was the guest appearance of the Chordettes, a Sheboygan quartet, that has appeared on Mr. Waring's radio program in New York. It is composed of Virginia Cole Osborn, Dorothy Hummitzsch, Alice Mae Buschmann and Janet Buschmann Ertel."

"In announcing their opening number, "I'd Love to Live in Loveland," Mr. Waring said, "Need me? I'll be right there." Their second number was "Carolina In The Morning" and it is needless to say that they were one of the big hits of the show."

Later the article reported, "Prior to the evening program, Mr. Waring and his entire troupe were guests of the Manitowoc and Sheboygan chapters of the Preservation and Encouragement of Barber Shop Singing in America, at a dinner and program at the Heidelberg Club." The Heidelberg Club

Leonard Kranendonk, born in Oostburg, was a professional singer and soloist.

19

was located on the top floor of the Security Bank Building located on the northeast corner of North 8th Street and Center Avenue.

Above is a postcard photo showing the private dining room of the Heidelberg Club. Fred Waring and the Chordettes were here for a dinner and program on March 15, 1947, before appearing at the Sheboygan Armory. (From the author's collection)

"O.H. "King" Cole, president of both chapters, was a capable mater of ceremonies, and the unrehearsed humor that was exchanged between Mr. Cole, Mr. Waring, Charles Faulhaber and others on the program, was as fast and funny as any Bob Hope show."

(Sheboygan) "Mayor Willard M. Sonnenburg presented Mr. Waring with a key to the city, and they also made Mr. Waring an honorary member of the two barber shop chord chapters during the course of the fun. The Manitowoc and Sheboygan choruses performed, Milton Detjen of Manitowoc did a remarkable piano number, the Chordettes sang, and some of Mr. Waring's did specialty acts to make the occasion a most successful event."

The Chordettes gave only two other shows in March. On March 1st, they appeared in Madison, Wisconsin and on the 17th, they were in Fond du Lac, Wisconsin

Fred Waring, at left, is presented with the key to the city of Sheboygan, 17 March 1947. *Sheboygan Press* photo.

Postcard from author's collection.

On April 1ˢᵗ, the *Milwaukee Journal* ran an article in their Green Sheet. The Green Sheet was a popular section in their daily paper, Monday through Saturday. This section received its name from being printed on one sheet of paper (four pages) that was dyed a light green. The Green Sheet always contained the comics and special interest news. The headline for the article was, "Chordettes of Sheboygan Are Cinderella's of Barbershopping" and was written by Don Dornbrook. Dornbrook's article started out, "Men have always raised their voices in song "to the ladies." Witness the multitude of songs with girls' names in titles-to say nothing of the tunes singing the praises of mother. But to those incurable addicts of four part harmony who belong to the Society for the Preservation of Barbershop Quartet Singing in America, Inc, women, for the most part, are people to be seen, and not heard."

"Not that the boys of S.P.E.B.S.Q.S.A. are women haters. Far from that. They hold that women are fine-in their place. The society's national organ, "The Harmonizer" even went so far as to dedicate a recent issue "to the ladies" pointing out that male quartets have been made because of feminine influence ranging from arranging music to arranging nights out for the members. Nevertheless, women have never been admitted to membership."

Later, the article continued, "Sheboygan's Chordettes are the Cinderella girls of the barbershoppers. In eight short months these harmonizing honeys have appeared with Fred Waring twice-once on his regular, national hookup radio show; the second time at a Waring concert in Sheboygan. They also have done radio stints on the Don McNeill "Breakfast Club" radio show and the Morris B. Sachs "Amateur Hour" another Chicago radio program. After they had entertained some Chicago S.P.E.B.S.Q.S.A. members, the following note was published in the "Pitch Pipe" the Chicago chapter's official organ:

"We now can see the infinite wisdom of our founder, O.C. Cash, in framing bylaws that prevent women from belonging to our organization. He anticipated the Chordettes and was afraid they'd show us up."

"There is more truth than fiction in that handsome compliment. Some day a talent scout, with the ability to recognize a pretty voice when he sees it, is going to offer the Chordettes a contract. For the present they'll remain amateurs." Three years later, after the Chordettes signed a professional contract, Dornbrook would remind everybody that he had written this.

Next was a brief review of how the Chordettes were formed. "The Chordettes were organized last August. O.H. (King) Cole, vice president in charge of sales at the Kingsbury breweries in Sheboygan and Manitowoc and a barbershopper to end all barbershoppers, was making arrangements for the annual "parade of quartets" in Sheboygan. He left his music on the piano and his daughter, Virginia Cole Osborn, picked it up. She recalled that her dad once had booked a girls' trio at a Sheboygan quartet parade. She reasoned that if a girls' trio would go over, why not a girl's quartet?"

"You can't get a good girl bass, that's why," her father told her. But Ginny did get a good girl bass; she got a dandy-Janet Buschmann Ertel. She also rounded up a baritone, Janet's sister, Alice, and a lead, Dorothy Hummitzsch. Ginny sings tenor."

"A month later, the Chordettes practically brought down the 1,300 capacity house at the Sheboygan (North) high school auditorium. That started their personal parade to barbershop parades-and the end is not in sight. They appeared in Manitowoc; Madison; Green Bay; Omaha, Neb.; Jersey City, N.J., and got bids to appear in Louisville, Ky.; Evansville, Ind.; Topeka, Kas.; Grand Rapids, Mich., and Chicago."

"That was last September. Two months later, King took the girls to Chicago to appear at the National Beer Wholesaler's convention, and a famous son of Sheboygan, radio's Don McNeill, was in the audience. He invited them to appear on his show. Ole Olson of Olsen and Johnson heard them and sent a note to Fred Waring."

"When the girls later went east to sing for a barbershop show in Jersey City, Dave Murray, former personal manager for Olsen and Johnson, was in the audience. He had gone to their hotel to audition them-he's organizing his own talent bureau-and stayed to observe their stage presence before the 2,500 persons at the Jersey City concert. The Fred Waring appearance followed. That in itself was unusual, for radio reporters say Waring is not given to arranging guest appearances for amateurs on his program."

The article continued, "These girls are a bit bewildered by the enthusiastic reception they have received. They've had their share of unscheduled experiences. When they played Madison, the bass (Janet) lost her voice at a dinner party before the show. They were snowed in at Sheboygan for two days before the Jersey City program and wore down their long fingernails worrying about whether they'd make it. The day of the Don McNeill show, they discovered they had left their skirts in Sheboygan. Replacements were found, however. The Chordettes costume consists of green and brown sport jackets and brown skirts."

"The girls use standard barbershop quartet arrangements, practice a couple of hours a day, and all read music. Their reading ability was a pleasant surprise for Fred Waring, most quartets sing by ear. Milton Detjen, director of the Manitowoc barbershop quartet chorus, has been working with them since they started."

"When the Chordettes took first place on the Morris B. Sachs show, last December, they won a $75 girls' wrist watch. Without saying a word to Milton, they traded it for a men's model and gave it to him at the Waring concert."

The article ended with, "The Chordettes spent an entire Saturday afternoon recently going from ward to ward at the soldier's home here (Milwaukee)." (A photo of the Chordettes visiting with one of the soldiers, John R. Kluck of Milwaukee, appeared with the article). "They are scheduled to return in June for the international contest of the singing society with the long name. And if the male quartets aren't on the beam, it won't be because the Chicago chapter didn't warn them."

The Chordettes started out April of 1947, with no shows for the first 11 days. But, then they performed seven shows in 16 days in five different states. On the 12th, they performed in Grand Rapids, Michigan, followed by a show in Chicago, Illinois the next day. Travel was not the easiest in 1947. Air travel was still in its early days and the planes were small and propeller driven and many places did not have airports. Car travel was also slow, as there were no interstate highways and even some of the major highways were not paved, but were gravel or even dirt and if it rained, these dirt roads turned to mud, where cars could get stuck in the ruts, once the mud dried. The most comfortable and easiest way to travel was by passenger train.

Four days later, on the 17th, the Chordettes were in Kansas City, Missouri for a barbershop show sponsored by the Kansas City Chapter of the S.P.E.B.S.Q.S.A. This show was held in the Windsor Room of the Phillips Hotel. An ad for this show, announced, "You are Cordially Invited to See and Hear the Chordettes, Singing the Songs that Mother Sang – But Better." The ad also stated, "This remarkable quartet is being currently billed as the "Cinderellas of Barbershopping." The last part of the ad, said, "We assure you you will go away saying, "Those girls are out of this world."

Two days after the Kansas City show, they were doing another barbershop show, this time in Oklahoma City, Oklahoma. After the show, an Oklahoma City newspaper reported, "More than 5,000 barbershop singing fans applauded enthusiastically during a three-hour songfest Saturday night at the Municipal auditorium when the championship barbershop quartets of the nation paraded across the stage." Later the same article stated, "The show was almost stolen by a girls quartet, the Chordettes, of Sheboygan, Wis. Singing "I'd Love to Live in Loveland," "Beautiful Isle of Make Believe," and "Carolina in the Morning."

The next day, April 20, the Chordettes were invited to a barbecue. The headline in the Oklahoma City newspaper said about this event, "Barbershoppers Haven't Had Enough, Sing at Ranch Party." The article that followed reported, "A lot of democrats and, so it was whispered, even a few Republicans showed up at the Flying L Ranch near Davis, Sunday as Bill and Alice Likins played host to the visiting barbershop quartets. While nobody bothered to count noses, there was an estimated 1,000 persons on hand to eat barbecue, look at Herefords (cattle) and sing barbershop harmony."

"The barbecue was given by the Likins in honor of the quartets that sang here in the Municipal auditorium Saturday night in the annual parade of champions. And there was a lot of singing, too. Every time four people would get together, they would stop and sing a song. While it wasn't all good, it was loud.

Later the article added, "After the many guests had finished eating a half ton of barbecue at noon, they journeyed over to Gov. (Oklahoma Governor Roy Turner) Turner's ranch near Sulphur to look at more Herefords."

After leaving the barbecue, the Chordettes did not get much of a chance to rest. The next evening, they took part in a barbershop show in Tulsa, Oklahoma. The show in Tulsa was held in the Topaz Room of the Hotel Tulsa where, "The Chordettes, a nationally known quartet of women barbershop singers from Sheboygan, Wis. were guests of honor at a joint meeting of the Society for the Preservation and Encouragement of Barbershop Singing in America and the Sweet Adelines;" according to a Tulsa, Oklahoma newspaper.

The Chordettes finished April of 1947 with two shows in Wisconsin. On April 26, they were in La Crosse for a Barber Shop Parade of Stars, which was held at the Vocational Auditorium. Two days later, they were in Two Rivers.

Most of May saw an easy schedule for the Chordettes. On May 3, they appeared at a barbershop show held in Appleton, Wisconsin, at the high school. The *Appleton Post-Crescent* of May 5, said about the Chordettes appearance, two days earlier, "Into the strictly masculine sanctorum of the barbershoppers came the Chordettes of Sheboygan, four girls in smart black faille suits, whistle-provoking ankle-strap sandals and bright corsages, who demonstrated capably that anybody can sing barbershop harmony-if they have good enough voices. Their four numbers were well-suited to their individual talents, "Loveland," "When Day is Done," "Mean to Me" and "Carolina in the Morning."

However, the second week of May from the 7th to the 15th, saw the Chordettes performing six times in eight days. But, of these six shows, five were in their hometown of Sheboygan. On the 7th, the Chordettes took part in a scholarship concert in the Sheboygan North High School auditorium, sponsored by the North High School Alumni Association. The money raised went towards scholarships for three graduating students of North. In an interesting note, the Chordettes did not receive top billing in the program that evening. They were listed third in the program, out of eight. The *Sheboygan Press* said about the Chordettes, in the next day's newspaper, "Then came the much-traveled Chordettes- Alice Mae Buschmann, Janet Buschmann Ertel, Dorothy Hummitzsch and Virginia Cole Osborn. Their numerous appearances throughout the United States and the resulting enthusiasm for harmonized singing was matched in their home city. "I Had A Dream, Dear, " "When Day Is Done" and "Carolina In the Morning" were their program offerings, but they added another, "I'd Love to Live in Loveland" because the

24

crowd wanted more. Their voices have beauteous blend, and they know how to captivate with smiles and mannerisms."

This ad appeared in the *La Crosse (Wisconsin) Tribune* of April 24, 1947. Notice how the Chordettes got top billing. The black lines in the ad are from scratches in the microfilm. Author photograph of ad.

Three days later, on May 10th, the Chordettes were 30 miles north of Sheboygan, in Manitowoc for a barbershop show. This show was held in the auditorium of the Lincoln High School. Then it was back to Sheboygan for shows on May 12, 13, 14, and 15. The show on Tuesday, the 13th was a small "Evening of Entertainment" sponsored by members of the Girls' guild of St. John's Evangelical and Reformed Church. The show was held in the church hall, which was located on the corner on North 13th Street and Lincoln Avenue. The first part of the entertainment was a one-act play titled, "Madame's Hat Shop." After the play, two barbershop quartettes performed. First were the Four Clippers, followed by the Chordettes, which completed the "Evening of Entertainment."

The remainder of May wasn't as busy. On the 17th, they gave their only show for the month, not held in Wisconsin. For this show, they were in Iron Mountain, Michigan. Their final show for the month was on May 28 in Kenosha. The Kenosha show was the first barbershop parade held in Kenosha and was hosted by the Kenosha chapter of the SPEBSQSA and it was quite a success. The show was held at the Kenosha High School and was sold out three days before the event.

But, between their final two shows of the month, there was both a happy event and sad event. On May 24, Alice Mae was married to Roy W. Spielvogel and announced that she would be leaving the group.

Eighth Street in Sheboygan during the 1940s and 1950s. Above, the Sheboygan Theater and Janet's Hat Shop.

Below, H.C. Prange, the center of the community.

CHAPTER 3
ON THE ROAD, 1947-1949

The Chordettes are shown here singing at the National Barbershop Convention, held in Milwaukee, Wisconsin, June 13-15, 1947. New Chordette, Carol Hagedorn is shown second from the left. Notice that she had not yet been fitted with costumes to match the other Chordettes. The other Chordettes are, left to right, Janet Ertel, Dorothy (Dottie) Hummitzsch, and Virginia Osborn. Alice Mae also sang with the group in Milwaukee.
(Photo courtesy of Dorothy Schwartz)

From June 13 to 15, 1947, the annual international barbershop contest finals of the Society for the Preservation and Encouragement of Barber Shop Quartet Singing in America was held in Milwaukee, Wisconsin. This was just 50 miles from the Chordettes' hometown of Sheboygan.

The *Milwaukee Journal* ran an article about the barbershoppers on the front page of their June 12th newspaper. Part of the article gave a brief background of the barbershop singing group. The Journal reported, "Barbershop quartet singing, born in the leisurely days of horse cars and handlebar mustaches, was almost extinct in 1938 when the SPEBSQSA was founded. The society was intended to do just what its zany title says-preserve and encourage the home-spun glory of the male quartet, getting together on a nostalgic song. Chapters, clubs and quartets sprung up all over the country, but in all its 91,000 membership today (1947), the society has not a single soloist. It is still all harmony."

"Each year the chapters hold contests to determine the best quartet. The winners sing against other winners in sectional contests and this year (1947), out of 200 sectional contestants, 30 quartets were selected to compete for international supremacy in the manly art of "Mmmmm.""

"Thursday (June 11) at the Schroeder Hotel, the international officers held business meetings. There were new officers to be chosen, business and organizational problems to discuss. Then, too, the society heard that the U.S. Army forbade singing by American soldiers of occupation in Germany, and the membership decided it was morally bound to pressure the army into rescinding the order." One of the new officers chosen was O.H. "King" Cole of Sheboygan, who was elected vice-president.

The Journal continued, "By Thursday night, 2,000 barbershoppers are expected to be in town. By Friday morning, another 1,000 are expected. Friday the contest will start. The top 30 quartets will be judged by experts. Ratings based on 30 points for originality of song arrangement, 30 for harmony, 30 for voice expression and 10 points for stage presence will be given. The top five quartets will be chosen. Saturday night the five will compete at the Auditorium for the final honors." The Mutual Broadcasting (Radio) Network also broadcast the finals live, coast-to-coast.

The winning quartet was the "Doctors of Harmony" from Elkhart, Indiana. The second place group was the "Lions Club Serenades" of Kansas City. This was the fifth consecutive year that this group finished in second place.

The Chordettes also performed at the convention. The big news for the Chordettes was a new member, making her first public appearance with the group, as Carol Hagedorn sang with the group. She would be taking Alice Mae's spot in the group.

Carol was also a Sheboygan girl, born and raised. She attended Bethlehem Lutheran Grade School and graduated from Sheboygan Central High School in 1945. At Central, Carol was active in the school choir, forensics, oratory, debate team, and drama, taking part in the school play, her junior and senior years. She was also a member of the honor society.

In a December 1999 interview for the "Both Sides Now" newsletter, Jinny said the following about Carol joining the group, "Alice Mae wanted to leave the group, and Dottie knew Carol from high school. By that time, we were fairly well organized, with scheduled singing engagements and everything. Before we auditioned her, we wanted to know what Carol looked like. The first time I ever laid eyes on Carol was at the railroad station. She had a job in Chicago, (working for the publisher of the World Book Encyclopedia) and was going down to Chicago on the train. She was wearing a red coat and a little red hat to match, and she really looked great, very classy. She was as classy as she looked, and became my best friend – and still is. She replaced Alice, and my father (King Cole) got really carried away and took us to Milton Detjen."

Carol added in the same interview, "There was a fellow, Milton Detjen, who was the Chorus Director (of the S.P.E.B.S.Q.S.A.) in Manitowoc, just about 25 miles north of Sheboygan. He was an excellent musician. Jinny's dad wanted us to go to him to have him polish our singing. He used to coach us, with dynamics and such, and we practiced a lot. He kind of gave us our barbershop style."

Jinny added, "Milton was a pianist who had some very fine training in Europe. We added to our repertoire, and he told us what notes we should be singing, where to breathe and when to breathe, about crescendo and all that sort of stuff, and whipped us into a fairly nice singing group. In the meantime, everybody thought we were just cute as bug's ears, because we were all kids at that time, and nice girls. They kept asking us to be on their barbershop shows, and we'd go to one and get four invitations to other shows. After about six months, we were all over the place. My mother even drove us to Oklahoma City on one of these, which was a long, long drive." This was before interstate highways and many roads in the United States were not paved. Many areas still had gravel roads and in some places roads were still dirt, which turned into mud holes, where cars would get stuck when it rained or snow melted. The interstate highway system was the idea of President Eisenhower, who took office in January 1953, after seeing the autobahns of Germany at the end of World War II.

Carol Hagedorn

Carol Hagedorn's graduation photo from the 1945 Sheboygan Central High School Lake Breeze yearbook.

By the time Carol joined the Chordettes, she was no longer working in Chicago, but was working for the Telephone Company in Sheboygan. Like Dorothy, before her, Carol also had to leave her job at the Phone Company in order to be a member of the Chordettes. Years later, Jinny would say in an interview, "We were rough on the phone company."

The remainder of June and July 1947, saw the Chordettes staying within 50 miles of Sheboygan, with a performance in Two Rivers, Wisconsin on June 19 and on June 24, the Chordettes made their third appearance of the month in Milwaukee.

The Fourth of July saw the Chordettes performing in the tiny village of Oostburg, as part of the village's Independence Day celebration. This was an outdoor performance in the Village Park. Oostburg was 10 miles south of Sheboygan and in 1947 had a population of about 750 people. Oostburg would be the smallest town the Chordettes would perform in during their history.

The 12th of July saw the Chordettes in Fond du Lac, Wisconsin and the 20th saw them in Oshkosh, Wisconsin for the second annual picnic of the Land of Lakes District of the S.P.E.B.S.Q.S.A. Over 1,000 people were in attendance. Bleachers and park benches were set up for this event with the steps of the American Legion clubhouse being used as the stage. The following day in the *Oshkosh Daily Northwestern* newspaper, an article about this event was printed. One paragraph reported, "The Chordettes of Sheboygan, famed all-girl quartet, was warmly received at the evening session. The group is recognized as one of the outstanding women's quartets in the nation and has appeared with Fred Waring's Orchestra."

The Chordettes ended July of 1947 performing in Manitowoc on the 25th. They started out August of 1947 in Neenah, Wisconsin on Saturday, August 2, where the Chordettes took part in the second annual chorus and quartet festival, sponsored by the Neenah-Menasha chapter of the Society for the Preservation and Encouragement of Barbershop Quartet Singing in America (S.P.E.B.S.Q.S.A.). According to the Neenah-Menasha Daily News of August 4, 1947, nearly 2,000 people attended this event. This event was held outside at the Neenah swimming pool and before the singing, there was an exhibition of swimming and diving.

For the barbershop singing portion of the show, there were eight barbershop quartets. According to the newspaper, "Sharing honors for top billing (with the Mid States Four of Chicago, Illinois State Champions) were the Chordettes of Sheboygan, as pretty a quartet as ever set foot inside a barbershop. These four attractive girls, Dorothy Hummitzch, Virginia Osborn, Alice Phelps, and Janet Ertel, have had radio engagements and only recently were guests on a Fred Waring show. The only feminine barbershoppers in the state, they did a good job with "Moonlight Bay" and "Carolina in the Morning." Notice that Alice Mae was still listed as Phelps, even though she had recently been married.

Later in the same article, a mention was made of a problem during an outdoor show, as the newspaper reported, "All during the evening, swarms of fluttery insects competed with the singers for the spotlight, even though the stage committee made frequent raids with spray guns. But, since "the show must go on," the barbershoppers did their best to ignore the winged pests, and adroitly warded off all but the most persistent bugs."

During an evening on the same day, the Chordettes performed before a football game in Green Bay. During the afternoon show, Alice Mae sang for the final time as a member of the Chordettes and Carol officially took Alice Mae's place. Alice Mae would become the "Pete Best" of the Chordettes, as the Chordettes would reach the top of their field, but she would be forgotten. Pete Best was with the Beatles at their beginning, an original Beatle, but left before they reached the peak of their success and was replaced by Ringo Starr. Or maybe it could be said that Pete Best was the Alice Mae of the Beatles.

On August 13, 1947, the Chordettes were in Elkhart, Indiana to take part in the annual Elkhart Music Festival, which was held at Rice Field. According to the *Sheboygan Press*, this event was "the last preliminary celebration of the Chicago Tribune's 16th Summer Music Festival. At this event were various bands, choral groups, vocal soloists, baton twirling, and a community sing. There were also two "name acts" that were not part of the competing acts. These two name acts in the program were "Dennis Carroll, Tenor of Stage, Screen, and Radio" and the Chordettes, according to the program. The Chordettes performed near the end of the evening. After the Chordettes sang, the American Legion Drill Team of Jackson, Michigan performed for the crowd. After the drill team finished, the evening ended with fireworks.

The final event for the Chicago Tribune's Summer Music Festival was held at Chicago's Soldier Field on August 17. The Chordettes were not there, but one of the bands that did take part was the Kohler Band under the direction of Miss Joyce Gerlach. The Kohler Band finished in third place out of 20 bands that took part in the band portion of the festival. The Kohler Band was from the village of Kohler, Wisconsin. Kohler, Wisconsin is just west of the Chordettes home city of Sheboygan. Kohler is so close to Sheboygan that a person could stand facing either north or south and have one foot in the city of Sheboygan and the other foot in the village of Kohler.

On August 15, 1947, the city of Manitowoc, Wisconsin started a 10-day celebration of its Marine and Malting centennial. Manitowoc was one of the major ports on Lake Michigan and during World War II was the only site on the Great Lakes to build submarines. The malting part of the centennial was for its beer brewing history. One of these breweries was Kingsbury, of which King Cole was president. In the *Manitowoc Herald-Times* of August 15, there was a large full-page ad advertising all the events for the first day. Out of 12 different types of entertainment, the Chordettes were the only one to have their name in capital letters. Also, included in the ad was a photo of the Chordettes with Fred Waring.

The *Manitowoc Herald-Times* said in their August 16, 1947 edition, "Later the festivities swung to South Eighth Street, between Jay and Washington Streets. Two orchestras provided music for street dancing. There were numerous musical specialties, with Gordon Barner acting as master of ceremonies. Among those participating was the famous Chordettes of Sheboygan, a girl quartet, which specializes in barbershop harmony. Police estimated that during the course of the evening between 8,000 and 10,000 persons gathered."

The Chordettes finished August of 1947 with performances in their hometown of Sheboygan on the 18th, Chicago, Illinois on the 20th, and Neenah, Wisconsin on the 26th. The Chordettes had only one performance during the month of September 1947, with a show in Milwaukee on the 16th.

The beginning of October saw the Chordettes again on the East Coast. On October 3, they performed in Rochester, New York, followed by North Hampton, Massachusetts the next day. The *Sheboygan Press* gave some information on this Chordettes' trip in their Monday October

Village Park — Oostburg, Wisconsin

The above postcard photo shows the Village Park in Oostburg, Wisconsin where the Chordettes performed on the Fourth of July, 1947. The bandstand where they sang from can be seen in the center of the photo. (From the author's collection)

7, 1947 newspaper. The headline was "Chordettes On Waring's Show Wednesday." The article that followed stated, "The Chordettes are putting Sheboygan in the limelight again. This time it is in the east. Later it will be in different sections of the country because the singing quartet has bookings at intervals for one and one-half years."

"Wednesday morning over NBC, on the Fred Waring show, they will be guest stars. It will be recalled that they were on a similar broadcast from New York last February (1947), and in March were featured on the program presented by Fred Waring at the local (Sheboygan) Armory."

"Last Thursday, the four went East to sing over WMAM (radio) in Rochester, N.Y., on Friday. They arrived in Northampton, Mass., Saturday afternoon, and that evening took part in the Barbershop Parade of Quartets, given in Smith College auditorium."

The article ended, "Their trip continued to New York, where they are spending from Sunday until their radio appearance tomorrow. Personnel of the quartet is Virginia Cole Osborn, tenor; Dorothy Hummitzsch, lead; Carol Hagedorn, baritone; and Janet Buschmann Ertel, bass. Miss Hagedorn, daughter of Mr. and Mrs. Otto J. Hagedorn, 2116 S. Seventh Street, replaces Alice Buschmann Spielvogel, who is no longer a Sheboygan resident." This was the first mention made in the *Sheboygan Press* that Carol had joined the group and that Alice Mae was no longer part of the group.

The Chordettes did even more traveling later in the month. On October 22, the Chordettes were in Milwaukee, Wisconsin for a show, followed by a performance in Fort Wayne, Indiana, three days later on the 25th. On the 28th, they were again back in Wisconsin, this time in Wisconsin Rapids. The *Wisconsin Rapids Daily* Tribune reported about this event in their October 29, 1947 newspaper. Under the headline, "Elks Supper Club Ladies Night Held" the article stated, "Over 200 Elks, their wives and friends attended the first Ladies' Night dinner meeting of the of the year, sponsored by the Elks supper club Tuesday evening. A special program of barber shop music was presented by the "Chordettes" of Sheboygan, a group of four girls, who have appeared as guest artists on the Fred Waring program."

November of 1947 was a busy month for the Chordettes, in both number of shows and travels, as they did eight shows during the month in six different states. The month started with the Chordettes in Flint, Michigan on the 1st, followed by shows in Milwaukee, Wisconsin on both the 5th and 11th. Four days later, on November 15th, they were in Omaha, Nebraska and three days later; they were again in Wisconsin for a show in Madison. The 22nd saw the Chordettes in Louisville, Kentucky. The Chordettes ended the month with shows in La Grange, Illinois on the 29th and the next day, they were in Wilmington, Delaware.

One interesting story from 1947, about the Chordettes success was supplied by S.P.E.B.S.Q.S.A. In information they sent, they reported that at the Madison show in 1946, "The girls, the Chordettes had their hotel paid by the district (of S.P.E.B.S.Q.S.A.), $30.00. A year later (November 1947) they were getting $1500 for a commercial appearance." Today, $1,500 may not appear like much, but in 1947; a person could have bought a brand new top of the line, 1947 Chevrolet Fleetline Sportmaster four-door sedan for $1,371.

On November 15, 1947, the Sheboygan chapter of the SPEBSQSA held their second annual parade of barbershop quartets. As in 1946, this event was again held in the auditorium of North High School. But, the Chordettes were not there. Instead they were in Omaha, Nebraska for a barbershop show. The Omaha World-Herald had an article in their newspaper of November 15 about this show. The headline read, "Nation's Top Quartets Sing to Help Children's Hospital" but you almost had to go to the end of the article to find out who these "top quartets" were other than the Chordettes. The Chordettes were also shown in a photo taken by the newspaper. The beginning of the article reported, "Omahans who may have wondered what the art of barbershop harmony is all about have a treat coming at 8 p.m., Saturday at the City Auditorium. It's the Parade of Barber Shop Quartets sponsored by the Ak-Sar-Ben Chapter of the Society for the Preservation and Encouragement of Barber Shop Quartet Singing in America."

"By train and plane, quartets arrived here Saturday. Heedless of Omaha's snowy weather, they gathered in hotel rooms to rehearse their favorite chords."

"The Chordettes — four girls from Sheboygan, Wisconsin were up early. There has been a change since they appeared here last January. Carol Hagedorn has replaced Alice Phelps who got married. The girls delighted the audience at their last appearance."

"Profits of the show are being turned over to the Children's Memorial Hospital."

After leaving Delaware, the Chordettes had a few days off, until December 5. But then within three days, they did three shows in three different cities in two different states. On the 5th, they were in Sturgis, Michigan; the 6th found them in St. Charles, Illinois, for the third annual concert of the Fox River Valley Barber Shop Chorus, which was held at the St. Charles Community High School. The next day, December 7th found the Chordettes doing a show in Chicago. This was followed by one day off before appearing in Milwaukee, Wisconsin on December 9th and again on the 19th. In between these two Milwaukee dates, the Chordettes appeared in Evansville, Indiana on December 13.

Before the Chordettes appeared in Evansville, one of the local newspapers printed a lengthy article about the Chordettes and their upcoming appearance in the Evansville Chapter of the SPEBSQSA Parade of Champions. The article included a publicity photo, which still included Alice Mae, but Alice Mae was identified as Carol Hagedorn. The newspaper article reported as follows, "True barber shop harmony is the blending of MALE voices in song, using close harmony chords known to devotees as "changes," "slides," and "swipes."

"When the SPEBSQSA was first formed, the boys were determined to keep the Society on a high level, and therefore, banned the singing of "Sweet Adeline" on the grounds that it was associated in the public mind with drunks and barrooms."

"After an acid battle via the press, written and spoken criticism by all the lovely ladies named "Adeline" the boys gave in, and admitted "Sweet A." back to the fold. Never underestimate the power of a woman."

"When the girls found out how much fun the boys were having with their barbershopping, they wanted in, too. The SPEBSQSA put a firm foot down but the girls are still putting up quite a fight. In fact, the "Sweet Adelines, Inc." is now a full-fledged society and is planning on annual conventions and champions."

"Perhaps no musical group in the country has gained such meteoric heights in such a short time as four young ladies from Sheboygan, Wisconsin, known among barbershop enthusiasts as "The Chordettes.""

"Considered the finest girls' quartet, singing the difficult barbershop type of harmony, the "Chordettes," organized only a year ago, have sung in feature spots at many of the leading Barbershop Quartet Parades given by various Chapters of the Society for the Preservation and Encouragement of Barbershop Quartet Singing in America, Inc., throughout the nation."

The previous article spoke about the Sweet Adelines, Inc. and the success of the Chordettes. The Sweet Adelines may not have even been formed if not for the success of the Chordettes. But, there are two interesting items about this. One, the Chordettes never joined the Sweet Adelines and two; Sheboygan did not get their own chapter of the Sweet Adelines until five years later, in October 1952.

The Chordettes had a nice Christmas break in 1947. After doing a show in Milwaukee, on December 19, they did not have to make any public appearances for 30 days, until January 18, 1948.

During this break, the new Hotel Hamilton in Two Rivers, Wisconsin ran large ads in both the Manitowoc and Two Rivers' newspapers, under a large heading, "Announcement." The ad then announced, "In line with our aim to give the residents of Two Rivers, Manitowoc and vicinity the finest in entertainment in our beautiful cocktail lounge, we are extremely proud to have obtained the services of the brilliant Milton Detjen, widely known Manitowoc concert pianist and organist, who will play nightly except Mondays on our Hammond Electric Organ."

"Mr. Detjen, nationally known as the director of the famous male chorus of the Manitowoc County Chapter of the Society for the Preservation and Encouragement of Barber Shop Singing in America, has just completed an extended engagement in the Hotel Antlers new mirror bar in Milwaukee. In securing Mr. Detjen, we feel confident that we have obtained for your approval Wisconsin's Finest Organist, whose musical repertoire is extremely large. If you have any particular favorite, Mr. Detjen will graciously respond to your request."

"Enjoy an evening in an atmosphere of hospitality, visiting our handsome Cocktail Lounge beginning Sunday, December 21 (1947), at 9 p.m." The ad also included a photo of Milton Detjen.

In the history of the Land of Lakes Chapter of the S.P.E.B.S.Q.S.A., the following was said about Milton Detjen, "The dean of the early directors was probably Milton Detjen of Manitowoc who was a through musician who at the same time understood the needs of barbershoppers. He was the first director at Manitowoc and was a quartet coach along the Lake Michigan shore. Included among his quartets were the 1951 champion Schmitt Brothers (of Manitowoc) and the Sheboygan Chordettes."

Shortly after Mr. Detjen started working at the Hotel Hamilton, the Two Rivers newspaper ran an article after one of his shows. The headline was "Chordettes in Surprise Call On Instructor." The article started, "Four unique singing Misses," the Chordettes from Sheboygan have recently soared to meteoric heights on the wings of fame, paid a surprise visit to their teacher, Milton Detjen last night as the latter played the organ at the Hotel Hamilton here."

"It was Milton Detjen who tutored the talented young ladies in the intricate and difficult barbershop type of harmony when they first banded together last August. Today, Mr. Detjen, an accomplished musical personality in his own right, feels the inner glow of satisfaction in knowing that the girls are popularly accepted as the finest girls' quartet in America."

"The four dropped in last night about 10 p.m. with the alert young master of the piano and organ not having the least inkling of their coming, guests not only from this city, but from Manitowoc as well, all friends of Mr. Detjen, gathered in the lounge awaiting the girls' coming."

"Their arrival at the hotel was announced from the lobby as they swung into the familiar strains of "Are You From Dixie" as a greeting to teacher Detjen."

"The first few bars, we must admit, made the Detjen jaw drop slightly, then his face beamed and his eyes lit up happily as he recognized his pupils standing in the doorway."

"The following three hours witnessed the Chordettes being called time and again to the fore by the assembled guests to sing the old barbershop melodies, such as "Sweet Sixteen," "The Man in the Moon," and "I'd Like to Live in Loveland with a Boy Like You," and many other favorites."

The article ended with a brief history stating, "The Chordettes, comprising Virginia Cole Osborn, tenor; Dorothy Hummitzsch, lead; Carol Hagedorn, baritone; and Janet Ertel bass, came into being when Virginia, daughter of King Cole, international vice-president of the Society for the Preservation and Encouragement of Barber Shop Quartet Singing in America, assembled the three other talented Sheboygan young ladies. They began singing the barbershop numbers belonging to Virginia's father and their natural blend was readily apparent." Notice that this paragraph makes it sound like these four women were the original four and Alice Mae was already forgotten.

"Following a period of expert coaching by Detjen, the services of the Chordettes were soon in demand in this area. A short time later, they were singing at Barbershoppers' parades in many distant points and followed with appearances with Fred Warring, at Don McNeil's Breakfast Club, and guest starred with the Olson and Johnson Show in New York."

The article ended, "Today, their engagement books are full, which is a fine tribute to their instructor, Milton Detjen."

When the Chordettes surprised Detjen, he was 39 years old, having been born in Manitowoc, Wisconsin on February 11, 1908. He died in Manitowoc on November 23, 1983, and according to his obituary, he was very involved in music his entire life. His obituary reported, Mr. Detjen "was employed with the Manitowoc Ship Building Company as a timekeeper and also served as director of the Sub Mariner's Band which played for all submarine launchings at Manitowoc." (During World War II, submarines were built in Manitowoc.) "Mr. Detjen was the first director of the Society for the Preservation of Barber Shop Quartet Singing in America. For 42 years, Mr. Detjen had served as organist for Grace Evangelical Church. Mr. Detjen was a very active member of the Manitowoc Senior Citizens where he was head of the Warblers singing group. Mr. Detjen also had his own printing company where he printed and published 31 organ music books for church use, which is played in more than 200 churches in the United States and Canada. He was also a member of the Musicians Music Union."

After a month off, the Chordettes started doing shows again on January 18, 1948, but didn't travel very far. Their performance on January 18 was in their hometown of Sheboygan, as was their next performance on January 22. No location was found as to where they performed on the 18th.

On January 22, 1948, the *Sheboygan Press* ran a lengthy article about the Kool-Aid Bottling Company of Sheboygan, which had started production in Sheboygan on August 27, 1947. The article stated "Initial steps were taken here (Sheboygan) today to launch a nation-wide $25,000,000 business when Heronymus and Associates, Inc., announced preliminary plans for the bottling and distribution of Kool-Aid (soda) through thirty-nine bottling corporations with headquarters strategically located throughout the nation."

"For the occasion, 50 securities dealers from Chicago, leading Wisconsin cities, and other cities throughout the Middle West were guests of the Sheboygan concern. After inspecting the Sheboygan Kool-Aid bottling plant at S. Twelfth Street and Indiana Avenue, the visitors were taken by bus to Rutherford's New Surf Hotel at Centerville." (Centerville was about midway between Sheboygan and Manitowoc.)

The article continued, "There the guests enjoyed a steak dinner after which they were addressed by John Heronymus, president of Heronymus and Associates, Inc., who explained the entire project." Later in the article, Heronymus stated, "When the shortage of sugar ended (due to World War II) and the Sheboygan plant started operations, it was so successful and Heronymus and Associates, Inc., became so enthusiastic over its possibilities that the Perkins Products Co. has made us franchise manager for Kool-Aid bottled carbonated beverages." Flavors of Kool-Aid soda included, club soda, lemon-lime, punch, orange, cherry, ginger-ale, grape, perk up, kola, cream soda, and Hawaiian royal.

An interior shot of the Kool Aid bottling company, June 1953.

The final paragraph stated, "Entertainment was provided for those present in the form of musical numbers by the Chordettes, famous for appearances on Fred Waring's and other well-known radio programs."

The big plans for Kool-Aid soda did not go as planned. Sheboygan was one of only a handful of places in the United States that actually bottled Kool-Aid soft drinks. The Sheboygan plant would be one of the last plants to close and would close 10 years later, in 1958.

The final appearance for the Chordettes in January 1948 was in Fort Atkinson, Wisconsin on the 24th, where they took part in a barbershop show. While January did not see much traveling for the Chordettes, February did. The Chordettes only appeared in three cities during February, but the cities were spread out. On February 7, the Chordettes appeared in Tulsa, Oklahoma, followed by Rochester, New York from the 12th to the 14th. The Chordettes finished the month in Des Moines, Iowa on the final day of the month.

The *Sheboygan Press* reported in their February 5, 1948 issue, "This evening the Chordettes are leaving for Oklahoma, where on Saturday they will sing at a Barbershop parade honoring O.C. Cash, founder of the S.P.E.B.S.Q.S.A. Members are Virginia Cole Osborn, tenor; Miss Dorothy Hummitzsch, lead; Janet Buschmann Ertel, bass; and Miss Carol Hagedorn, baritone." The local Tulsa, Oklahoma newspaper reported about the barbershop parade held at Tulsa's Convention Hall, in their February 7, issue. One paragraph was devoted to the Chordettes and stated, "Four lovely young women comprising the Chordettes of Sheboygan., stole the show with their rendition of the hitherto "reserved for men" ballads. The Chordettes have made several personal appearances on nationwide radio programs, having appeared twice with Fred Waring and his Pennsylvanians."

The Sheboygan Press of February 11, 1948 reported, "The Chordettes will be in Rochester, N.Y., Thursday, Friday, Saturday, and Sunday, to sing for the opening of the new million and one-half dollar F.M. radio station, WHFM."

Also while in Rochester, the Chordettes also appeared at a meeting of the Rochester Ad Club. In the club's Bumblebee weekly newspaper of February 12, 1948, Neil A. Gallagher did a short article about the Chordettes and made the Chordettes sound as if they were the greatest thing on Earth. Gallagher wrote, "Let's talk about the Chordettes first. Your reviewer heard these gals first during last fall's Chamber of Commerce membership campaign."

"The Chordettes are an all-girl barber shop quartet and, for my money, infinitely better than any male aggregation I've ever heard. As a convincing proof, let me state only that, during their last visit here, their singing was studied by local chapters of SPEBSQSA as an object lesson in how numbers can be rendered! They've been on Fred Waring's show, on the Breakfast Club program, the Olsen and Johnson broadcast, and are in Rochester to take part in the inaugural broadcasts of WHAM's new Radio City. They look like movie stars and they sing like angels-what more can mere man ask for?"

For their show engagement on February 29, in Des Moines, Iowa, the Chordettes appeared before 3,000 people at the KRNT Radio Theater, for a barbershop parade, sponsored by SPEBSQSA. The Des Moines Register newspaper reported after the event, "Four Sheboygan, Wis., girls, the Chordettes, put "beauty" in place of "barber" in the corporation's name. Their "Moonlight Bay" would be the delight of any "shop" quartet, and their "Thoity-thoid and Thoid" (Thirty-third and third) was one of the better sung comedy pieces."

March of 1948 saw the Chordettes in Milwaukee, Wisconsin on the 6th. On Tuesday, March 8th, the *Sheboygan Press* reported, "Miss Carol Hagedorn and Dorothy Hummitzsch were in Chicago on Monday. On Tuesday they joined Virginia Cole Osborn and Janet Buschmann Ertel, other members of the Chordettes, in Grand Rapids, Mich., for a singing engagement. They will fly back from Michigan on Wednesday. Their Michigan show was actually in Saginaw, Michigan.

The day before the show, the Saginaw newspaper ran a seven-paragraph article about "Female Barber Shoppers On Auditorium Program" and also included a photo of the Chordettes. The article started out, "A variety show it will be, March 13 at the auditorium, and one of the main reasons for the variety will be the appearance of the Chordettes, a girl's barber-shop quartet, no foolin'!"

"Founder O.C. Cash of Oklahoma never dreamed of anything like this when he organized the Society for the Preservation and Encouragement of Barber Shop Quartet Singing in America a decade ago."

"Out of Sheboygan, Wis., they come-four young ladies singing harmonies steeped in the atmosphere of the barber pole, the pot-bellied stove and the cracker barrel, "Wait For Me, Mary" "Way Down Yonder In The Corn Field" "On The Banks Of The Wabash" "My Mother Was A Lady." The male monopoly on these songs has been questioned, and, at latest report, the girls are doing all right."

"Two recent appearances with Fred Waring's Pennsylvanians have climaxed a busy 18 months since the Chordettes organized."

"The Chordettes are the brainchild of Virginia Cole Osborn, daughter of King Cole, international vice president of the SPEBSQSA."

"Now Mrs. Osborn is no husky-voiced lass with a masculine manner. In fact, she is very much a soprano, and sings the "tenor" part in the group. Among her equally feminine friends she discovered a "bass", a "baritone", and a "lead" songstress. Soon they were surprising neighborhood audiences by lending a feminine twist to "When You Were Sweet Sixteen", "Sweet Adeline" and the rest."

The article ended, "The Chordettes have made quite a name for themselves through appearances on just the type of show being sponsored by Saginaw Chapter No. 6 of the SPEBSQSA at the auditorium March 13. They have made hits in several Midwest states. Their radio appearances have been the outgrowth of their stage success."

After the show, the Saginaw, Michigan newspaper reported that a capacity audience attended the sixth annual Barber Shop Variety Show at the auditorium. About the Chordettes, the newspaper reported, "The Chordettes, girls' quartet from Sheboygan, Wis., won the audience completely. Adding a feminine flourish to the traditional barbershop style, they sang "Moonlight Bay", "Sweet Sixteen" and "I'm Looking Over a Four-Leaf Clover" as these old favorites have never been sung before."

On March 15, the newspaper in Wauwatosa, Wisconsin ran a photo of the Chordettes. Under the photo, the caption stated, "The irrepressible members of the Society for the Preservation and Encouragement of Barber Shop Quartet Singing in America, Inc., like to sing about the girls, but they don't take them into the society. However, there are times when the boys will bend an ear to a sweet girl quartet-and when the girls are as easy to look at as these honeys of harmony, the men are bound to look to. The girls call themselves the Chordettes, they come from Sheboygan, Wis., and they'll be guests at the parade of barbershop quartets at the Wauwatosa High School auditorium Saturday night (March 20)." No follow up article to this event was found.

The Chordettes started the month of April 1948 in Kansas City. The *Sheboygan Press* of Saturday, April 2nd reported, "On Friday, the Chordettes left for Kansas City, Mo., where they will spend several days. The girls will sing at a barbershop show." After the show, the Kansas City Star newspaper, in their April 4, 1948 edition, said about the Chordettes, "The Chordettes, a feminine aggregation from Sheboygan, Wis., have been heard on Fred Waring's radio program, and certainly proved that barbershop singing does not have to be confined to men. Virginia Osborn, Carol Hagedorn, Dorothy Hummitzsch, and Janet Ertel chose such nostalgic items as "Moonlight Bay" and "Kentucky's Way of Saying Good-Morning" among their selections, and their delivery was tuneful and artistic to a high degree."

The Chordettes were also busy the following weekend, doing a barber shop show in Minneapolis, Minnesota on Saturday, April 10. The next evening, they were in Three Lakes, Wisconsin, doing a show at the Northernaire, a luxury resort.

On April 1, 1948, the weekly *Three Lakes News* newspaper ran an article about the Chordettes and their upcoming appearance at the Northernaire on the front page of their paper. The article started by calling the Chordettes "One of the finest quartets in the country."

The News went on to say, "Fortunately the girls were able to get to the Northernaire between engagements and will stop at the famous Three Lakes Hotel on their way from Minneapolis, Minn., Sunday afternoon (April 11) and stay the night. In order that residents of this area can enjoy hearing the girls sing, the Northernaire has arranged for a special dinner concert Sunday evening. Those who are unable to come for the dinner are invited to hear the girls sing Sunday evening in the Cy Williams Lounge."

Cy Williams was the person responsible for building the Northernaire and was the owner. But, he had another claim to fame. Williams played 19 seasons of major league baseball, from 1912 to 1930. From 1912 to 1917, he played for the Chicago Cubs and from 1918 to 1930; he played for the Philadelphia Phillies. He also led the National League in home runs, four times. In 1916, during the dead ball era, he led the league with 12 home runs and in 1920, hit 15 home runs to again lead the league. In 1923, he had his career high in home runs with 41 to again lead the league. In 1927, he led the National League with 30 home runs. That same year, Babe Ruth hit 60 home runs to lead the American League.

The article concluded with a six-paragraph history of the Chordettes. Also, in the same issue, was a large ad announcing in large letters, "The Chordettes America's Finest Girls' Quartette will sing in the Marine Dining Room, Sunday evening, April 11 and in the Cy Williams Lounge later that same night. Reservations for deluxe dinners at $3.50 per plate are now being accepted for this special occasion." The same article and ad also appeared in the April 8th edition of the Three Lakes News.

After their shows at the Northernaire, the Chordettes had almost two weeks off. On April 23, according to the *Sheboygan Press*, they spent the day in Chicago, before continuing to Dayton, Ohio, where they performed at the Memorial Hall, as part of a parade of barbershop quartets concert, sponsored by the Dayton chapter of the S.P.E.B.S.Q.S.A.

The Chordettes finished April of 1948, performing in Milwaukee, on the 30th. Two weeks later, they were in the Upper Peninsula of Michigan. On May 14, they were doing a barbershop show in Marquette, Michigan. The next day, they were performing in a barbershop show in Iron Mountain, Michigan.

On the 21st of May, they were in the Lower Peninsula of Michigan, performing in Holland, Michigan. This was the second year in a row that they were in Holland, Michigan for the Holland Tulip Time Music Festival. The Chordettes did not get much of a chance to rest, as the Chordettes were the final act in the festival, which started at 8:15 p.m. The next day (May 22), they had to do a barbershop show in Rochester, New York, followed by shows in Syracuse,

Post card image from Holland, Michigan's Tulip Festival in 1946.

New York on the 23rd, 24th, and 25th. Tickets for the Chordettes show at the Lincoln Auditorium of the Central High School on the 25th were $1.00, tax included. By this time, the ads for the Chordettes appearances were referring to them as the "World's Championship Female Barbershop Quartet."

The *Sheboygan Press* reported in their May 28th issue, "On Thursday afternoon (May 27), the Chordettes returned to the city after a week's trip. The quartet was in Holland, Mich., for the Tulip Festival, and from there went to Rochester, N.Y., for a barbershop parade. The group then went to Syracuse, N.Y., for a series of radio shows, and Wednesday evening appeared at a barbershop parade in Kenosha (Wisconsin)."

After this whirlwind schedule, the Chordettes took a week of vacation before heading to Oklahoma City, Oklahoma, for the International Convention of the Society for the Preservation and Encouragement of Barber Shop Quartet Singing in America. Even though the Chordettes were from Sheboygan, they were not the top story relating to Sheboygan at the convention. At this convention, Ginny's father, King Cole of Sheboygan, was elected president of the S.P.E.B.S.Q.S.A. He would be re-elected the following year. But, the *Sheboygan Press* would not report on this honor, until August 23, more than a month after it occurred.

On June 11, after King Cole was elected president of the S.P.E.B.S.Q.S.A., the Oklahoma City newspaper ran a 19-paragraph article, including a photo, on King's wife, Kay. The article started by saying, "One of the happiest women in Oklahoma City Friday was Mrs. O.H. "King" Cole, Sheboygan, Wis., when she heard her husband had been elected international president of the Society for the Preservation and Encouragement of Barber Shop Quartet Singing in America."

"I am more thrilled than if he had been elected president of the United States," Mrs. Cole beamed. "Although it is a hobby with him, King works at being a member of the organization."

"Cole has served as international vice-president the last year and has headed several committees."

"The first lady of SPEBSQSA, her blue eyes sparkling, recounted the story of barbershop singing in the Cole family."

"I met King at the University of Washington, where he was a member of a quartet," she explained. "Then when he took me home to meet his family, the first thing they did was group around the piano for some old fashioned harmony."

"All members of the family, including a married daughter, Virginia, 21, are harmony fans. Virginia and three friends who organized the Chordettes in Sheboygan came along for the tenth annual convention here."

"I have gone to nearly all the conventions and district meetings with my husband," Mrs. Cole said, "and I would rather hear a barber shop quartet, than see a New York stage play. That's how interested I am!"

"She never spends her time during conventions going to picture shows (movies) or reading magazines."

"We have so many friends in the organization and the convention gives us the opportunity for a reunion," she said. "I like to met wives of other barber shoppers, and I particularly enjoyed again meeting Mrs. Turner, wife of the governor."

"Mrs. Cole said she was impressed by Oklahoma because nowhere else had she found the Sooner brand of hospitality and Courtesy."

"When I get to a place with well stocked stores, such as in Oklahoma City, I always do a little shopping," she said, "but if there are any old friends coming in or leaving, King and I make it to the train. Nothing interferes with our renewing old acquaintances on these trips."

"She feels the SPEBSQSA is like no other organization in that she meets persons from all walks of life."

"The democratic principal is certainly carried out with these groups," she explained. "I have listened to many quartets where the town's distinguished doctor stood next to the garbage collector . . and enjoyed it immensely."

"When Mrs. Cole's husband is busy during conventions, she ferrets out the wives of other members for lengthy chats on new songs, arrangements and customers, and every other pie in which the harmony boys have their fingers."

"Even though gardening is my hobby, I think I am just as interested in quartets as King." She continued. She added that most wives are just as enthusiastic as she and that they were 100 percent in attendance here."

"Some of the Coles' best friends are those they met in the harmony organization. Mrs. Cole gave an example of the closeness of these ties."

"Last Sunday, the Stop the Music program called our number. King guessed the title of the song played, and consequently we won a radio console with a record attachment. It had been no more than announced than we began getting congratulatory calls from singers as far away as

Chicago."

The article concluded, "Concluding there is no other entertainment which has given her and King such pleasure, Mrs. Cole said, "Our home is always open to barbershop quartets. We love the musical harmony plus fellowship we share with the boys when they meet."

In the *Sheboygan Press* of Friday, June 18, 1948, more information was given about the Chordettes time during the S.P.E.B.S.Q.S.A. convention. The Press reported, "The Chordettes, Virginia Cole Osborn, Dorothy Hummitzsch, Janet Buschmann Ertel and Carol Hagedorn, accompanied by Mrs. O.H. King Cole, returned Wednesday from a 10-day trip to Oklahoma City, where they appeared on programs of the international convention of the S.P.E.B.S.Q.S.A. They were the only girls' group on the program given on the capital grounds, and participated in the jamboree Saturday afternoon. Sunday morning, they sang on the breakfast program with the champions. The honor of having been entertained by the state executive, Governor Roy Turner, an ardent barbershopper, and his wife, Saturday evening at dinner was another thrill of their stay in Oklahoma."

Following their trip to Oklahoma City, the Chordettes returned home to Sheboygan for a well-deserved rest. Between June 16 and August 11, a period of seven weeks, the Chordettes only did three shows, and two were close to home and the third one was unplanned. On June 24, the Chordettes traveled to Elkhart Lake, Wisconsin. Elkhart Lake is in the northwestern part of Sheboygan County and today is most known for the Road America racetrack. But, in 1948, Elkhart Lake was known more as a resort town for conventions. In June of 1948, the Wisconsin State Bar Convention was held at the Hotel Schwartz. The *Sheboygan Press*, said about part of this convention, in their Friday, June 25th paper, "A dance at the pavilion at Schwartz' resort, where the convention is being held, was the wind-up of activities Thursday. As entertainers, Bar Association members and their wives, had the Chordettes, Sheboygan's feminine counterpart of a barbershop quartet, and Bob Neller of Appleton, a ventriloquist."

On Friday, July 2, the *Sheboygan Press* reported, "The Chordettes visited in Chicago on Thursday. Members are Virginia Cole Osborn, Janet Buschmann Ertel, Dorothy Hummitzsch and Carol Hagedorn."

On July 13, the Chordettes were in Manitowoc to perform. On July 18, the Chordettes traveled to Oshkosh, Wisconsin for the S.P.E.B.S.Q.S.A. Land O' Lakes district barbershop chorus concert and picnic, which was held at the Oshkosh American Legion clubhouse." The Wisconsin Rapids Daily Tribune newspaper, the next day reported, "The day's activities were climaxed by an impromptu parade of quartets. Appearing on this part of the program were the district champions, the Madison Cardinals, and the Chordettes, girls' quartet from Sheboygan."

The Chordettes vacation ended in August, when they did five shows in five different cities within 10 days. On August 12, when they did a show in Green Bay, followed by a show two days later in Neenah, Wisconsin. The following day, the Chordettes were in Chicago, for a show.

The 22nd of August saw the Chordettes performing in Milwaukee. The day before the Milwaukee show, the Chordettes took part in a party, in Sheboygan, honoring King Cole. The *Sheboygan Press* reported on this celebration in their newspaper of Monday, August 23, 1948. The headline stated, "Barber Shoppers Honor King Cole At Party Saturday Night."

The accompanying article started, "The Sheboygan Chapter of the S.P.E.B.S.Q.S.A., Inc. was host to a party Saturday evening at the Grand Hotel in honor of O.H. King Cole, who was recently elected to the International Presidency of the Barber Shoppers. A buffet luncheon and entertainment was enjoyed during the evening."

"Ed Heidenreiter, vice president of the Sheboygan Chapter, gave the address of welcome in the absence of President J.A. Sampson who underwent an emergency appendicitis operation on Friday afternoon. He introduced Henry Beyer who acted as master of ceremonies for the remainder of the evening."

"The Sheboygan chorus, under the direction of Henry Beyer, opened the program with three songs and during the program, the Sheboygan Troubadours, Pigeon River Four, Harmonomaniacs and the Chordettes also performed." (Note: the Pigeon River flows through the northern part of Sheboygan.)

The article continued, "Speakers included Ed Smith of Wayne, Mich., second vice president of the International and president of the Michigan district; Jerry Beeler of Evansville, Ind., first vice president of the International and director of the 125-voice Evansville Chorus; Carroll Adams of Detroit, Mich., International secretary: John Means of Manitowoc, Land O' Lakes district president; and O.H. King Cole, International president. The Sheboygan chorus concluded the program and the luncheon and a social hour was enjoyed by the guests and members of the Sheboygan Chapter and their wives."

"A meeting of international and local officers was held during the afternoon at the home of O.H. King Cole, with John Heronymus in the role of chef at the outdoor fry." The article concluded by listing the various guests at the fry including the Chordettes.

The next day (August 22), the Chordettes were in Milwaukee, Wisconsin, where they sang as part of Barbershop Harmony Day at the Wisconsin Centennial Exposition. This was in honor of the 100th anniversary of Wisconsin becoming a state in 1848.

On August 25, the *Sheboygan Press* ran an article on their opinion page about King Cole, under the headline, "A Great Day For The King" and went on to say:

"Saturday was a big day in the life of the Barber Shoppers, and more especially of O.H. King Cole, International President, when the local chapter honored his election to the highest office within the gift of the organization."

"During the evening the chapter held a reception at the Grand Hotel at which First Vice President, Jerry Beeler, Evansville, Indiana; Edward Smith, Wayne, Michigan, Second Vice President; and Carroll Adams, Detroit, Michigan, International Secretary, were present to honor their chief."

"While it was an affair strictly within the chapter, still we feel warranted in breaking faith to the extent of recounting the tributes that were paid Mr. Cole. He was referred to by the three executives as one of the hardest working presidents that this international body has had in years past. He has built up more chapters, not only in the United States, but in our possessions such as Alaska and Hawaii than any previous executive." (Note: at this time, Alaska and Hawaii were not states, but United States territories. They did not become states until 1959.) "From one end of the country to the other, the barber shop quartettes and choruses have become the backbone of entertainment features."

"During the evening, the Sheboygan chorus rendered three songs and the Sheboygan Troubadors and Chordettes also were features on the program. The latter is another achievement of President Cole and the four young women: Virginia Cole Osborn, Carol Hagedorn, Janet Buschmann Ertel, and Dorothy Hummitzsch, are winning fame for Sheboygan. They have appeared on some of the biggest radio programs and are scheduled ahead for the coming year as topliners in numerous cities throughout the country."

The article ended, "President King Cole deserves all the credit that is coming to him for his

The Northernaire Resort, located in Three Lakes, Wisconsin is shown above in a postcard view from the mid 1950's. This building was built in 1947 and the Chordettes performed in this building on April 11, 1948. (From the author's collection)

outstanding work as International President."

In the above paragraph, it says that the Chordettes "have appeared on some of the biggest radio programs" but TV programs are not listed. The reason for this was that there were not many people with TV sets and very few TV stations. A newspaper article from July 1948, explained the new thing called television. During World War II, which ended in 1945, there were a total of six TV television stations in the country and they were all experimental. By 1948, when this article was written, there were only about 30 television stations in the country and another 100 had been approved by the Federal Communication Commission to start in business.

The article also reported, "Television got off to a kind of stumbling start right after the war for several reasons. This is one of them:

Manufacturers of television receiving sets were a little about making them until a number of television stations were operating. And the people who wanted to set up television broadcasting stations were a little nervous about starting till enough people had receiving sets. This problem has been ironed out."

Next the article mentioned that in the United States there were about 350 thousand TV sets. These television sets ranged in price from $169.00 to $2,500, not counting the cost to install them. A television set was very expensive in 1948, especially when you consider that the minimum wage was 40 cents an hour. In 1948, the most expensive Chevrolet was the Fleetmaster convertible, which cost $1,750 or $750 less than a top of the line television. Also, in 1948, all TV sets were black and white. There were no color TVs.

The article also told about other problems facing television in its early days. According to the article, "There are four television broadcasting networks, but most of their network operations are being done up and down the heavily-populated part of the Atlantic Coast. There is no transcontinental network and won't be for some time."

"This will explain the problems of getting a coast-to-coast network going. There are three ways of sending television broadcasts:

(1) Direct television. This is when a station broadcasts a television show, but can only do so in its own local area. So it doesn't travel far.

(2) Piping television through a special conductor in a cable from a station in one city to a station in another city. Then the receiving station re-broadcasts the show, but only locally. This is called the co-axial method, so named because the cable through which the television conductor runs is called a co-axial cable.

Shown here is a photo of O.H. "King" Cole and his wife, Kay. In June 1948, King Cole was elected president of the S.P.E.B.S.Q.S.A. (Photo courtesy of Kay Hunt)

(3) Micro-wave broadcasting. Television waves, sent through the air, are picked up and relayed by a series of special relay stations. These are really pumping stations, probably 30 miles apart, which push the micro-waves from one to the other until they reach a regular television broadcasting station, which then sends the show out in its own area."

"Co-axial cables for television are being laid across the country now, and pumping stations are being built in certain areas. But it will be some years, probably at least two, before there is any coast-to-coast broadcast of a television show"

"For example:

Right now, (1948) because of the co-axial or micro-wave system already set up in the area, a televised event can be sent up and down part of the Atlantic seaboard. Which means that the Democratic Convention in Philadelphia next week (July 15, 1948) can be seen simultaneously in Washington D.C. and New York. But people in St. Louis or San Francisco can't see it at the same time. That's because the network hasn't reached that far West."

"People in San Francisco will see it (the Democratic Convention) if films are rushed there by plane and then televised from a San Francisco television station to the people in that area."

The article ended, "Right now alltelevision broadcasts are in black and white. Someday television will be in color. That's being worked on for now. Some time ago, the FCC (Federal

Communication Commission) decided commercial color television wasn't far enough along in its development to okay it for broadcasting. But that will come in time."

On September 7, 1948, the Sheboygan Indians held their annual season ending banquet at the Hotel Foeste in Sheboygan. The Indians played in the Wisconsin State League and were the league champions again. Sheboygan were league champions in three of the six years (1942, 1947, 1948) that the league was in existence. The Sheboygan Indians' manager was Joe Hauser and were a minor league team for the Brooklyn (now Los Angeles) Dodgers.

On September 8, the *Sheboygan Press* ran a lengthy article about the banquet. Part of the article reported, "An appetizing dinner was followed by entertainment, both by the harmony-singing "Chordettes" of Sheboygan, as fine a group of feminine vocalists as can be heard any-where, and by a number of speakers who dwelt on the humorous side of baseball and the serious as well."

On September 15, the *Sheboygan Press* reported, "Rotarians Hold Regular Meeting At Girl's Camp." The beginning of the article stated, "Sheboygan Rotarians held their meeting Monday evening (September 14) at the Girl Scout Camp near Crystal Lake as guests of the Girl Scouts and the Girl Scout Council. Ninety members attended." Crystal Lake is in the northwestern part of Sheboygan County.

"Evening activities included a tour of the camp, which is located on 200 acres of wooded hills south of Crystal Lake, a dinner at the main lodge, entertainment by the Sheboygan Chordettes, and discussions of camp life."

The Chordettes also stayed close to home for their third appearance of September 1948. On Saturday, September 18, the Chordettes took part in the Sheboygan Chapter of the Society for the Preservation and Encouragement of Barber Shop Quartet Singing in America's third annual Parade of Quartets, which was again held at North High School. Tickets were $1.80, which included tax.

After the event, the *Sheboygan Press* ran a brief article about the program, which was held before a full house. Part of the article reported, "O.H. King Cole, international president of the SPEBSQSA and master of ceremonies Saturday evening, gave the program continuity with apt comments and droll humor. The audience became participants instead of listeners in a round of community singing of barber shop tunes led by Charles Faulhaber."

Also included with the article were four photos from the evening's entertainment. The four photos showed O.H. King Cole, the Sheboygan Harmomaniacs, the Sheboygan Chorus, and the Chordettes.

On September 25, 1948, King Cole was in Rhinelander, Wisconsin, where more than 200 people were in attendance, as the Rhinelander Chapter of the S.P.E.B.S.Q.S.A. received their charter. This event started at 3:00 in the afternoon with a musical program, dinner, and an "after glow." According to the Rhinelander newspaper, the following day, "During the "after glow" members of the various quartets sang for the fun of it, and not just because they are a scheduled part of the program."

The newspaper also listed the various quartets that took sang during the afternoon program. The first quartet listed were "The Chordettes, well-known girls' group from Sheboygan."

On Wednesday, September 29, the *Sheboygan Press* reported, "On Tuesday, the Chordettes, Virginia Cole Osborn, Dorothy Hummitzsch, Janet Buschmann Ertel, and Carol Hagedorn, left for Spencer, Iowa, where they will sing at a Barbershop Parade. On Thursday evening (September 30), they will be featured at a benefit concert in Manitowoc (Wisconsin), and their next appearance will be at Lafayette, Ind., over the weekend" (October 2). This meant that they were doing three shows in four days in three different states.

Also, on September 29, the newspaper in Spencer, Iowa ran two articles. One article carried the headline, "Season's Song Highlight At High School Tonight" and reported on the second annual parade held by the Spencer Chapter of the S.P.A.B.S.Q.S.A. Part of the article stated, "and as special guests of the men, the Chordettes of Sheboygan, Wis.-an all-girls quartets, considered one of the top girls' quartets in the country, having sung with Fred Waring."

The second article was five paragraphs long under the headline, "Parade Preview Given This Noon." The headline was a bit misleading as all five paragraphs were about the Chordettes. The article stated, "A short preview of the Barbershoppers' Parade in the form of an impromptu number by the Chordettes, during lunch at the Tangney Hotel this noon, gave promise to a big evening at the high school auditorium."

"The Chordettes, a girls barbershop quartet imported from Sheboygan, Wis., for tonight's affair, are the only nationally known girls barbershop group in America."

"The girls have appeared throughout the east and Midwest during the past two years as a top attraction at parades and other special functions. They have made two network broadcasts with Fred Waring as well as many other radio appearances."

"Two of the girls, Virginia Osborn and Janet Ertel are married. Dorothy Hummitzsch and Carol Hagedorn are single. Miss Hagedorn, newest member of the group joined the group when their original baritone married and left Sheboygan."

"Judging from the reception their rendition of "A Night in June" received from barbershoppers lunching with the girls today, they are due for a great reception tonight."

The next day, the Spencer newspaper reported that over 1,400 people attended the program. About the Chordettes, the newspaper said, "The Chordettes, the sugar and spice of the show and mighty fine looking young women, received a royal welcome from the moment they came into town. At an informal noon luncheon for them at the Tangney Hotel, they answered a request to sing and soon had everyone within range clustered around to hear. On the night show, wearing black ballerina skirts with a bit of red plaid petticoat showing and with blouses of the plaid, they made a cheery entrance with "Kentucky's Way of Saying Good Morning!" Then, "Beautiful Isle of Make Believe" and "Got No Time" won more applause. They closed bringing down a bid laugh with an East Side comic, "Thirty Thurd and Thurd." No wonder Fred Waring wanted them on his program."

The article ended with a comment about the end of the show. According to the newspaper, "And then the grand finale: the big chorus and all of the quartets on the stage (with the Atomic Bums juggling positions to get next to the pretty Chordettes) ended the show with "The Old Sings."

On October 2, 1948, the Chordettes were in Lafayette, Indiana for a barbershop show held at Jefferson High School. The Tippecanoe County Chapter of S.P.E.B.S.Q.S.A. presented this show in co-operation with the Band and Orchestra Parents' Club of Jefferson High School. "Proceeds will go towards the school band and other musical organizations to finance trips to school music contests," according to the Lafayette Journal and Courier newspaper. Before the show, the newspaper described the Chordettes as "Probably the most outstanding women's group of its kind in the country. The famous girls' quartet to appear is "The Chordettes," of Sheboygan, Wis., which has won many local laurels. This group will feature "Sweet Sixteen," "Nothing Could be Finer," "Thoity-Thoid and Thoid," and other songs."

Shown here is a postcard view of the Grand Hotel in Sheboygan. On August 21, this hotel was host to a party honoring O.H. "King" Cole. This hotel was located on the south side of Center Avenue, between 7th and 8th Streets. (From the author's collection)

On October 4, 1948, the *Sheboygan Press*, hometown newspaper of the Chordettes ran an article, under the headline, "Barbershoppers Doff Hats to Sheboygan Chordettes." The article included a photo of the Chordettes and a smaller photo of King Cole. The unusual thing about this article was that it was the first article in the *Sheboygan Press* that gave any information on the success of the Chordettes, and most of what was in the article was copied word for word from articles that appeared in other newspapers more than one year earlier. The Chordettes were formed two years and two months earlier in August 1946, but this article reported, "The "Chordettes" came into being a year ago last August," showing that very little effort was made to update the article.

October 12 saw the Chordettes in Milwaukee for a show, followed two days later by a show in their hometown of Sheboygan, on the 14th. Two days later, they were in Escanaba, Michigan for a show, followed by another show, two days later in Beaver Dam, Wisconsin, on the 18th. On October 23, the Chordettes were in Chicago, Illinois for a barbershop show.

The Chordettes ended the month of October in Wisconsin Rapids for a barber shop show on the 30th. Three weeks before this show, the Wisconsin Rapids Daily Tribune was already running ads for this barbershop program, named "Moonlight Bay" to be held at the Lincoln Fieldhouse in Wisconsin Rapids. The most expensive tickets were $1.50 plus tax (remember this was when the minimum wage was 40 cents an hour). The Chordettes were the second act listed in the ads and were described as "Four girls as lovely as their voices singing the songs you like to hear."

On October 23, 1948, the same Wisconsin Rapids newspaper ran an article under the headline, "Page Sweet Adeline." The article reported about a woman from Chicago and her efforts to join the men's only S.P.E.B.S.Q.S.A. group. Even the Chordettes were mentioned in the article. The

In August 1948, O.H. King Cole was honored in Sheboygan for being elected president of S.P.E.B.S.Q.S.A. (Photo courtesy of Kay Hunt)

article said, "According to a recent news release from Chicago, some gal is not only pining to join the Society for the Preservation and Encouragement of Barber Shop Quartet Singing in America, Inc., but she has taken concrete steps towards this objective and is suing the organization for entrance. Spokesmen for the society have retaliated with the word that they will contest the case to defend the stronghold, which they describe as housing the art of harmonizing, "the last vestige of masculine rights."

"In case there are those unfamiliar with the primary rule of the SPEBSQSA, no female is allowed on the membership roster. The Chicago girl claims that singing is not strictly a hobby for males and adds that women also like to indulge in a little harmonizing once in a while too. In addition, she might point out that even the barber chair is no longer a haven for men because in some localities, the girls are putting their money on the line for a close trim of the curly locks."

The article continued, "But back for a few more digs at the poor men who are trying to defend their organization against the entrance of women. People who attend the (barber shop) Parade, October 30, will be interested to note that while the barber shoppers are limiting their membership, they along with the audience, will be very enthusiastic about one of the program numbers which happens to be the Chordettes."

The next paragraph was about the Chordettes and said, "These four young ladies from Sheboygan have developed their own versions of barber shop harmony and have gained considerable recognition in many states. They are so well known in fact that they have appeared as guest artists with Fred Waring. Official Barber Shoppers? Oh no! Just to show how rigidly the rules are enforced, the pappy (father) of one of the girls is old King Cole himself, international president of the SPEBSQSA, and even that didn't make a particle of difference to the board of directors."

No further articles were found about this lawsuit. But, one clue about the outcome is that more than 55 years after this lawsuit was filed, the SPEBSQSA is still for men only.

Following the barbershop show on the 30th, the Wisconsin Rapids newspaper reported, "A pleasing interlude in the parade of male quartets was the appearance of the Chordettes, four young women from Sheboygan who have not only entered the field of barbershop harmonizing, but have sung in many parades throughout the country. Dorothy Hummitzsch, Virginia Osborn, Carol Hagcdorn, and Janet Ertel presented a number of selections, which included, "I'd Love to Live in Loveland" and "Me Too." The girls were attired identically in checkered Gibson girl blouses and black skirts which featured checked frills at the hemline."

The first appearance by the Chordettes for November 1948, occurred on the 3rd in Fond du Lac, Wisconsin. They appeared at Bernwood Hall for a meeting of Kingsbury Brewery dealers from Sheboygan and Manitowoc.

Three days later, the Chordettes were in Mississippi for their first appearance in that state, appearing in Jackson, Mississippi. The day after their appearance in Jackson, they were doing a show in Chicago, on the 7th. The *Sheboygan Press* reported in their Wednesday, November 10th edition, "The Chordettes returned Tuesday from Jackson, Miss. where they had been attending a Barbershop parade. The group flew to Chicago from Jackson, en route home. Members are Mrs. Virginia Osborn, Miss Dorothy Hummitzsch, Miss Carol Hagedorn, and Mrs. Janet Ertel. The latter had her daughter, Jackie with her." Jackie at this time was eight years old.

November 9th saw the Chordettes in Manitowoc and that weekend found them in Milwaukee for a Barbershop parade. The following weekend, November 20, the Chordettes were in Louisville, Kentucky for another Barbershop show at the Memorial Auditorium.

After the show, the Courier-Journal newspaper in Louisville said about the Chordettes, "Honest-to-goodness pulchritude hit the stage with the appearance of the only female quartet, the Chordettes, of Sheboygan, Wis. Dressed in bright taffeta, they received a good hand for "Me Too."

The Chordettes ended November with another appearance in Chicago on the 26th and 27th, followed by an appearance in their hometown of Sheboygan, on the 29th.

On December 2, the Chordettes did a show in Milwaukee, followed by a stretch of 11 days off. During these days off, the Chordettes spent one day posing for pictures, in where else, but a barbershop. The barbershop was Al Schroeder's Barber Shop, which was located on the southwest corner of North 14th Street and Michigan Avenue, in Sheboygan. The building had originally been part of Born's Park in Sheboygan

Following their 11 days off, the Chordettes traveled to Madison, Wisconsin for a barber shop show on December 13. Four days later, on the 17th, the Chordettes were in Chicago for a show. The *Sheboygan Press* reported in their Saturday, December 18th, edition, "The Chordettes were in Chicago on Friday, where they appeared at a banquet, and today are in Milwaukee, singing for another banquet."

On Wednesday evening, December 22, at 7:30, the Sheboygan Barber Shop Chorus under the direction of Henry Beyer presented a half-hour concert of Christmas music over radio station WHBL. The program originated from the First Methodist Church in Sheboygan. The Sheboygan Troubadours, the Harmomaniacs, and the Chordettes assisted the chorus. Immediately after the program, the Chorus and quartets went to Sheboygan's Fountain Park Band Stand, where the program was repeated over loud speakers for the late Christmas shoppers who were unable to hear it on the radio. The Chordettes sang "Christmas Island" for their part of the program.

The Chordettes finished 1948 in Chicago, on New Years Eve, for a show at the Drake Hotel. This was the Chordettes fourth appearance in Chicago in less than three months.

On January 5, 1949, the *Sheboygan Press* reported in their personal column, "On Sunday, Otis Osborn, Miss Karen Vollrath, and Martin Widdifield motored back to Madison (Wisconsin) to resume their studies at the University of Wisconsin. The first mentioned had spent the holidays with his wife and son at the home of her parents, Mr. and Mrs. O.H. King Cole, 2727 Highland Terrace." Otis Osborn was married to Jinny (Virginia) of the Chordettes.

The next day, January 6th, would be the first 1949 public appearance for the Chordettes. This show was in their hometown of Sheboygan. Unknown to the Chordettes at the time was that by the end of the year, none of them would be living in Sheboygan anymore.

FOUNTAIN PARK, SHEBOYGAN, WIS.

During the evening of December 22, 1948, the Chordettes took part in an outdoor Christmas concert, designed to entertain holiday shoppers. The group sung from the bandstand in Sheboygan's Fountain Park. In the background on the left is the Sheboygan Clinic. The Foeste Hotel is seen in the background on the right. (From the author's collection)

On Saturday, January 15, 1949, the *Sheboygan Press* reported, On Friday, the Chordettes left for Toledo, Ohio, where they are appearing at the Mid-Winter Barbershop convention. They will then go on to Flint and Detroit, Mich."

January 15th saw the Chordettes in Toledo, Ohio for a barbershop parade in the Museum of Art Peristyle. Before this event, the Toledo newspaper had a four-paragraph article about the show. The Chordettes were not named in the article. The final paragraph of the article reported, "A 30-voice chorus of the local organization, which will include the chapter's four quartets, will participate in the program as will a woman's quartet from Sheboygan, Wis." While the Chordettes were not named in the article, a photo of them accompanied the article, under the title "Glamour."

Also, on January 15, the same newspaper reported on "How the Chordettes keep slim. At the Buckeye Breakfast, so many people came to talk to them that they had no opportunity to eat before taking their turn on stage. So many encores that breakfast was cold and appetites gone when they finally returned to their table."

Monday, January 17th saw the Chordettes in Flint, Michigan, home of General Motors, for a program. The Flint Industrial Executives Club held the program at the IMA Auditorium. A few days before, the Flint newspaper said about the Chordettes, "The girl singers have gained fame in a short time. They hail from Sheboygan, Wis., and are considered one of the first girls' quartets in America in their specialty."

The following day, on the 18th, the Chordettes were in Detroit. Their next shows were back in their hometown of Sheboygan on the 25th and 26th of January. On the 29th, the Chordettes traveled to northern Wisconsin for a show in Rhinelander. For their final show of January 1949, the Chordettes went back to Detroit, Michigan, where they had appeared less than two weeks earlier.

February was a very busy month for the Chordettes as they did 12 shows in 28 days. Their first show of the month was in Evansville, Indiana on February 2. On January 26, 1949, the Evansville newspaper printed a photo of the Chordettes and reported, "The Chordettes, one of the nation's outstanding quartets and winner of the 5th annual Parade of Harmony in Chicago last October, are coming to Evansville to sing at the Sales Convention of Sterling Beer Distributors, February 1 and 2. They will also be heard on (radio station) WGBF next Wednesday, February 2, at 11:30 a.m."

The next day, the Chordettes were in Chicago for a show. Two days later they were back in Michigan for a show in Lansing, on the 5th. February 9th saw the Chordettes again in Detroit, for their third appearance in that city in less than a month. Abraham Lincoln's birthday, February 12, saw the Chordettes back in Wisconsin, for a show in Milwaukee.

On February 15, 1949, the *Sheboygan Press* reported, " Mr. and Mrs. Ray Wagman left today to be gone until the latter part of March. Last week, they were in Detroit, Mich. Attending the national convention of Club Managers, and were delighted to have the Chordettes of this city entertain the group at a formal dinner-dance on the last evening of the convention. The Wagmans manage Pine Hills Country Club."

Three days later, on Friday, February 18, the *Sheboygan Press* announced, "The Chordettes left Thursday for Wichita Falls, Tex., where they will appear on a barbershop parade. From there they will fly to Galveston, for another performance. The group plans to be gone for a week. Members of the singing quartette are Virginia Cole Osborn, Dorothy Hummitzsch, Janet Buschmann Ertel and Carol Hagedorn."

The Chordettes appeared in Wichita Falls on February 18 and 19, for the second annual barbershop parade in that city. But, the Chordettes had been featured in the local Wichita Falls newspaper way back on January 9. Their photo appeared under the title, "Show Stoppers." The accompanying article said about the Chordettes, "Considered the finest girls' quartet in America, singing the tricky barbershop arrangements of favorite tunes, "The Chordettes" literally stopped the show every time they swung out of the wings to the mike. They've been singing together only a little more than two years, but they've already had top-billing at SPEBSQSA parades throughout the entire nation."

"The captivating harmonizers have had guest appearances with the Fred Waring Pennsylvanians, the Breakfast Hour, and with the Olson & Johnson Show in New York. "The Chordettes" started when Virginia Cole Osborn, daughter of President King Cole of the International SPEBSQSA, collected three of her friends, borrowed her dad's book of songs, and went at it. They clicked. Theirs was a natural blend, and within a few weeks, their unending "parade" was under way."

Following their show in Wichita Falls, the gals traveled to Galveston, Texas. The Galveston newspaper of Tuesday, February 22 reported, "H.S. Autrey, president of the Galveston-Houston Brewery, was host to the brewery's 240 salesmen and their wives at a dinner at the Hotel Buccaneer Monday Night."

The Chordettes, one of the nation's outstanding quartets and winner of the 5th annual Parade of Harmony in Chicago last October, are coming to Evansville to sing at the Sales Convention of Sterling Beer Distributors, February 1 and 2.

They will also be heard on WGBF next Wednesday, February 2, at 11:30 a.m. The girls, left to right, Virginia Cole, Dottie Hummitzsch, Carol Hagedorn and Janet Ertel.

The above photo of the Chordettes appeared in an Evansville, Indiana newspaper on January 26, 1949, for their appearance there on February 2. Notice that Virginia (Ginny) is identified by her maiden name. (Photo courtesy of Dorothy Schwartz)

"Mr. Autrey arranged for a fast moving floor show to follow the dinner, and, as a last-minute surprise, for the Chordettes of Sheboygan, Wis., only feminine barbershop quartet in the country, to sing. The girls, Mrs. Jinny Osborn, Janet Ertel, Dorothy Hummitzsch and Carol Hagedorn, are making only two appearances in Texas this spring. They sang at Wichita Falls Saturday and plan to fly back to Sheboygan Tuesday."

The Chordettes finished February 1949, with appearances in two cities that they had been to earlier in the month. The *Sheboygan Press* of Saturday, February 26, stated, The Chordettes were in Chicago Friday evening, and are in Detroit, Mich., today. They performed at both places."

March of 1949, saw the Chordettes performing in only five cities. They started the month in Pontiac, Michigan on March 5, before returning home to Sheboygan for a show on March 7th. On March 7th, the Sheboygan Kiwanis Club held a district meet at the Hotel Foeste in Sheboygan. "Approximately 150 Kiwanians from Manitowoc, Chilton, Plymouth, West Bend, Kewaskum, and Port Washington were guests of the Sheboygan Kiwanis Club," according to the *Sheboygan Press* of March 8th. After dinner, the speaker was Dr. J.H. Nickell, governor of the Wisconsin-Upper Michigan district of Kiwanis International. He speech was about "the danger of communists actively undermining our way of life in the United States and Wisconsin." After the speech, "Entertainment was provided by the Chordettes, Sheboygan's feminine barbershoppers."

On March 12, the Chordettes were in Oshkosh for a Parade of Quartets program held at the Recreational Gymnasium. The *Oshkosh Daily Northwestern* newspaper described the Chordettes as "Vocalovelies."

The rest of the month saw the Chordettes in Michigan for shows. On the 15th, they were in Grand Rapids and on March 29, 30, 31, and April 1, they were back in Detroit. This was the third month in a row, where the Chordettes final show of the month was in Detroit.

On Friday, April 8th, the Chordettes were in Chicago for a show. The *Sheboygan Press* of that date, stated, "Miss Dorothy Hummitzsch visited in Chicago on Thursday. Today she was joined by the rest of the Chordettes, Virginia Cole Osborn, Janet Buschmann Ertel, and Carol Hagedorn, and the four went on to Lincoln, Neb., where they will appear at a barbershop show over the week end. Last week they were in Detroit, Mich." The show in Lincoln was held at the University of Nebraska Coliseum and was sponsored by the Cornhusker Chapter of SPEBSQSA. Money raised was to go to the Cedars Home For Children. The Chordettes received top billing in the newspaper articles about the show.

One week later, on the evening of Saturday, April 16th, the Chordettes were back in Wisconsin. This time in Waukesha, where they took part in Waukesha's Society for the Preservation and Encouragement of Barbershop Quartet Singing in America's second annual Parade of Barbershop Quartets, which was held in the auditorium of the Waukesha High School. Among the quartets at the show, in addition to the Chordettes, were the Mid-States Four of Chicago, 1948 second place International Champions; the Cardinals of Madison, Wisconsin, 1947 Wisconsin State Champions; Harmony Limited of Green Bay, Wisconsin, 1948 Wisconsin State Champions; Antlers of Flint, Michigan, 1948 Michigan State Champions, plus local quartets.

On April 20, 1949, The *Sheboygan Press* had a small mention about the Chordettes on the Personals page. The newspaper reported, "The Chordettes today are in Vincennes, Indiana, where this evening they will appear on a barbershop show."

Three days later, the Chordettes were back in Manitowoc, Wisconsin for another Barbershop Parade. The *Manitowoc Herald-Times* newspaper reported on the program in their Monday, April 25 edition. Their article started out by saying, "The good citizens of Manitowoc turned out 1,100 strong for the Barbershoppers fourth annual night of harmony, Saturday evening at the Lincoln High School auditorium. A mock television program gave the crowd a peek into the future. A television program, accompanied by noisy commercials on atomic cereal, was presented with the quartets appearing on the screen of the huge television set built on the stage." Unknown to the people in the auditorium that evening, was that in just a few months, one of the acts in the show, would be appearing as regulars in a real television program.

Sheboygan was well represented at this show. The newspaper reported, "The Sheboygan Troubadors appeared for a tryout and entertained with "You'll Never Know What A Good Fellow I've Been" and "Hello, My Ragtime Girl." They were very nattily dressed in tan coats, dark trousers and bright kelley green ties." In the second half of the show, they sang, "Sweetheart of Sigma Chi," Kentucky Babe," and "Sheboygan."

"An added attraction, not on the program, was the appearance of the Four Scholars of Mission House College." Mission House College is now known as Lakeland College and is located about 15 miles northwest of Sheboygan.

"The Chordettes, famous girl's quartet from Sheboygan, gave forth with "Alexander's Ragtime Band" in the television show and reappeared in the second half to sing, "When Day is Done" and "Cruising Down the River." For an encore they sang, Moonlight Bay."

Also taking part in the show was the Manitowoc Choir under the direction of Milton Detjen. As you may recall from earlier in this book, the Chordettes were students of Detjen.

The end of the month found the Chordettes, in where else but Detroit. This was the fourth consecutive month where the Chordettes' final show of the month was in Detroit. They were in

Easy on the Eyes and the Ears!

— The Chordettes —

Just ONE of the many attractions

TOMORROW NIGHT at 8:00 SHARP

Manitowoc Chapter SPEBSQSA's 4th Annual

Night of Harmony

Lincoln High Auditorium

YES—TICKETS AVAILABLE

Reserved seats and a few "rush" seats are still available at Pleuss Realty Co., 807 Jay St. Latecomers will be accommodated at the door up to the capacity of the auditorium.

You can SEE and HEAR from ANYWHERE
in this fine auditorium

DON'T STAY AWAY!

The ad at left was found in the *Manitowoc Herald-Times* newspaper of April 22, 1949. Notice the top where it says, "Easy on the Eyes and the Ears!"

Detroit for appearances April 29 through May 2.

About two-thirds into the article about the Brewers railroad trip, the newspaper reported, "Come noon, some of the boys (Brewers) head for the diner (car) but some sit tight to save meal money. Breakfast was late and dinner will be early. Passing through the club car, the boys hear some close harmony. Four girls are playing cribbage and singing in low voices. We sit down to listen."

"Don't know what we've got here," offers a passenger. "The girls are all dressed alike. Maybe they're with a band."

"The inquiring reporter quickly learns that these are the Chordettes, from Sheboygan, Wis., bound for a barbershop quartet convention at Abilene, Texas. The girls give out with one song after another and everybody sticks around. They're good."

"The Elks ought to get them to sing at the baseball dinner next spring," suggests somebody, and all hands agree. The girls are willing and hand over their manager's card."

On Wednesday, May 11, the *Sheboygan Press* had a brief article about the Chordettes in their newspaper. The Press reported, "The Chordettes returned to the city on Monday, from Abilene, Tex., where they had been since Thursday, appearing on radio shows and giving other performances. Wednesday (May 11), they will be in Detroit, Mich., and Thursday (May 12) in Chicago, to audition for television shows."

Saturday, May 14 saw the Chordettes in Marshfield, Wisconsin for a barbershop parade at Purdy High School Auditorium. One week earlier, the *Marshfield News-Herald* printed an article about the upcoming barbershop parade, under the headline, "Famous 'Chordettes' to Appear Here Next Week." Seven of the nine paragraphs in the article were about the Chordettes. The photo accompanying the article also showed the Chordettes.

After the show, the newspaper reported, "The nationally famous girls quartet from Sheboygan, the Chordettes, lived up to their advance billing as the top girls' quartet in America by giving out with a slate of songs that mixed popular hits of today with old time favorites like "Alexander's Ragtime Band." Over 750 people attended this show, which was the first annual parade of barbershop quartets sponsored by the Marshfield Chapter of SPEBSQSA. Also in-

54

cluded were two photos. One showed the Chordettes with the caption, "Good Looking Too. The Chordettes as they appeared Saturday night at the Marshfield SPEBSQSA parade, proved just as nice to look at as they are to listen to. The girls, along with the Troubadours were among the eight quartets that presented a pleasant two-hour session of barbershop singing at the Willard D. Purdy auditorium. Both of the quartets hail from Sheboygan." The Troubadors were also pictured under the Chordettes photo.

News on the Chordettes for the next few months was hard to find, as newspaper articles were unavailable. The remainder of May found the Chordettes in performing in Milwaukee on the 19th and in Wauwatosa, Wisconsin on the 21st.

The Chordettes did not have many show dates in June, but they did a lot of traveling for the shows they did have. They were in Kenosha, Wisconsin on the 8th, and the next day, June 9th, found the Chordettes in Buffalo, New York. They stayed in Buffalo, making appearances through the 12th. June 15, found the Chordettes back in the city that was becoming their second home, as they were again in Detroit. Two days later, they were back in Wisconsin, for a show in Madison.

The Chordettes finished the month in Kentucky. *The Sheboygan Press* of Tuesday, June 21, 1949, reported, "The Chordettes left Monday evening for Louisville, Ky., where they will be until Saturday, when they will go to Frankfort, Ky., for another appearance. Members are Virginia Cole Osborn, Dorothy Hummitzsch, Janet Buschmann Ertel, and Carol Hagedorn."

The twelfth of July found the Chordettes in Flint, Michigan for a show, followed the next day with a show in Chicago. On July 28, the Chordettes were in Kalamazoo, Michigan, before returning home to Wisconsin for a show, close to home on July 30 in Kohler, Wisconsin. The village of Kohler borders the city of Sheboygan.

On July 14, 1949, *The Kohlerian* newspaper featured a photo of the Chordettes under the heading, "CHORDETTES TO APPEAR HERE." The article stated, "On Saturday, July 30, the KWA (Kohler Workers Association) is sponsoring its annual open-to-the-public, day-and-night picnic at the Kohler ball park. The official opening is at 10:00 A.M. and the Picnic Committee predicts that, providing we have good weather, this year's outdoor festival of fun and frolic will be the biggest ever."

"On this gala-day fun is promised everyone-young and old alike…Ferris Wheel…Chair-O-Plane…Merry-Go-Round…Kiddie Autos…Miniature Train…Ponies…Game of Skill…Prize Contests for the Kiddies…Novelties…Fishpond…Photo Gallery…Ice Cream…Candy…Popcorn…Gum…Peanuts…Lunches…Drinks for Young and Old…Free Vaudeville (6 acts)…Free Dancing."

"Included in the high-class vaudeville program are the CHORDETTES, Sheboygan's nationally famous girl barbershop quartet, appearing through the courtesy of the Kingsbury Breweries Company. This special, top-notch attraction, highly acclaimed at its every appearance throughout the country, is one that nobody can afford to miss. And it's for free, too."

The remainder of the article was about something equally important for a picnic in the Sheboygan area. The article continued, "And what's more, this year's beer bar (Yep! Ten-cent beer in 7-ounce bottles!) will for the first time be housed in a monstrous 40 x 100 ft. tent. So, no matter how hot the weather may be, you will be able to drink in comforting shade, beer cooled to just the right temperature."

"Remember the day and date: Saturday, July 30."

"Remember the time: 10:00 A.M. to 1:00 A.M. the following day."

On August 23, 1949, the *Sheboygan Press* reported on the Chordettes activities, saying, "The Chordettes returned last Wednesday from appearing at a show in Asheville, North Carolina, and then drove back with John Ertel, husband of one of the group, going through the Smoky Mountains and other spots of interest enroute home. The four then went to Ashland, Wis., for a three-day stay. On Friday the singers will leave for Watch Hill, Rhode Island, where they will appear at a wedding luncheon and reception, and then will be in New York and New Jersey for another week. Members are Virginia Cole Osborn, Dorothy Hummitzsch, Janet Buschmann Ertel and Carol Hagedorn."

The Rhode Island wedding and trip to New York turned out to be the start of something special for the Chordettes. In a letter dated, October 17, 1949, the Chordettes' Business Manager, Clara Weber, had this to say about their experiences on this trip. Weber wrote, "The "Chordettes" were filling an engagement in Rhode Island-- when they decided to return home via New York to renew some old acquaintances. One of these acquaintances, whose company had engaged the "Chordettes" to sing at some of their sales meetings, had contact with a Godfrey Talent Scout, and was able to arrange an audition on September 5th. The girls felt that if they were fortunate enough to be selected to appear on the Talent Scout Program, the attendant publicity would be very helpful in the acquisition of additional singing dates, and since the girls had decided to make singing their career instead of just a hobby, this opportunity was not to be overlooked."

"After the audition, they were leaving the Studio with the feeling that they apparently had missed their chance, when a voice came out of the loud speaker asking them to stand by for further instructions. They were then informed that they should be in New York on September 26th to appear on the first Talent Show of the new season and which was to be televised."

The Chordettes returned to Sheboygan to practice for the show. But, they also made one appearance in Sheboygan. On September 17, the Sheboygan Chapter of SPEBSQSA held their fourth Parade of Quartets, which was again held at North High School.

After the show, the *Sheboygan Press* reported in their September 19th newspaper, "The audience suffered not a bored moment from the time the Four Corners of Eau Claire, tripped onto the stage in white togas and other accouterments of Roman dress, until Sheboygan's lady barbershoppers, the Chordettes, brought evening gown glamour to the platform."

Later the same article added, "The Chordettes, especially sweet and winsome by contrast with the raucous Carpenter Brothers, were the last quartet on the scheduled program. The Chordettes, already known throughout the country, are Virginia Cole Osborn, tenor; Janet Ertel, bass; Carol Hagedorn, baritone; and Dorothy Hummitzsch, lead. They received a big ovation from the audience with "Alexander's Ragtime Band," "Cruising Down the River," "Night in June," and "Ballin' the Jack." One week later, on September 26th, the Chordettes would be singing "Ballin' the Jack" on a nationwide TV show.

After the show, the *Sheboygan Press* reported in their September 19th newspaper, "The audience suffered not a bored moment from the time the Four Corners of Eau Claire, tripped onto the stage in white togas, and other accouterments of Roman dress, until Sheboygan's lady barbershoppers, the Chordettes, brought evening gown glamour to the platform.

Later the same article added, "The Chordettes, especially sweet and winsome by contrast with the raucous Carpenter Brothers, were the last quartet on the scheduled program. The Chordettes, already known throughout the country, are Virginia Cole Osborn, tenor; Janet Ertl, bass; Carol Hagedorn, baritone; and Dorothy Hummitzsch, lead. They received a big ovation from the audience with "Alexander's Ragtime Band, " "Cruising Down the River," "Night in June," and "Ballin the Jack." One week later, on September 26th, the Chordettes would be singing "Ballin the Jack" on a nationwide TV show.

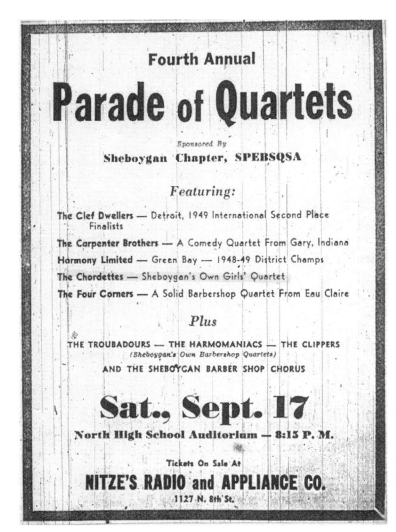

This ad appeared in the *Sheboygan Press* for the fourth annual Sheboygan SPEBSQSA Parade of Harmony. This turned out to be the Chordettes last appearance in Sheboygan before hitting the big time, nine days later.

Above: Eighth Street between New York and Center. West side of the street. The Bank of Sheboygan, Greek Revival in style, was built in 1910 for $80,192.

Below: Citizen's Bank, architecturally much like the Bank of Sheboygan, designed by W.C. Weeks, it opened in March 1910. Citizens Bank merged with the Bank of Sheboygan in 1955 and moved into the new Citizens Bank of Sheboygan, located on the northeast corner of Seventh Street and Wisconsin Avenue in 1957.

CHAPTER 4

THE ARTHUR GODFREY YEARS

1949 TO 1953

On Monday, September 26, 1949, the Chordettes appeared on the Arthur Godfrey Talent Scouts program. It was the first show of the new TV season and Godfrey had just returned from a one-month, 18,000-mile tour of South America, as a guest of Captain Eddie Rickenbacker. Rickenbacker was president and general manager of Eastern Airlines. During the 1920s, Rickenbacker was the head of a car company, which included a car named after him and during World War I, he was an ace, having shot down 26 enemy planes in only two months. The format of the show was that there would be four different acts that would compete against each other and the winner would win a chance to perform on the Arthur Godfrey Radio and TV shows for the next three days.

After the opening of the show, Godfrey took his seat at his desk, which was covered with Lipton signs and products. Lipton sponsored the Godfrey's shows. The second guest on the show was Ted Rau, who was a Western Electric Plant Inspector from Hasbrouck Heights, New Jersey. The following conversation went on between Rauh and Godfrey:

Godfrey: "Hasbrouck Heights, My hometown. That's where I went to school."

Rau: Everybody talks about it up there, Arthur."

Godfrey: "Why, I paid off all the bills. They don't have to talk anymore. I was nine years in the kindergarten over there. I had a wonderful time."

Godfrey: "Are you married?"

Rau: "Very much, 25 years."

Godfrey: "25 years married. To the same woman?"

Rau: "Same woman."

Godfrey: "Any hobbies?"

Rau: "I sure do."

Godfrey: "What do you do?"

Rau: "Barbershop singing.

Godfrey: "Do you belong to that outfit? What's the name?"

Rau: "S-P-E-B-S-Q-S-A, Incorporated."

Godfrey: "S-P-E-B-S-Q-S-A"

Rau: "Incorporated."

Godfrey, "We gotta put inc. on the end of it."

Godfrey: "I'm a member of that group too!

Rau: "What chapter?"

Godfrey: "Manhattan chapter."

Rau: "That's our largest chapter."

Godfrey: "I never attended any meetings yet. But one day, I'm going to do it. I love to hear you guys sing. Your just wonderful."

Godfrey: "What did you bring for talent? Not a barbershop quartet?"

Rau: "Not a men's barbershop quartet, but a ladies barbershop quartet."

Godfrey: "Go on, a ladies barbershop quartet? Wow, that's wonderful. You mean they use the same techniques, same harmony?"

Rau: "Well, they try to. One of the girls, her father is president of SPEBSQSA, Inc. (Laughter)

Godfrey: "He's the president, right?"

Rau: "That's right."

Godfrey: "Tell me who these girls are. What do they call themselves?"

Rau: "They call themselves, the Chordettes."

Godfrey: "Chordettes?"

Rau: "From Sheboygan, Wisconsin."

Godfrey: "Sheboygan, Wisconsin, my, my, my."

Godfrey: "How did you meet this gang of gals from Sheboygan?"

Rau: "We met them out in Milwaukee." (Laughter) At one of these barbershop quartet affairs. This is strictly a men's organization, understand."

Godfrey: "How did these girls get in there?"

Rau: "Well Ginny found some of her father's music around the house. She got some girls act together and I have them with me here tonight."

Godfrey: "Oh, wonderful. The Chordettes. Let's get them on out here. Have they done anything professionally?"

Rau: "They've toured all over the country, Arthur."

Godfrey: "Good, good, let's get them on out here. The Chordettes. Thank you ever so much, Mr. Rau. We'll have the Lipton spotlight on them right now, the Chordettes.

The Chordettes then sang, "Ballin' the Jack."

After the Chordettes were done singing, Godfrey went right on to the next guest. The final guest of the show was a comedian named Wallace Cox, who would go on to fame as Wally Cox.

After all four acts performed, the audience was able to choose who the winners were for the evening. The Chordettes were judged to have received the loudest applause, using an applause meter.

The next day, Tuesday, September 27, 1949, the Chordettes hometown newspaper, the *She-*

boygan Press, ran a photo and article about them on the first page of the second section. The photo was their standard publicity photo and above the photo, in a box were the words, "Sheboygan Chordettes In National Spotlight." Under the photo, the Press caption stated, "This quartet of Sheboygan girls has come a long way since singing their first time together more than two years ago. Their climb to prominence as one of the outstanding feminine quartets in the country was climaxed last night when they took first place on the popular "Talent Scout" show presented by Arthur Godfrey. They will appear on Godfrey's (radio) morning show on the CBS network each morning this week and will make a television appearance on Wednesday evening."

Next to the photo was an article, topped by the headline, "Chordettes" Take First In Network Talent Scout Show." The accompanying article reported, "A quartet of pretty, talented young ladies from Sheboygan today found themselves basking in the limelight as guest stars on a trio of radio and television shows on national networks." The "Chordettes" answered the knock of opportunity last night when they walked off with first place in the "Talent Scout" program staged by Arthur Godfrey in New York."

"They won the acclaim of a large studio audience and millions of listeners to the network show by singing, "Ballin' the Jack." The girls, including Virginia Cole Osborn, Carol Hagedorn, Janet Buschmann Ertel, and Dorothy Hummitzsch, won first place on the show and with it the right to appear on the Arthur Godfrey morning show on a national network each morning this week."

"This morning they repeated, "Ballin' the Jack" at Godfrey's request and followed with a rendition of "Cruising Down the River." The reception accorded the "Chordettes" prompted Godfrey to invite them to make an appearance on his television show on Wednesday evening."

"Within a matter of minutes following their successful appearance Monday night, a flood of telegrams began to arrive at their homes here bearing congratulatory messages from friends throughout the country."

"The ability of the "Chordettes" has long been recognized in Sheboygan and in many cities in the country where they have appeared on programs staged by the Society for the Preservation and Encouragement of Barbershop Quartet Singing in America. Their success story has paralleled the growth of the S.P.E.B.S.Q.S.A. in Sheboygan and the nation."

"The original "Chordettes" were organized in 1946, but the current group has been together about two years. Since that time, they have made countless appearances in the state and Midwest as well as on radio shows such as the Fred Waring program and Morris B. Saxe's Talent Show in Chicago. On Saturday, the quartet will take part in a Parade of Quartets at Omaha, Neb."

"The fact that two of the quartet members are married and the mothers of a boy (Virginia) and a girl (Janet) has limited their ability to travel throughout the country."

"The group was introduced by Ted Rau of Hashbrouck Heights N.J., on the "Talent Scout" show. Mr. Rau is the tenor of the Garden State quartet, 1946 International S.P.E.B.S.Q.S.A. champions."

It did not take long for at least one Sheboygan business to try to capitalize on the Chordettes success. The same day that the Press reported on their win on the Godfrey Show, the Sheboygan Dry Goods store ran an ad advertising new 16-inch televisions for $399.95. For the TV, a person could pay $10.00 down and make weekly payments as low as $3.50. At the bottom of the ad, in capital letters, was "SEE YOUR LOCAL GIRLS "THE CHORDETTES" ON ARTHUR GODFREY'S TELEVISION PROGRAM, SATURDAY, OCT. 8."

Not to be outdone, the following day's (September 28) edition of the *Sheboygan Press,* contained an ad for Willie's Bar. The top of their ad, said, "Just Installed, NEW CROSLEY TELEVISION, COME OVER." Under this, was a large box in the center of the ad. Inside the box, were the words, "SEE SHEBOYGAN'S OWN **Chordettes On Television Tonight.**"

In 1950, one of the songs on the Chordettes' first album was "Ballin' the Jack" shown above. This was the song they sang on the September 26, 1949 Arthur Godfrey show. (From the author's collection)

It didn't take long for some businesses in Sheboygan to capitalize on the Chordettes appearing on the Arthur Godfrey show. Willie's Bar, located on the northwest corner of North 12th Street and Michigan Avenue, ran this ad in the September 28, 1949 edition of the *Sheboygan Press*. One of the Chordettes, Dorothy, played softball for Willie's Bar and in one game reached base 10 times in 10 plate appearances and scored 10 runs.

The Chordettes prize was to sing on Godfrey's Tuesday, Wednesday, and Thursday radio shows and also his Wednesday evening TV show. But, on Thursday, Godfrey asked the Chordettes to stay around for another day, to also sing on his Friday radio show. The Chordettes and other cast members would do their parts of the show from New York, while Godfrey would be broadcasting his part from Chicago.

Friday, September 30, 1949, again saw the Chordettes with their picture in the *Sheboygan Press*. Only this time, they appeared on the front page, under the headline, "Chordettes Join Godfrey Show." Smaller headlines reported, "Announcement Made By Arthur With A Fine Tribute To The Girls" and "Members Of His Staff Assist And Urge That Sheboygan's Pride Be Made A Part Of Their Daily Show And On Television Each Wednesday Night."

The article that followed and which was one and three quarters long, reported, "Announcement was made this morning by Arthur Godfrey on his morning show over CBS that the Sheboygan Chordettes would be a part of his daily program in the future and appear on his television show on Wednesday nights."

"Mr. Godfrey was broadcasting from Chicago. He said the members of his cast had voluntarily taken a cut in wages so that the Chordettes could be included in the show, inasmuch as the budget had already been set for the year. This fine spirit on the part of the Godfrey cast is not only a wonderful tribute to themselves, but to our Sheboygan Chordettes as well." (The *Sheboygan Press* liked to refer to the Chordettes as the "Sheboygan Chordettes" but that was never their official name. Their official name in the beginning was "The Chordettes" and they never changed it.

"In a further announcement, Mr. Godfrey said that never had he been more impressed with a quartette, and one composed of not only excellent singers, but lovely and beautiful girls as well. Being in Chicago, he talked directly with members of the Chordettes, and their reply was that they are to be in Omaha on Sunday to attend the Omaha meeting of barbershop quartettes with singers present from all over the country. It will be a parade of stars and the Chordettes will appear on the program. Mr. Godfrey inquired when they would be coming to New York and arranged for them to meet him in Detroit and fly back east in his plane. "According to the *Sheboygan Press*, "It has always been predicted and was our thought, that some day these girls would reach the top. Virginia Cole Osborn, tenor: Carol Hagedorn, baritone; Janet Buschmann Ertel, bass; and Dorothy Hummitzsch, lead, having been singing together for two years and on each appearance were more polished and finished in their work."

According to the *Sheboygan Press,* "It has always been predicted and was our thought, that some day these girls would reach the top. Virginia Cole Osborn, tenor; Carol Hagedorn, baritone; Janet Buschmann Ertel, bass; and Dorothy Hummitzsch, lead, have been singing together for two years and on each appearance were more polished and finished in their work."

Following a recap of Monday's show and their first place finish, the *Press* continued, "The girls have signed a contract with him (Godfrey) for 26 weeks and will be heard each morning, Monday through Friday."

"The Redskins (A Sheboygan pro football team that once lost to the Green Bay Packers 87-0), the Indians (A minor league baseball team of the Brooklyn Dodgers), Don McNeill, all have brought acclaim to Sheboygan and now the Chordettes will appear on the roster of fame in Sheboygan's history."

On Friday, September 30, 1949, the *Sheboygan Press* printed the above photo on the front page of their newspaper. Above the photo, in a box, were the words, "Our Chordettes Win Fame." Under the photo, the caption read, "This is a picture taken recently of the Chordettes in a barber shop in this city. Note the barber licenses in the background." The Press did not identify the Chordettes, who from left to right are, Ginny, Dorothy, Carol, and Janet. (Photo courtesy of Dorothy Schwartz) *Sheboygan Press* photo

"Usually, Mr. Godfrey doesn't "rave" about individuals on his program, but he said wonderful things about these Sheboygan girls, both in Chicago this morning and each day this week when they were presented."

"We can imagine the feelings of O.H. King Cole, international president of the Barbershoppers and father of one of the Chordettes. He has led his international association to new heights, and now Mr. and Mrs. Cole have a new honor through their daughter and three other members of the quartette, achieving national fame."

"In a party flying to Omaha to welcome and congratulate the girls will be Virginia Cole Osborn's parents, Mr. and Mrs. O.H. "King" Cole; her husband, Otis Osborn and small son, Keith; Janet Buschmann Ertel's husband, John Ertel; and Mrs. Louis Weber Jr., of Manitowoc, business manager of the Chordettes."

The article ended with information on how the group started. This included their appearance on the Fred Waring show. The *Press* ended, "The Chordettes' star has been on the up swing ever since, and they have become one of the leading barbershop singing features in the country."

Two weeks later, *Newsweek* magazine ran a short article about "Godfrey's Girls" on their

Radio-Television page. The article included a photo of the Chordettes with Arthur Godfrey. The article read as follows:

"The girls, composing one of very few genuine female barbershop quartets, called themselves The Chordettes. For three years at home in Sheboygan, Wis., Virginia Osborn (tenor), Dorothy Hummitzsch (lead), Carol Hagedorn (baritone), and Janet Ertel (bass) had sung together, mostly "for something to do on Sunday afternoons." Inevitably a few professional engagements led to a spot on Arthur Godfrey's talent Scouts (CBS and CBS-TV, Monday, 8:30-9 p.m. EST) on Sept. 26, where a close-harmony version of "Ballin' the Jack" won The Chordettes top honors and a crack at three appearances on Godfrey's morning show (CBS, Monday-Friday, 10:15-11:30 a.m. EST)." EST is short for Eastern Standard Time zone. "Usually, Mr. Godfrey doesn't "rave" about individuals on his program, but he said wonderful things about these Sheboygan girls, both in Chicago this morning and each day this week when they were presented."

The above photo of the Chordettes (Left to right, Virginia (Ginny), Dorothy, Carol, and Janet) with Arthur Godfrey appeared in the October 17, 1949 issue of Newsweek magazine
(Photo courtesy of Dorothy Schwartz).

The article continued, "Ordinarily The Chordettes would have sung out their three days, then vanished back into the hinderland of show business, leaving the time to other Talent Scout winners and the regular singing of Janette Davis, Bill Lawrence, and the Mariners (all-male) quartet. But the girls' unaccompanied chords hit a soft Godfrey spot. Unable to reach agreement with his five sponsors (Spray-A-Wave, Wildroot Hair Tonics, Gold Seal Products, National Biscuit Co., and Chesterfield cigarettes) fast enough, Godfrey went to Miss Davis and the Mariners. Would they, for the time being, give up a song a week and the accompanying salary? They would-and did cheerfully. With their money and a kick-in from Godfrey's own pocket, The Chordettes last week got a full time job on the morning program."

With the Chordettes getting hired for the Arthur Godfrey show, it also meant other major changes in their lives. This included moving from their small hometown of Sheboygan to the large city of New York. For a while, the Chordettes were living in a hotel, while they each found a home to live in. For Janet and Ginny, it also meant that their husbands had to quit their jobs in Sheboygan and find new jobs in New York. Janet also had the added responsibly of finding a new school for her daughter, Jackie.

In addition, the Chordettes had to cancel some appearances at some of the barbershop shows that they had agreed to attend. The Chordettes' business manager, Clara Weber sent out a three-page letter to various barbershop societies. The letter also gave a detailed account of how the Chordettes got on the show and what happened after their first appearance. Dorothy was kind enough to share a copy of this letter. In the letter, Weber said:

"Although I wired you in regard to the inability of the "Chordettes" to appear on your show, I have wanted to follow this up with a letter giving full details."

"The "Chordettes" were filling an engagement in Rhode Island—when they decided to return home via New York to renew some old acquaintances. One of these acquaintances, whose company had engaged the "Chordettes" to sing at some of their sales meetings, had contact with a Godfrey Talent Scout, and was able to arrange an audition on September 5th. The girls felt that if they were fortunate enough to be selected to appear on the Talent Scout Program, the attendant publicity would be very helpful in the acquisition of additional singing dates, and since the girls had decided to make singing their career instead of just a hobby, this opportunity was not to be overlooked."

After the audition, they were leaving the Studio with the feeling that they apparently had missed their chance, when—a voice came out of the loud speaker asking them to stand by for further instructions. They were then informed that they should be in New York on September 26th so appear on the first Talent Show of the new Season and which was to be televised."

"Four happier girls never existed. They hurried home to Sheboygan and put in many hours of diligent practice, such as only true barbershoppers can appreciate, in order to polish their number, with the idea of trying to top the show. The ambition to succeed became an obsession with the girls, so when they returned to New York for the show, the four young hopefuls were ready to put everything they had into it."

"On the same program were other very talented artists—an accordianist, of renown—a very clever comedian—and a soprano that sounded like she belonged at the "Met" in operatic roles."

"Little did our girls dream that when the applause meter registered its reaction – they would be declared the winner. This is now a matter of history. By virtue of their winning top honors—the girls earned the right to appear for three days on Godfrey's Morning program. On the second morning Godfrey asked the girls if they would like to sing on his televised Chesterfield Supper Club Program, Wednesday evening. They accepted with alacrity. At the end of their three day engagement, Godfrey asked the girls to stay over and sing on his Friday morning program as he was going to Chicago and he said he wanted to hear them from Chicago. He intimated that something was stirring."

"Then on Friday morning—came the thunderbolt—Godfrey announced from Chicago after the girls had sung, that he was adding the "Chordettes" to his permanent staff, as of October 3rd, with a nice contract from C.B.S. This was only the second time that he has ever taken any of the winners on his talent Scout Program and added them to his permanent staff. They have since been singing each morning Monday through Friday, as well as on the Wednesday night televised Chesterfield Show."

"These four young ladies, with as much love for barbershop harmony in their hearts as any member of the SPEBSQSA Inc., realized that they would have to forego the enjoyable gatherings at the many Barbershop Parades where they were booked to sing. It was not without many pangs that they advised me to wire each Chapter canceling out their barbershop Parade dates as well as the dates for other appearances, necessitated by the terms of the contract."

"We realize that this would cause considerable inconvenience to the Chapters who had completed their bookings for their shows, particularly those that were close at hand. The girls sincerely regretted this, as they have never failed to appear once they were scheduled. However, they felt that under the circumstances, all their Barbershop friends would understand and gladly release them so they could continue their climb to greater heights. They felt that they would be in a position to give the SPEBSQSA considerable publicity which has been fully borne out as you may have noticed, if you are listening to any of these programs."

"If the Society was paying for a Commercial plug on this National Broadcast, it wouldn't get as much publicity as what Godfrey is giving it for free."

"While some of the individual Chapters will be denied the privilege of having the Chordettes appear on their program—the Society itself gains through all this free publicity."

"All but a very few of the Chapters, where the girls were booked to sing have expressed their admiration for the girls and wished them all the luck in the world in their new field. We therefore hope that everyone in your Chapter will understand and if there is any ill-will remaining from the necessity of canceling out, we hope it will be washed away so that the girls can continue to hold the respect and best wishes of every true barbershopper."

"Little did we realize on the start that our four girls from Sheboygan would reach such a pinnacle of fame, although with their meteoric rise it was almost certain that they would eventually land somewhere near the top. Now they are working harder than ever to justify Godfrey's faith in them and to win the general public's favor—as they have won the favor of most of the barbershoppers."

"Pardon me for the length of this letter. I thought if you had the full details, you would understand better."

"Chordette"-ly yours,

One week after this letter was sent out, the *Sheboygan Press* reported on another change for one of the Chordettes, in their October 24th newspaper. The headline was, "Engagement Of Chordette To A Green Bay Man." The short article reported, "Mr. and Mrs. Arthur Hummitzsch, 1435 Superior Avenue, are announcing the engagement of their daughter, Dorothy, to William Schwartz, son of Mrs. Sam Schartz, Green Bay, Wis."

"The future bride now is residing at the Hotel Dryden in New York, N.Y., where she is singing the lead part with the well-known Sheboygan Chordettes, currently appearing on Arthur Godfrey's morning radio show and television. Mr. Schwartz is affiliated with the Morin-Schwartz Artists Representatives in Milwaukee."

Even though The Chordettes were now living in New York they still came back to Sheboygan. On Tuesday, November 15, 1949, the *Sheboygan Press* reports, "Three of the Chordettes, Virginia Cole Osborn, Janet Buschmann Ertel and Carol Hagedorn, flew from New York on Friday to spend the weekend in the city (Sheboygan). They returned to the metropolis on Sunday afternoon."

Eleven days later, on Saturday, November 26, the *Press* reported that the only Chordettes that didn't visit Sheboygan two weeks earlier was in Sheboygan. *The Press* said, "Miss Dorothy Hummitzsch, a member of the Chordettes, arrived in Milwaukee by plane Friday evening and then continued on to Sheboygan for a weekend stay with her parents, Mr. and Mrs. Arthur Hummitzsch, 1435 Superior Avenue. She will return to New York on Sunday afternoon.

The *Mansfield News Journal* from Mansfield, Ohio on December 4, reported on a barber-shop quartet show held in that city the night before. A separate article reported, "On hand to hear the barbershop singing two members of another famed quartet, the "Chordettes," of the Arthur Godfrey show."

"Janet Ertel and Carol Hagedorn, en route to New York after a Columbus (Ohio) appearance, stopped in Mansfield for the all-star show here. The other two members of the Chordettes continued on to New York.

On December 14, 1949, the *Sheboygan Press* reported that O.H. "King" Cole had been named president and general manager of Kingsbury the day before. The unusual thing is half the article was about his interest in the SPEBSQSA and that he was also president of the organization.

A little more than two months after announcing their engagement, Bill and Dorothy were married on New Year's Eve 1949. An article in the *Sheboygan Press* of January 4, 1950 contained the headline, "Marriage Takes Place Saturday in Milwaukee." The article said, "Announcements were received by relatives and friends on Tuesday of the marriage Saturday of Miss Dorothy Hummitzsch, daughter of Mr. and Mrs. Arthur Hummitzsch, 1435 Superior Avenue, to William Schwartz, Milwaukee, son of Mrs. Sam B. Schwartz, Green Bay, and the late Mr. Schwartz."

"The marriage ceremony was performed by Rabbi Harry Pastor in Temple Emanu-El in Milwaukee, and the bride was given in marriage by her father. Attendants were Mrs. Edward Nelson of Sheboygan and William T. Rother, business associate of the bridegroom."

"Guests, numbering 25 persons, had a wedding dinner at the Wisconsin Hotel. Following the meal, the newlyweds flew to New York, N.Y., where the bride will resume her work, singing with the Chordettes on the Arthur Godfrey radio and television shows over CBS, and her husband will open a New York office for his firm, in the Morin-Schwartz Agency, theatrical booking office. He will also take a special course on television production."

"Mr. and Mrs. Schwartz are at home at 23 Terrace Avenue, Hasbrouck Heights, N.J." The remaining part of the article listed the guests.

Congregation Emanu-El, 2419 East Kenwood Boulevard, Milwaukee, site of the 1949 marriage of Dorothy Hummitzsch and William Schwartz.

February 1, 1950 saw a small article in the *Sheboygan Press* about moving. The article reported, "This morning, John Ertel Jr., and daughter, Jacqueline, left for New York, where they will reside, with their wife and mother. Mrs. Ertel, a member of the Chordettes, has been living in the metropolis since September, when the quartet began singing on the Arthur Godfrey show,"

For the Chordettes, being on the various Arthur Godfrey shows meant that weekly schedules now changed and they had to do many things that they had not done before. In February 2008, the Sheboygan County Museum held a special program on music of the 1940s and 50s. Both Dorothy Schwartz and Carol Buschmann took part in the event. Carol was interviewed for "A Day in the Life of a…Chordette." In the interview, Carol said, "This would be a typical Tuesday while we were on the Arthur Godfrey show, which was almost four years, but the beginning of our professional career. We would be at the studio at 8 a.m. The radio show went on the air at 10 a.m. Eventually it was simulcast, which means it was also on TV at the same time as on radio. The studio was on the lower level of the CBS building, which Arthur regularly referred to as the "basement." Archie Bleyer and his musical group were in the studio. The singers congregated in another room to try to warm up our voices and wait for our turn to rehearse in the studio on the microphone. The director and soundman were in the booth. Sometimes your voice would take a lot longer to wake up than your body. There was a lot of singing and weird noises in that back room to help your voice wake up. A couple of the Mariners had unusual voice exercises, so it wasn't necessarily a place you'd want to spend time listening to.

A radio performance of "Oh Mo'nah" by The Mariners

The Mariners were a male quartet consisting of two black men and two white men. At that time, the early fifties, there were a few TV stations in the south that would not carry our show because of the racial situation. The female singer was Janette Davis who sang mostly popular songs of the time, but I particularly remember her for her rendition of "I Didn't Know the Gun Was Loaded," which she could really belt out. Our male singer was Julius LaRosa, who became one of the most popular singers from that show. We also had the Hawaiian girl, Haleloke. Arthur would make yearly trips to one of his favorite places, Hawaii. One year he brought Hale back with him and she became a regular part of the show. When the show started, the singers remained in the back room until it was their turn to participate. There were four sponsors of 15 minutes each and one half hour, which was sponsored by Chesterfield cigarettes. On Monday morning, we would each receive a carton of Chesterfields."

"Arthur used a different singer or singers for each segment of the show. You knew which segment you were on and would wait "in the wings" until he called your name. The audience of about 250 wouldn't see you until you came out to sing. Then you'd usually chat with Arthur before you performed."

"One time when the Sheboygan Redskins (our basketball team) was in New York to play, they all came to see our show. Since we were on the lower level (the basement), there was a fairly low ceiling. Arthur introduced them and they all stood up. They didn't quite hit the ceiling, but they made a very impressive sight. It was another plug for Sheboygan. He almost always introduced as, "The Girls from Sheboygan.""

"After a morning show, we had a quick lunch at Colbys, which was in the CBS building. Then we got together with our arranger, Walter Latzkom who Arthur referred to as the 5th Chordette. Most days we'd spend our time learning new material. When we originally signed this long-term contract with CBS, I figured we would run out of songs to sing in about three weeks. But with Walter arranging and rehearing with us, and getting into the studio at 8 every morning, we got ourselves into a routine and managed almost four years."

"Since we had an hour TV show on Wednesday night, we would have all new material to work on. Sometimes we would have a new song that would go with the theme of the show. Sometimes it would be a western show, a circus, or one time it was a French show. Not only did we have to learn a new song, but, we did it in French. There was a Dutch show where we wore authentic wooden shoes that were custom made for us by a man that came here from Holland for the show. Then there were the ice skating shows where we had to practice on the top floor of Madison Square Gardens after 10 p.m. because that was the only time available for us. This is where the New York Rangers hockey team practiced. Most of the people on the show had never been on ice skates. Sometimes we would do a number with Arthur, sometimes with Julius, and there were always a couple numbers with the whole cast. So we were very busy on Tuesday rehearsing new things."

"Also on Tuesdays, we would have to be fitted for whatever costume or outfit we would be wearing on the Wednesday night TV show. Then to the theatre to lay out all the movements that would be used on the show. You would sit in the theatre to wait till they did a number you were in, or go upstairs in another room and keep going over our songs with Walter. After the TV rehearsal on Tuesdays, we would all go to another studio and view our TV show from the previous week. Wasn't always the easiest thing to watch yourself on television, but of course the idea was to help you for the next time. That was finally the end of our Tuesday, which was our busiest day of the week."

"On Wednesday was a similar routine, with our dress rehearsal in the afternoon till the show was on the air at 8 p.m. Arthur would always spend winter weekends in Florida and occasionally he would take us with him. Sometimes we would leave after our Thursday morning show and fly with him in his plane and do the Friday morning show from Florida. After that show, we could swim, sun bathe, and eat good food for the weekend. This was a special weekend. Other times there were personal appearances on the weekend but back to the 8 o'clock routine on weekdays."

February 23, 1950 *Sheboygan Press*

70

Another new thing the Chordettes had to add to their busy schedules was recording records. Less than five months after being hired to be on the Arthur Godfrey show, their first record was released. Actually, it was a record by "Arthur Godfrey with the Chordettes." On February 23, 1950, the *Sheboygan Press* contained an ad for the Sheboygan Radio and Record Center, located at 1210 North 8th Street. The top of the ad contained in all capital letters, "FIRST RECORD HERE BY 'CHORDETTES' SHEBOYGAN NATIONALLY KNOWN QUARTER." The word "Chordettes" was in large letters, three times larger than the rest. After this, in small, non-capital letters, the ad said, "Godfrey sings along, too." The odd thing about the ad, was that no where in the ad, did they mention the name of the record.

At the end of March 1950, the Grand Rapids, Michigan newspaper reported, Barbershop quartets from throughout the nation will merge on Grand Rapids April 15, for the seventh annual Great Lakes Invitational Barbershop Quartet Show. The remaining six paragraphs of the article was all about the Chordettes. No other barbershop group was mentioned. Also included with the article was a large picture was that they misidentified Janet as Carol and Carol as Janet.

In 1950, newspapers were using more and more photos, but they were almost all black and white. Color pictures were just starting out and it was expensive to print color photos in newspapers. But, on Sunday, April 9, the *Milwaukee Journal* printed a full page, color photo on the front page of their entertainment section. The photo was of the "Barbershop Cinderellas," the Chordettes.

The beginning of the article stated, "Someday a talent scout, with the ability to recognize a pretty voice when he sees it, is going to offer the Chordettes a contract." That's what we wrote in the April 1, 1947 Green Sheet, after hearing the four harmonizing honeys of Sheboygan, Wisconsin for the first time."

"Almost a year and a half later on September 26, 1949, the comely quartet won first place on the "Arthur Godfrey Talent Scout" radio program. Their singing brought tears to the eyes of a talent scout with eyes as his ears, the one and only Arthur Godfrey. After the show he called them aside and said, "Have you made any radio commitments yet? You haven't? Good. Don't sign anything until we get a chance to talk to you."

"For the next three mornings, as part of their prize, the girls appeared on Godfrey's daily radio show. When they were through, the nation's No. 1 talent scout signed them as a permanent feature of his weekday program."

"The day we signed that contract was the biggest day in our lives," the girls told us when we visited with them in New York a short time ago." The rest of the article gave a background of their career.

In May 1950, Columbia Records released the Chordettes first album. The name of the album was "Harmony Time, the Chordettes." Records at the time were undergoing a big change. 78 RPM records which had been the only type of record for 50 years were being challenged by two new types of records, 33 1/3 RPM, 10-inch albums and 45 RPM, 7-inch records. RPM was the abbreviation for Revolutions Per Minute. The Chordettes album was released in all three versions. The cover of the album was the same except that in the center of the album was a barber pole with a red circle on top of the pole. On the 78 version, this was a solid red ball, while the 33 1/3 version contained the letters "LP" in the center. LP stood for Long Play. Inside the ball of the 45 version was "45" RPM.

The album contained the following songs: Ballin' The Jack; When You Were Sweet Sixteen; Moonlight Bay; Carry Me Back To All Virginny; Shine On Harvest Moon; Tell Me Why; I'd Love To Live In Loveland; and When Day Is Done." The 33 1/3 version (CL 6111) contained all the songs on one record.

The 78 version, contained a four record set, numbered C-201. Record one contained "When You Were Sweet 16" (C-201-1) and "Moonlight Bay" (C-201-2). Record two contained, "Carry Me Back To Old Virginny" (C-201-3) and "Ballin' The Jack" (C-201-4). Record three contained, "Shine On Harvest Moon" (C-201-5) and "Tell Me Why" (C-201-6). The final record contained, "I'd Love To Live In Loveland" (C-201-7) and "When Day Is Done" (C-201-8). Many times these four records are now found as singles, instead of as a set.

The 45 RPM set (B-201) also contained four records. This version contained the songs on the same records as the 78s, but used the letter "B" at the front of the number instead of a "C".

For many years, Sheboygan's most popular store was the H.C. Prange Company store, which stood on the corner of North 8th Street and Wisconsin Avenue. On May 25, 1950, Prange's ran an ad in the *Sheboygan Press* announcing that the Chordette's new album was available. (From the author's collection)

On May 25, 1950, the H.C. Prange store ran an ad in the *Sheboygan Press*, announcing that they were the "First in Sheboygan" to have "The Chordettes, Sheboygan's Own" new album. According to the ad, "You've heard about this album on Arthur Godfrey's program (and have probably been waiting anxiously to hear it.) It's here now, and we advise you to hurry right down. You know the "Chordettes" and their recordings are definitely destined to be "best sellers" everywhere!" The price for the album was $3.95.

On the back of the record album was information on the Chordettes. Part of this information included "the 'tenor' part in the quartet is sung by Virginia Osborn, a Seattle girl who moved to Sheboygan in 1934. Attending Downer Seminary and Frances Shimer College, she majored in music and dramatics. Dorothy Hummitzsch, who sings leads roles in minstrel shows staged by

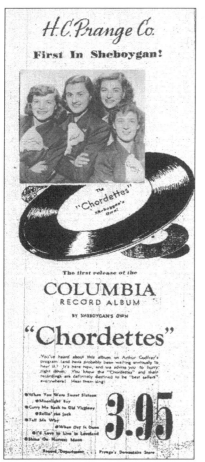

The ad that the H.C. Prange store put in the *Sheboygan Press* for the Chordette's first record is shown here.
(From the author's collection)

her brother. Carol Hagedorn, the 'baritone' was also born in Sheboygan and specialized in singing and dramatics during her high school days. A member of a barbershop quartet while in school, she also studied drama and speech in Chicago. And Janet Ertel, the 'base' left Sheboygan early to tour with a dramatic company, and later appeared on stage with her aunt before returning home and joining forces with the Chordettes."

"In this collection, the Chordettes are heard in eight familiar melodies, favorites of quartets and soloists all over the country. These are songs almost always heard when group singing occurs, and their well-known melodies are always welcome. As sung by the Chordettes, they take on added interest from the careful harmonization and the unusual qualities of female voices singing in four part arrangements." The songs on this album included, "When you Were Sweet Sixteen," "Moonlight Bay," "Carry Me Back to Old Virginny," "Shine On Harvest Moon," "Tell Me Why," "I'd Love to Live in Loveland," "When Day is Done," and "Ballin the Jack," which was the song they sang the first time they appeared on the Arthur Godfrey Show.

In the May 27, 1950 issue of *TV Forecast* magazine, a photo of the Chordettes appeared and under the photo it said, "NEXT WEEK 'Godfrey's Chordettes'. Read about four young ladies from Sheboygan, Wisconsin, who were discovered by Arthur Godfrey. Boss man of this popular CBS-TV show. Their story is in next week's TV Forecast on sale Friday at your favorite newsstand.

"The Chordettes Bring Fame to Sheboygan" was the headline of a lengthy article in the December 2, 1950 issue of the *Sheboygan Press*. The article also contained two large photos of the Chordettes that were three newspaper columns wide. The article state, "The Sheboygan Chordettes broke into print on a national scale in September 1949 when they won the honors for a three day program on the Godfrey broadcast after an audition on the Talent Scouts program. Three days went by and the girls were made a permanent feature of the show and appear five mornings a week on radio (CBS) and Wednesday nights on television.

"Now they are in their second year and more popular than ever. When they were first signed Arthur Godfrey remarked, "When they hit those harmonies, the tears just roll out of my eyes." A short period back, the girls were singing "Down on Thirty-third and Third," and preceding the song, the girls mad an announcement: "We came from Sheboygan to visit the city and now we're staying for good. Since we have been here we have been training our ear to talk like all city folks should. Since we have arrived in New York, here is how they taught us to talk."

"Then they went into their song, and not only Arthur Godfrey, but the whole nation applauded. These Sheboygan girls are one of the outstanding features on both radio and television. And to think they started on a small scale here in Sheboygan.

In July 1950, Radio and TV Mirror devoted their entire issue of their magazine to Arthur Godfrey and the members of his show. One page, as expected, was on the Chordettes. The headline said, "Mention their Names in Sheboygan. And you can tell them where they're at for the girls are known as the Chordettes are a credit to anybody's home town."

The story then split into four separate articles, one on each of the Chordettes. First was Dottie (Dorothy) Schwartz, followed by Jinny Osborn, Janet Ertel and finally Carol Hagedorn. But, throughout the article and with Janet's picture, they spelled her name wrong, as Erlet instead of Ertel.

The Chordettes Bring Fame To Sheboygan

At Ease On A Television Program

Left to right, Virginia Osborn, Dorothy Schwartz, Carol Hagedorn and Janet Ertel.

How They Appear On Television

Bottom row, left, Janet Ertel, right, Virginia Osborn, top row, left, Carol Hagedorn, and right, Dorothy Schwartz.

The article continued, "Virginia Osborn, who sings 'tenor' organized the Chordettes. She was born in Seattle, Washington and moved to Sheboygan with her parents in 1934. . . . Went to Downer Seminary in Milwaukee and completed her schooling at Frances Shimer College in Mt. Carroll, Illinois, majoring in music and dramatics. Had leading roles in college plays and was soloist with the chapel choir."

"Dorothy Schwartz, 'lead'. Born in Sheboygan. Sang with quartets during high school days and played lead roles in minstrel shows staged by brother."

"Carol Hagedorn, 'baritone'. Born in Sheboygan. Educated there and specialized in singing and dramatics. Was member of a barbershop quartet while in school. Completed a course in drama and speech at Columbia Radio School, Chicago.

"Janet Ertel, 'bass'. Born in Sheboygan. Always interested in music and drama as a child. Toured the country with a stage troupe, later was on stage with aunt."

"The Chordettes have recorded, "If It Wasn't For Your Father," and "Candy and Cake," with Arthur Godfrey. They also have a Columbia Records album titled "Harmony Time," which consists of favorites from their barbershop quartet repertoire.

"Pleased by their harmonies, they stuck together and launched a career which was climaxed when Arthur Godfrey made them permanent members of his television and daytime radio cast, after they had copped top honors on his CBS radio-television "Talent Scouts." They are heard with the "Little Godfreys" five mornings a week on radio (CBS, 10:00-11:30 a.m., EST,. Monday through Friday), and Wednesday nights on television (CBS-TV, 8:00-9:00 p.m. EST)." EST stands for Eastern Standard Time Zone.

"They feel like four Cinderellas now, but success and recognition came only after hard work, in perfecting their own style of barbershop harmony . . . Or maybe, in their case, it should be called beauty parlor harmony."

Arthur Godfrey released one song on Columbia Records in 1951 titles, "Dance Me Loose" and it became one of the top songs for the year, making it into the top 10 on the record charts. The song "Dance Me Loose" had both the record label and sheet music listing the artist as "Arthur Godfrey with the Chordettes."

The release of the Chordette's second album, again for Columbia Records, also occurred in 1951. Since their first album, "Harmony Time" sold fairly well, the second album was simply titled, "Harmony Time Volume II."

Like their first album, "Harmony Time Volume II" was issued as a four record set of 78 RPM records, along with a four record set of 45 RPM records, and a single 10 inch 33 1/3 record. In the four record sets, record #1 (B241-1 and B241-2) contained songs, "Runnin Wild" and "Alice Blue Gown." Record two (B241-3 and B241-4) contained songs, "Love Me And The World Is Mine" and "Lonesome—That's All" while record three (B241-5 and B241-6) contained the songs, "Moonlight On The Ganges" and "Let The Rest of the World Go By."

The final record (B241-7 and B241-8) contained songs, "The World Is Waiting For The Sunrise" and "Love's Old Sweet Song."

Shown here is the cover of the sheet music for Arthur Godfrey with the Chordette's "Dance Me Loose."

Pictured left to right are Carol, Arthur, Janet, Jinny and Dorothy.

(Photo of cover from the author's collection.)

This album contained the song, "Alice Blue Gown." In September of 1951, the Chordettes received a fan letter from a fan, for Alice Blue Gown. The letter read as follows:

"Dear Girls,"

"Everybody likes to get fan mail, especially if it's laudatory, and you deserve some for Alice Blue Gown. Your record of which I heard up here in the fastnesses of northeast Nevada, is a fine rendition and beautifully balanced."

"Say hello for me to Pops Godfrey. We hear him, too, up here."

"Yours"

"Bing Crosby"

At the time, Bing Crosby was one of the most popular recording and movie stars. His recording of "White Christmas" is still the best selling record of all time.

At left is a photo of the cover of the second Chordettes album.

Like their first album, it was issued in three versions, 78 RPM, 45 RPM, and 33 1/3 RPM. The cover was the same for all three versions, except for the center of the white ball on the bottom of the barber pole.

On the 45 version shown here, it contained "45" RPM. The 33 1/3 version contained the letters LP, while the 78 version was blank.

(From the author's collection.)

In February of 1951, the second journal (newsletter) of "The Chordettes Time" was issued to members of the Official Chordettes Fan Club. This issue contained 25 pages and was dated February-March-April 1951 and looking at a copy of this newsletter, shows that a lot of effort was made in putting this issue together. The cover had color added, which was done by hand. In addition a small photo of the Chordettes was attached to the bottom of the cover, using photo mounts on each corner of the photo. This allowed a person to remove the photo if they so desired. Inside were many drawings on the various pages. The first page included the names of the various editors of the journal, along with the names and addresses of the club officers, both active and honorary. The Chordettes were honorary presidents.

The second page featured nicely done sketches of Jinny and Carol wishing them a happy birthday on April 25 (Jinny) and May 13 (Carol). Some of the other pages featured current movie and record reviews, meet your members, poems, letters to the editor, contests, member's birthday's, Cook's Nook, other fan clubs, and articles about Joan Evans and Doris Day. Also, included was an article written by Joanne Sidle titled, "Meeting the Chordettes" and told about her first trip to New York City where she got to meet the Chordettes and also have lunch with them. In addition, there were a few pages about the Chordettes, titled "Ask The Chordettes" and "Spotlighting The Chordettes."

"Ask The Chordettes" was a section where fan club members could ask the Chordettes various questions. There were 20 questions asked. Among the questions asked were, "What is your favorite dish?" The answer was, "Jan(et) loves steak, Dottie never tires of spaghetti, Carol would rather eat her Mother's Irish stew than anything else, and Jinny likes clams, lobster and food in general."

Another question was, "Do you think you will like color TV when it comes out?" To which the answer was, "Have no idea about color television, but Carol and Dottie have seen some colored television and thought it was wonderful." (Note: The Chordettes would later be on the first show to be broadcast in color.)

One other question was, "What is the color of your hair and eyes, height and weight?" "Jinny has light brown hair and hazel eyes. She's 5'4" and weighs 122 pounds. Dottie has blonde hair and blue eyes. She's 5'7" tall and weighs 130 pounds. Carol has dark brown hair and eyes. She's 5'9" tall and weighs 130 pounds. Janet is 5'6" and weighs 126 pounds and has reddish brown hair and hazel eyes."

The next question was, "Were you friends when you were younger and still in high school?" The answer given was, "Dottie and Carol went to high school together and sang in a trio and a quartette while there." (Note: Dottie and Carol went to Sheboygan Central, while Jinny went to Sheboygan North and Janet had already graduated before the other Chordettes had even started high school.)

The second last question was, "What is your favorite recording that you have recorded?" "Our favorite recordings were the ones we made at Christmas time with Arthur, "Marshmallow World" and "Angie, the Christmas Tree Angel."

The final question was, "Do you always dress alike?" The answer given was, "We don't always dress alike, but we have about eight or ten matching suits and daytime dresses."

In the above mentioned newsletter, the Chordettes had been asked about color TV. A few months later, in the *Sheboygan Press* of June 11, 1951, the newspaper ran an article under the headline, "Colored TV To Begin In Two Weeks." The article went on to say, "The real chips-down battle of color television will start in about two weeks when the Columbia Broadcasting System begins the nation's first commercial telecasts in color."

"June 25, two weeks from today, now looks like the kickoff date for CBS' inauguration of color telecasts. The launching will feature Arthur Godfrey.

The next day, the *Sheboygan Press* had an article about the Schmitt Brothers of Manitowoc, who had just been crowned international barber shop quartet champions. Upon their return to Manitowoc the night before, they were met at the railroad depot and then took a motorcade to the Hamilton Hotel in Two Rivers. At the hotel they were honored with a ceremony where King Cole was master of ceremonies. They also received medallions for being champions. One paragraph stated, "One of the young ladies who pinned the medallions on the winning quartet was Virginia Cole Osborn, daughter of King Cole and a member of Sheboygan's famous Chordettes, stars of the Arthur Godfrey television and radio shows."

July of 1951 saw the Chordettes in Minneapolis, Minnesota for the 5th annual WCCO Aquatennial Radio Show at the Minneapolis Auditorium on Saturday the 21st. Other guests taking part in the show were, movie star Dennis Morgan, comedian Ken Murray, movie star and Coleen Gray. Ticket prices ranged from $1.20 to $3.60.

On July 21st, it was reported in a Minneapolis newspaper, "Chordettes Reach City, Minus One." The following article reported:

"Jinny missed the plane. The Chordettes arrived at Wold-Chamberlain airport Friday for Aquatennial festivities--minus their tenor."

"The tenor, Jinny Osborn, when last heard from, was stranded at the wrong New York airport. She was scheduled to arrive late last night."

"However, her three singing partners, Janet Ertel, bass; Carol Hagedorn, baritone; and Dottie

Schwartz, alto, had no worries."

"Jinny, they said, has done it before. But she always shows up in time."

"When the girls arrived, they were met and serenaded by Minneapolis members of the Society for the Preservation and Encouragement of Barbershop Quartet Singing in America."

The next day, July 22, 1951, the *Minneapolis Sunday Tribune* ran a photo of the Chordettes the afternoon of the previous day, where they sang at a luncheon for newspaper editors. 440 editors from Minnesota attended. The photo also showed all four Chordettes, including Jinny, who as the other Chordettes had said the day before, "always shows up in time."

On July 27 and 28, the sixth annual Wisconsin Spectacle of Music was held in South Milwaukee, Wisconsin. 19 drum and bugle corps, 13 bands and 400 baton twirlers competed in the event. But, the headliners for the event were the Chordettes, described as "Sheboygan's gift to the barbershop quartet singing world."

A couple of days before this event, on July 25, the *Sheboygan Press* reported that the "Wuerl Band To Participate In $5,000 Prize Competition." The first paragraph of the article, stated, "On Saturday, July 28, the Wuerl band, under the direction of Charles M. Faulhaber, will travel to South Milwaukee for the annual Wisconsin Spectacle of Music. In the largest instrumental music festival in the Midwest, the Wuerl band will be competing with 13 bands for a share of the $5,000 in prize money."

In July 1951, the Wuerl Band of Sheboygan under the direction of Charles Faulhaber, took first place in the Wisconsin Spectacle of Music. Special stars of this show were the Chordettes, shown here with Faulhaber. It was a reunion of sorts for Faulhaber and the Chordettes, as he was the high school music teacher of three of the Chordettes. Left to right are, Janet, Dorothy, Faulhaber, Jinny, and Carol. This photo originally appeared in the *Sheboygan Press* of August 3, 1951. (Photo courtesy of Carol Buschmann)

The last two paragraphs of the article added, "An added attraction from the standpoint of Sheboygan will be the appearance of the Chordettes as "stars" of the evening performance before a sell-out crowd of ten thousand. The quartet, composed of Virginia Osborn, Dorothy Schwartz, Carol Hagedorn, and Janet Ertel will be sponsored at the Spectacle by several South Milwaukee business firms.""

"Director Faulhaber is a former music instructor of three of the girls and he expects to have a happy reunion with his illustrious students on Saturday."

The Milwaukee Journal on Sunday, July 29, 1951 reported about "Wisconsin's Four 'Hick' Girls Sing Their Way to New York." The article included a photo of the Chordettes taken the evening before at the Wisconsin Spectacle of Music.

The article stated, "Four Wisconsin girls who have been called "hicks" on radio and television looked like anything but that Saturday. They did not seem a bit out of place in a large suite in the Schroeder Hotel, or in the Cadillac which took them to South Milwaukee behind a police escort."

"The four are the Chordettes, the women's barbershop quartet from Sheboygan, which is a fixture on Arthur Godfrey's radio and television shows. They were the headliners in South Milwaukee's "Wisconsin Spectacle of Music" Saturday night."

"Godfrey is always ribbing the girls on his show, asking them whether they are having difficulties getting along in "the big city," meaning New York."

"Five years ago, they were organized into a quartet by Virginia Osborn. She sings tenor and her father is King Cole, a Sheboygan brewery president and a barbershop quartet fan."

"The girls went on the road, singing all over the country, but they cashed in when they won first place on Godfrey's "Talent Scouts" program. Godfrey signed them up for his daytime show."

"The Chordettes live in New York now. Two are married-Janet Ertel, bass, to John Ertel, formerly of Sheboygan and now a New York furniture man, and Dorothy Schwartz, lead, to William Schwartz, formerly of Green Bay and now a New York booking agent. The fourth girl in the quartet is Carol Hagedorn, baritone."

"The girls recently recorded their second album-"Harmony Time No. 2," they chorused almost musically-and last week they got a fan letter from a ranch in Nevada."

"He said he liked our singing of 'Alice Blue Gown,'" said Miss Osborn. "Imagine-a fan letter from Bing Crosby." This letter is found earlier in this book.

———————————

On July 30, 1951, the *Sheboygan Press* reported, "Wuerl Band Wins Spectacle Of Music." The first three paragraphs reported, "The sixth annual Wisconsin Spectacle of Music, held Saturday and Sunday at South Milwaukee, attracted bands, drum corps, drill teams and marching units from all over the Midwest, but it turned into a one-city victory. Winners of just about everything, but the stadium where the festival was held, were Wuerl's Concert Band, and top feature attraction were the Chordettes, both the pride and joy of Sheboygan."

"Under the direction of Charles M. Faulhaber, Wuerl's band received the highest point total of any musical organization in the contest. This included 10 bands and 18 drum and bugle corps. Entered in class B, for units having less than 50 members, the local band out-scored even the top Class A entrant in the festival. For its victory, the band received a huge trophy and a $350 cash award. The trophy will be on display soon in the Bank of Sheboygan, Mr. Faulhaber announced today."

"Highlight of the evening program, were the Chordettes, stars or radio and television, who started in Sheboygan. Members of the girls' quartet are Janet Ertel, Dorothy Schwartz, Carol Hagedorn, and Virginia Osborn. The girls were escorted onto the field in a beautiful, yellow convertible and received a terrific ovation from a crowd of about 13,000 people."

Charles Faulhaber's music career in Sheboygan was coming to an end. Less than three months later, on October 15, 1951, the *Sheboygan Press* ran the headline, "Charles Faulhaber Buys Music Store At Madison." The article started, "Charles M. Faulhaber, long a leading figure in local school music circles, and for the past nine years director of the Wuerl Concert Band, has purchased the controlling stock in a Madison music company and will take charge of the firm this week."

CHARLES M. FAULHABER
Band Director

At left is a photo of Charles Faulhaber from the 1947 Central High School Lake Breeze yearbook.

Above right is an ad for Faulhaber's Music store from the *Sheboygan Press* of August 27, 1951, shortly before he moved from Sheboygan to Madison.

(Photos from the author's collection)

"Mr. Faulhaber announced today that a corporation, of which he is president and treasurer, is now the owner of the Ward-Brodt Music Company of Madison. Other officers of the corporation are Janet Faulhaber (his wife), vice president; Viola Ward, secretary, and L.O. Tuhus, director."

The following information about Charles Faulhaber was found in the article or supplied by his son, Michael. Charles Faulhaber was born in Lake Geneva, Wisconsin on May 2, 1911. He graduated from the Milwaukee State Teacher's College with a B.E. degree, studying music (French horn).

His professional study included instruction of the French Horn from outstanding instructors, as Trixis Justus of Chicago, Louis Dufrasne of the Chicago Civic Opera, and Max Pottage of the Chicago Symphony Orchestra.

His first teaching position was with the Milwaukee Public Schools, as a class instrumental instructor from 1930-1933. From 1933 to 1935, he was the band and orchestra director at Algoma, Wisconsin. In 1935, he came to Sheboygan where he was the director of the Sheboygan (later Central) High School.

In 1941, he married Janet Sprengel of Sheboygan. They had two children, Nancy and Michael.

While teaching at Central in 1942, he received his master's degree in music from Northwestern University in Evanston, Illinois. That same year, he was also named director of the Wuerl Band. During World War II, according to his son, Michael, "Unable to pass the physical, he was not able to serve during WWII. He really wanted to conduct a service band."

Faulhaber left Central High in 1947. In 1947, he opened and operated a music store in his home, which was located at 1227 Alabama Avenue and also worked as a traveling salesman, selling musical instruments to schools for a Milwaukee Company. From 1948 to 1951, he served as director of instrumental music at Mission House (now Lakeland) College located about 10 miles northwest of Sheboygan in Franklin.

Charles Faulhaber was the president of the Ward-Brodt Music Company in Madison, when he died in Madison on Sunday, October 19, 1969. He was only 58 years old. According to his obituary in the Capital Times, while in Madison, Faulhaber organized the Madison Muncipal Band in 1955 and served as its director until 1962. He also played trombone in the Madison Civic Symphony Orchestra and was a director of the Madison Music Assn. He was also a member of the National Assn. Of Music Merchants and served three years as its secretary, and was a member of the board of directors and chairman of the membership committee. In addition, he was a member of the Phi Beta Music multinational honorary band director's fraternity, the Wisconsin Bandmasters Assn., and an associate member of the American Bandmasters Assn. He was also very active with the Junior Achievement group in Madison. In 1962, he had served as membership chairman of Wisconsin for the National Band Assn.

He was survived by his wife, Janet; a daughter, Mrs. Thomas (Nancy) Schmelzer, Middleton, Wisconsin; a son, Michael in the U.S. Army Band (Pershing's Own) in Washington D.C.; a brother James in Washington D.C.; and two grandchildren.

Today, in 2013, the Ward-Brodt Music Company is still in business in Madison. It is run by Charles' son, Michael, who is president/CEO, having joined the business in 1973. Charles' widow, Janet was CEO until Michael took over.

During the first weekend of August 1951, on the 4th, the Chordettes were in Hershey, Pennsylvania at the Hershey Sports Arena. They were one of eight barbershop quartets taking part in the Festival of Harmony.

On September 7, 1951, the *Sheboygan Press* ran an ad telling its readers, "Here It Is-The Greatest Barbershop Quartet Show Ever Staged In This Area, When THE SHEBOYGAN CHAPTER OF SPEBSQSA Presents Its Sixth Annual PARADE OF QUARTETS, Featuring THE SCHMITT BROTHERS, 1951 International Champions of Two Rivers, and, THE CHORDETTES, Sheboygan's Own Stars of Stage, Radio, and Television." This event was scheduled for Saturday, September 29 at the Municipal Auditorium and Armory. Tickets were available at Nitze's Radio and Appliance Co., at 1127 North Eighth Street. Ticket prices were $2.40, $1.80, $1.50, and $1.20, tax included.

Here It Is—The Greatest

Barbershop Quartet Show

Ever Staged In This Area

—WHEN—

SHEBOYGAN CHAPTER OF SPEBSQSA

Presents its Sixth Annual

PARADE OF QUARTETS

—FEATURING—

THE SCHMITT BROTHERS

1951 International Champions of Two Rivers

THE CHORDETTES

Sheboygan's Own Stars of Stage, Radio and Television

The Villageaires
1951 Illinois District Champs
Palos Heights, Ill.

The Sing-Copates
1951 International Semi-Finalists
Appleton, Wis.

The For-Mor
One of Madison's Finest

The Tune Peddlers
of Sheboygan

SATURDAY, SEPTEMBER 29

MUNICIPAL AUDITORIUM AND ARMORY—8:15 P. M.

Tickets Now On Sale At

NITZE'S RADIO and APPLIANCE CO.

1127 North Eighth Street

ADMISSION: All seats reserved — $2.40, $1.80, $1.50, $1.20, tax included

This ad ran in the September 7, 1951 edition of the *Sheboygan Press.*

Notice that even though the Chordettes were returning to their hometown of Sheboygan for the first time in two years, they were only billed second.

(From the author's collection)

The *Sheboygan Press* of September 18, 1951 ran an article about the Chordettes being in Sheboygan for their first trip back since appearing on the Arthur Godfrey show. The final paragraph said, "Sheboygan has produced some bright, bright stars, but none have swept the nation like four young girls who have looks, charm, class, and above all-they can sing."

On Wednesday, September 26, 1951 (Two years to the day after the Chordettes first appeared on the Arthur Godfrey show), the *Sheboygan Press* reported, "Chordette" Days Proclaimed by Mayor Edward C. Schmidt." The short article that followed, stated, "Mayor Edward C. Schmidt today issued a proclamation designating Sept. 28 and 29 as "Chordette" days in Sheboygan, and urged all citizens to attend the Parade of Quartets at the Armory Saturday evening."

"Following is his proclamation:

Whereas, music and song are very properly part of the spirit and tradition of Sheboygan; and

Whereas, one of the fields of music which is enjoyed and appreciated by great numbers of our people is that highly specialized type of harmonizing known as barbershop quartet singing; and

Whereas; four young ladies from Sheboygan, known as the "Chordettes," have attained national recognition for their mastery of this particular style of singing and as a result have brought much favorable publicity to our city; and

Whereas, the said "Chordettes" are returning to Sheboygan for a homecoming and will be fea-

84

tured on the Sixth Annual Parade of Quartets presented by the Sheboygan Chapter of the Society for the Preservation and Encouragement of Barbershop Quartet Singing in America, Inc., to be held at the Municipal Auditorium and Armory at 8:15 p.m. Saturday, September the 29th, 1951,

Now, Therefore, I, Edward C. Schmidt, mayor of the city of Sheboygan, do hereby proclaim that the period of September 28th and 29th, 1951, shall be known and observed as "Chordette" days in Sheboygan. I invite all of our citizens who appreciate and enjoy the artistry and the close harmony of barbershop quartet singing, to attend the concert and thus give expression to our appreciation of the fine publicity which has accrued to our community by reason of the nation success attained by the "Chordettes" in the entertainment field."

EDWARD C. SCHMIDT, Mayor

The *Sheboygan Press* of Saturday, September 29, 1951 reported, "Hearty Welcome Given To Chordettes On Return Here." The article went on to say, "The Chordettes, the four girls who went from Sheboygan to win fame on the Arthur Godfrey radio and television programs, returned home as a group for the first time Friday evening. The popular quartet, which flew from New York to Chicago and then came by train on to Sheboygan, was greeted at the railroad station by hundreds of well-wishers who jammed the depot in an attempt to get a closer look at the girls who put Sheboygan on the musical map."

"The Sheboygan Barbershop chorus and members of the Wuerl band were on hand as the musical part of the welcoming committee, and both organizations serenaded the four stars— Carol Hagedorn, Janet Ertel, Virginia Cole Osborne and Dorothy Schwartz—as they alighted from the train. Other more formal members of the welcoming committee were E.F. Klozotsky and J. Murray Marks, president and secretary respectively of the Association of Commerce, and City Clerk Joseph Leberman who, in the absence of Mayor Edward C. Schmitt, represented the municipal government."

"The parents of the four Chordettes were, of course of hand for the warm reception afforded the girls. With a vanguard formed by motorcycle policemen, the Wuerl band and the Sheboygan Barbershop chorus, the Chordettes drove in a convertible slowly down Pennsylvania Avenue to Eighth Street and north on Eighth street to the Hotel Foeste where an informal reception awaited them."

"Friday night shoppers lined the streets on both sides, and the Chordettes waved to friends whom they recognized along the way. Upon arrival at the Hotel Foeste they were escorted into the main dining room, where refreshments had been prepared. Musical entertainment was again furnished by the Sheboygan Barbershop chorus and the Wuerl band.

"By popular demand, the Chordettes obliged with "Wait Till the Sun Shines, Nellie" and harmonized to "Sheltering Palms" for an encore."

Under the sub headline, "Extend Welcome" the article continued, "After the musical portion of the program, Mr. Klozotsky, in the role of master of ceremonies, introduced Mr. Leberman. Because Mayor Schmidt was unable to attend, Mr. Leberman welcomed the girls to the city of Sheboygan. The parents of the Chordettes, Mr. and Mrs. Cole (Virginia's parents), Mr. and Mrs. Hummitzsch (Dorothy's parents), Mr. and Mrs. Hagedorn (Carol's parents), and Mr. Buschman (Janet's father), also were called upon to take a bow."

The Hotel Foeste is shown in a postcard photo from about 1950. This is where the Chordettes stayed during their return to Sheboygan in September 1951. (From the author's collection)

"Walter Latzko, the Chordettes' arranger who made the trip along with husbands John Ertel and William Schwartz, was also introduced to the gathering. Mr. Latzko, in addition to taking a bow, added that because of his association with the girls, he is often called "Walter Chordette," a remark that brought laughter from the crowd."

"Choosing the right song for the girls to sing is a tough task, as there is always the boss to please. Mr. Latzko adds that the songs are sung "By the grace of God …and Godfrey.""

The Chordettes who will be featured at the Parade of Quartets tonight, will leave Sheboygan Sunday afternoon in time to fly back to New York for Monday's program. The sixth annual Parade of Quartets, sponsored by the Sheboygan chapter of the Society for the Preservation and Encouragement of Barber Shop Singing in America, afforded the Chordettes the opportunity to make a homecoming trip as a unit. The girls have been back many times individually, but this is the first time the four have arrived together."

"The girls themselves were happy to be back. They spent most of the time at the Hotel Foeste talking to their parents and friends and talking over old times. While Carol Hagedorn spoke to George Eisold and reminded him of how little she was when he played the piano during her dancing lessons, Dorothy Schwartz and Virginia Cole Osborne were surrounded by admirers."

"Janet Ertel, in an interview with a (Sheboygan) Press reporter, spoke for the quartet when she said that they were thrilled to be back. "We have been to many receptions, but none were anything like this. It's wonderful, and it certainly is good to be home," she said."

The article ended, "Charles Faulhaber, director of the Wuerl band, who is locating in Madison (Wisconsin) soon, received a promise from the girls that they would pay him a visit there sometime in the future."

"Meanwhile, Sheboyganites are making the most of the short visit as the response to the Parade of Quartets, which will be held tonight, indicates that it will be one of the biggest shows of its kind ever produced in this area."

Two days later, in their October 1, 1951 newspaper, the *Sheboygan Press* reported on the Saturday evening program, under the headline, "3,800 Hear Top Quartets In Parade of Quartets Saturday." The *Press* reported, "Talent Aplenty" could have been the name of the of the Saturday evening revue staged by some of the nation's top Barbershop quartettes at Sheboygan's Municipal Auditorium and Armory. There were quartettes lovely to look at, some with showmanship-plus but there were none that it wasn't a pleasure to listen to. Six quartets, each hitting on "all four," joined the Sheboygan Barbershop chorus in a two and one-half hour program that left the crowd of 3,800 clapping for more."

"The Parade of Quartets, sixth in the annuals of the local chapter of the S.P.E.B.S.Q.S.A., was unusual. There were none of the expected slow or weak spots. Each musical foursome appeared to be out to out-do the others and as a result the program was simply a succession of top-notch performances by such units as the Chordettes, the Schmitt Brothers, Madison's For-Mors, the Sing-Copates of Appleton, the Illinois champions, the Villagaires and Sheboygan's classy Tune Peddlers.

Shown here is a postcard photo of the Sheboygan Municipal Auditorium and Armory, where the Chordettes performed upon their return to Sheboygan in September 1951. This building was also the home of the Sheboygan Redskins Basketball team, which was one of the founding teams of the NBA (National Basketball Association) in 1950.

Later in the article, the *Press* reported, "Sheboygan's Chordettes, welcomed home Friday night, were back to take the spotlight and well-deserved bows for their meteoric rise to fame on radio and television. Mayor Edward C. Schmidt hailed their work as "ambassadors of good will for Sheboygan" and presented individual plaques to each as a token of the esteem of their fellow townsfolk. The plaques were hardly needed, however, as the large crowd broke out with a round of applause that assured the Chordettes of their status in the community."

A couple of paragraphs later, the *Press* printed, "The Chordettes popped out for their first appearance in lovely gowns and offered a musical "Hello to Sheboygan." Then came Mayor Schmidt's tribute and their renditions of "Peggy O'Neill" and "Lonesome, That's All." They closed with "Ballin the Jack," the tune that sent them on their way to national acclaim."

The second last paragraph in the article stated, "The Chordettes returned to sing, "Wait Till The Sun Shines Nellie" and "I Wonder Who's Kissing Him Now." Before they could leave the stage, the audience demanded three more numbers, "Down Among the Sheltering Palms" and Running Wild", as well as one of the original selections, "Tell Me Why." Also, included in the newspaper was one page of photos from the program, including one photo of the Chordettes.

A few days later, in their October 5, 1951 edition, the *Press* reported, "Rudy Finst Gets A Few Breaks On His Recent Trip." Finst was a Sheboygan insurance salesman. Part of the article read as follows, "Last Sunday (Finst) had an emergency insurance business call that necessitated that he go to New York. So what? He rode on the same plane with the Chordettes, went backstage with them in New York, and met most of the cast of the Arthur Godfrey show, not including, however, the great Godfrey. (How come he missed that?)"

On Saturday, October 13, 1951, the *Press* ran in their Editor's Mail Box, the following letter, addressed to Matt Werner, who was the publisher of the *Sheboygan Press*.

LOOKA HERE

New York, N.Y., Oct. 11, 1951

Mr. Matt Werner
The Sheboygan Press

Dear Sir:

We would like so much to thank everyone in Sheboygan for our grand weekend at home.

It was such a thrill to receive such a wonderful reception from all of our friends and neighbors.

Sheboygan will always be our home and we hope to be able to come back often.

We would be very grateful to you if you could find space to print this in order to show our appreciation.

Thank you.   THE CHORDETTES

The Chordettes wrote in the above letter, "We hope to be able to come back often." No one knew it at the time, but this event would turn out to be the first and only time they came back to Sheboygan to perform as a group. Members of the Chordettes would not appear together publicly in Sheboygan again for more than 50 years, until September 14, 2004 and then it would be for a program in their honor.

In the December 1951, "Chordettes Time" newsletter (Newsletter for the official Chordettes Fan Club) article, Ted Rau talked about "Chordette Day" in Sheboygan. Rau wrote "I told you about the people of Sheboygan declaring "Chordette Day." The girls were met at the station by the biggest band in Sheboygan with the mayor and notable people of Sheboygan to greet them. A banquet was given them and the following day the Sheboygan Chapter of S.P.E.B.S.Q.S.A. had a show in which the girls appeared. The place was packed to capacity with all standing room taken. Over 4,000 people were jammed into the place to hear the girls. They had a lovely time. One never to be forgotten."

"Janet's daughter, Jackie and Bob Buschmann, (Janet's brother) stayed at my house that weekend and all they kept saying was, "I wish I went along.""

While the Chordettes were in Sheboygan, they did grant one interview to Karl Krauss, a student at Central High School. The interview appeared in the Central High School student newspaper, the Lake Breeze on January 25, 1952.

Krauss wrote, "Karl Krauss, reporter and sports editor for the Lake Breeze bi-weekly had an opportunity to interview the famous Chordettes recently. Three of the members, Dorothy Schwartz, Carol Hagedorn, and Janet Buschman Ertel are graduates of Central High. Virginia Osborn attended North High during her sophomore and junior years."

"On Sept. 26, 1949, the Sheboygan girl's known as the Chordettes, appeared on the Arthur Godfrey Talent Scout show for an audition. When the four girls blended their voices in beautiful barbershop harmony, the audience became stifled and Arthur "the man" Godfrey couldn't hold the tears back, for they trickled down his freckled face."

"At the close of their audition, the applause became deafening and the show had to terminate. After their three-day run, the Chordettes were immediately chosen to Arthur's one and one -half hour broadcast. Now every morning over C.B.S. from 9 to 10:30 one can hear their hometown sweethearts.

"Dorothy, "Dottie" and Carol graduated from Central in 1945. In the interview when "Dottie" was asked what she remembered most about Central, her reply was, "All four years were wonderful and happy, but I'll always remember my senior year with a warm glow. That year the students gave "The Royal Rumpus" which was a big success-so much so that we were asked to give it for a bond drive at the Sheboygan Theater. It was a big thrill for all of us. I was lucky enough to sing in two trios and a mixed quartet with Carol."

————————————

The Royal Rumpus was held in Central High School's auditorium on March 16 & 17, 1945. It was so successful that it was held a third time, two months later at the Sheboygan Theater on May 29. For the show at the Sheboygan, admission was by purchasing War Bonds. A person received one ticket for the show with the purchase of $25.00 in bonds and two tickets if they purchased $50.00 or more in bonds. A person could not get more than two tickets.

According to the *Sheboygan Press* of June 1, 1945, "An estimated 1,300 bond-buyers loaded the spacious Sheboygan Theater to over-flowing to attend the first presentation of Central High School's musical extravaganza, "Royal Rumpus" outside of the school itself. Purchase of war bonds was the only means of admittance." Bonds were "available at all Sheboygan Banks and other War Bond issuing agencies," according to one newspaper ad.

Dorothy was very proud of the next part from the *Press* and read it to me, "According to

"Royal Rumpus" To Be Seen Tuesday Night For Bond Rally

The colorful costumes have arrived, the 18 songs and feature numbers of the show are ready, and the smooth swing band is definitely "in the groove" for the "Royal Rumpus," Central High school's hilarious musical comedy to be presented at the Sheboygan theatre tomorrow evening, May 29, at 8 p. m. as a benefit performance for the Seventh War Loan drive.

Final rehearsals are always exciting, and the "Rumpus" cast has been working overtime to stage a top-notch show for Uncle Sam and to push along the bond purchases that will help bring a lot of their friends and former classmates back home sooner.

Lights . . . music . . . and here we go for a preview. The court pages and guards step before the curtain. There's a fanfare of trumpets, and then a small figure dressed in aqua green reads the proclamation, "King Jerry Bologna, king of Bolognaville, and son of . . . ." The proclamation is finished, the minions of the court follow the parting curtains off-stage, and the show begins.

"The Royal Rumpus Swingsters" hold the stage in those first exciting minutes, and they continue to be important all through the entertainment. The 31 members of the band are artistically grouped on a step platform that lets the audience see each member. Girls are dressed in formals and boys in white dinner jackets, and for solo parts a spotlight picks out the individual who for the moment dominates the musicians. Song after song comes out sweet and true, with plenty of punch packed in the brasses and drums.

Act one sets the stage for act two, so that the audience knows that the talent to appear in the second act is that "super-colossal assortment of entertainment" collected by Count Derfert to help him win the hand of the beautiful princess. Almost 100 young singers, dancers, and musicians help to convince the king and queen (and the audience) — that here is the winning show, and for a grand climax the princess sings "I didn't Know About You."

People who have seen the show — and it has been given twice in Sheboygan, on March 16 and 17, at Central High, found it full of laughter and packed with talent. Nobody could agree on just what was the best part of it, or the most fun, for there was something for almost every taste, and an overall enthusiasm that made the "Rumpus" genuinely entertaining.

The same directors and an almost identical cast are putting on the same peppy show at the Sheboygan theatre tomorrow.

90

Girls' Vocal Trio . . .
Jeanne Gandre, Carol Hagedorn, Dorothy Hummitzsch

The photo at left is of a pre-Chordette trio performing at the Royal Rumpus show. Beginning at left, Jean Gandre, Carol Hagedorn and Dorothy Hummitzsch. Much about the event ran in the May 28, 1945 issue of the *Sheboygan Press.*

"Royal Rumpus" To Be Staged Here Tuesday Evening

Central High school's talent-packed 31-piece swing band, pictured above, will be featured throughout the rollicking musical attraction, "Royal Rumpus" to be presented on the stage of the Sheboygan theatre before local bond-buyers at 8 p. m. Tuesday. The all-student production is being sponsored by the Sheboygan Junior Chamber of Commerce in the interests of the Seventh War Loan campaign. Tickets, still available, can be obtained with the purchase of war bonds of any denomination from the bond booths in any local Warner Brothers theatre.

Tomorrow Night's The Night!

Central High's ROYAL RUMPUS Fun Show

★ Dancing!

★ Laughter!

★ Costumes!

Girls' Vocal Trio . . .
Jeanne Gandre, Carol Hagedorn, Dorothy Hummitzsch

★ Comedy!

★ Songs!

★ Entertainment!

Jeanne Zeinemann (Princess)
and
Arnold Gesch (Prince)
Love interest scene

Marimba Soloist,
Don Herman

Sheboygan Theatre
8:00 P. M.
Doors Open at 7:30 P. M.

Hurry for your Tickets!

They're going fast — so hurry, hurry, hurry! It's the one stage show you won't want to miss— chockful of laughter, songs and rollicking fun. Buy your war bonds at any authorized issuing agency—get your FREE tickets.

Sponsored by the Sheboygan Jaces and the War Activities Committee of the Motion Picture Industry

Admission by War Bond Purchase Only — Buy Your Bond

Carl W. Roth, executive manager of the bond campaign, the sale of $163,323.50 in bonds was directly attributable to the all-student talent production." Between the performance at Central and the performance two months later at the Sheboygan, the war itself had changed, with the war in Europe ending at the beginning of May, with Germany's surrender.

The Press article also reported, "Those who were unfortunate enough to have missed the performance, and there were hundreds of others clamoring for seats after the S.R.O. (Standing Room Only) sign was posted, missed one of the outstanding amateur musical comedy productions in Sheboygan's theatrical history. The show proved conclusively that "thar's talent in them rooms of Central."

Among the talent was a trio of Jeanne Gandre, Carol Hagedorn, and Dorothy Hummitzsch. This trio was pictured in an ad for the show, in the *Sheboygan Press* of May 28. Dorothy also took part in another trio with Joyce Schroeder, and Betty Kurtz singing, "The Very Thought of You." Dorothy and Carol also took part in a mixed quartet with Robert Roerdink and Anton Debevetz, singing, "Trolley Song."

After the show, the Central High School newspaper, the Lake Breeze reported, "A few of the acts were changed and new members added (from what was done at Central in March) to the show. A new trio of Carol Hagedorn, Jeanne Gandre, and Dorothy Hummitzsch put the audience in a romantic mood with their beautiful singing of "Dreams" and "Sentimental Journey."

Also part of the show was a 31-piece swing band. All together about 100 students from Central took part in the show. The show was sponsored by the Sheboygan Jaycees and the War Activities Committee of the Motion Picture Industry.

Returning back to the interview, "Carol immediately said, "The quartet in the talent show was the gay nineties style, and that is the closest I have ever come to the style we now sing."

"Turning aside, your reporter heard Janet giggling. "Well, what's so funny?" he asked."

"Janet replied, "Oh, I was thinking of my school days which are so far back that I remember practically nothing. However, I did graduate from Central, but I won't tell you when, for then you'd know my age. I have a faint recollection of being the shortest person in high school when I entered and one of the tallest when I graduated."

"Virginia, "Jinny" had been very quiet, so your reporter decided to give her the third degree. "Ginny," now let's her from you."

"Ginny" with a grin said, "I'm the traitor in the crowd, for I spent my sophomore and junior years at a good school—North."

"Janet quickly said, "Them's Fighting words, dearie." (Author's note: They may have been fighting words, but Jinny was correct about North being a good school.)

"Ginny" laughed and continued, "My freshmen year was spent at Milwaukee Downer Seminary and my senior year at Francis Shivier Junior College. I graduated in '45 and was active in glee club, dramatics and believe it or not, I was on the swimming and golf teams."

"The next question directed to the group was, "How did you gals get started?" Virginia popped up with, "My father encouraged me in barbershop quartet singing. He is now a past president of S.P.E.B.S.Q.S.A. I also talked with Mr. Faulhaber, a former music instructor at Central who encouraged me and who also gave me "Dottie's" name. Then I asked Alice Buschman Spielvogel who also brought her sister, Janet Buschman Ertel, to come to practice."

"We started singing just for fun and later it became a hobby. We began to sound mighty good, but soon Janet's sister Alice was married, so we accepted Carol into our tribe."

"When the girls were asked how they happened to get this "break" to sing for Arthur Godfrey, "Dottie" remarked, "It all happened so quickly. We went to New York to sing at a wedding reception, which resulted in our remaining for an audition on the talent show. From then on everything was very fantastic, and I guess, rather like a fairy tale.""

"Where did you give your outstanding performance?" was the next question asked. All of the girls agreed it took place when they performed at the Commodore Hotel on the same bill with Frank Sinatra, Ezio Pinza, and a crew of big name recording artists. The girls' only radio and TV appearances have been with Godfrey and his little Godfreys."

"Janet stated, "We have recorded two albums to date, "Harmony Time," volumes I and II. We haven't recorded any singles records by ourselves. We recorded "Candy and Cake," and "Dance Me Loose" with Ole Red-head Arthur.""

Relate Most Interesting Experiences

"Your reporter then inquired what their most interesting or humorous incident was which had ever happened to them. Both Carol and "Jinny" agreed being accepted as one of Arthur's "Little Godfreys.""

"Finally, Janet laughingly said, "I think one of the most harrowing experiences that has happened to me personally since we have been in New York, was the time "Jinny" and I missed the plane in Chicago after having done a New Year's Eve show. We tried desperately to charter a plane to New York for a morning show. Finally we arrived for the show at 11 a.m., which began at 10 o'clock. We went through some pretty tense hours. But when we arrived at the studio, Mr. Godfrey asked us to sing a duet which turned out to be an all-time "low" in music.""

"Dottie" related an interesting experience they had to Wichita Falls, Texas. "We were enroute—sleeping comfortably in our usual coach when the conductor woke us and informed us we had to get off the train as it didn't go to Wichita Falls. We dragged ourselves out and discovered we were in the middle of no-where at 5 o'clock in the morning.""

"Can you imagine four sleepy girls sitting on their suitcases along the railroad tracks? Well, that's what we did. After checking, we found that we could get a train at 8:30 so we went to the only coffee shop and ate many kinds of food to keep us awake and to waste time. It didn't seem funny at the time it happened, but now we can look back and laugh.""

The article ended, "In regard to their present plans, Carol replied, "We're kept much too busy with TV and radio to think about anything else, and Janet interrupted, "We wish for all of you some of the wonderful luck we have had.""

An undated "Chordettes Time" newsletter, which contained 24 pages and probably came out in early January 1952, the Chordettes wrote a letter about how they spent Christmas in 1951. The Chordettes wrote, "We all had a very nice Christmas. Jinny had her mother and her little boy with her in her brand new apartment." (Earlier in the year, Jinny and her husband, Otis were divorced.) "If you saw our Christmas television show, you know all the children of the members of the cast were on that show, so Jinny had a grand time. Janet's daughter was on the show too and Arthur gave her a lovely camera. Jinny's boy got an electric train which he loves."

"Dottie's parents flew out to New York to spend Christmas with her. They ran into some very bad weather – snowstorms and the like – and finally took a train, arriving almost a day late. In spite of the delay, they all had a wonderful Christmas. Carol was in Sheboygan for an early Christmas, but on Christmas Eve, we all got together at Janet's. We've spent our Christmas Eve's together ever since we started singing five years ago."

"On Christmas day we had our regular morning show and a very short television rehearsal. Right after the rehearsal, Janet and Carol went out to the home of our talent scout, Teddy Rau, for the rest of the day and had a very nice, homey Christmas."

"We hope you all had a very nice Christmas and we want to wish you all the best of everything for the coming year." The letter was signed, "Sincerely, Jinny, Dottie, Carol, Janet."

The *Sheboygan Press* on February 29, 1952 reported that the Chordettes had called King Cole and sang "Happy Birthday" to him over the telephone. This was in honor of his 13th birthday. Since he was born on February 29, 1896 and there was no February 29th in 1900, it was only his 13th year to actually celebrate his birthday on the day he was born.

The Chordettes were part of the Mirror's 18th annual American Ballad Contest for Barbershop Quartets held on June 11, 1952 in New York City's Central Park. There were 15,000 seats plus more room in surrounding green areas of the park.

In the August 13, 1952 issue of *People* magazine for Kohler Company employees, photos of the company picnic were shown. One picture showed Albert Buschmann and John Guetschow. The caption said, "John and Albert have a combined service record of 37 years. Al's daughter sings with the Chordettes, famous girl's barbershop quartet appearing regulary with Arthur Godfrey over radio and television."

At the beginning of summer 1952, another issue of Chordettes Time was issued and was dedicated to the Chordettes. The dedication said, "We dedicate this journal to the CHORDETTES FOR being so sweet and wonderful and for being so cooperative with their Fan Club." The summer 1952 issue contained 23 pages and included letters to the Chordettes, poems, a crossword puzzle, questions and answers with the Chordettes, and articles on Johnnie Ray and the Mariners.

About the Mariners, the newsletter said, "Four ex-U.S. Coast Guardsmen got their Christmas Present three days early in 1945 when they were invited to perform with Fred Allen. It was their first public appearance as civilians, and as the Mariners. Only three days before, they were known as the U.S. Coast Guard Quartet. They scored a hit and were invited to do guest appearances with Jack Smith, Paul Whiteman, and Eddie Cantor."

"Then, on Nov. 4, 1946, they joined the cast of CBS' "Arthur Godfrey Show" and have been with that program ever since. They are also featured on CBS TV's "Arthur Godfrey and His Friends.""

"The Mariners joined forces while they were stationed at Manhattan Beach N.Y., in 1942. They performed individually at camp functions until an officer asked them to sing as a group."

"We did," says tall, handsome James Q. Lewis, "and decided we'd better try to stick together. It was easy after the late Admiral Russel Waesche, then commandant of the U.S. Coast Guard, heard us. He decided that we should be attached to Headquarters Public Relations to do the whole Coast Guard Service what we were doing for Manhattan Beach. We were attached to the Third Naval District in New York and went to the Pacific in the summer of 1945."

"The Mariners are Thomas Lockard, James Q. Lewis, Martin Karl, and Nathaniel Dickerson."

"One of radio's best known quartets, the Mariners, play many benefits, club dates and recitals. Recently, they signed a contract to record exclusively for Columbia Records."

This journal also gave some information about the Chordettes recording future. Under questions, the Chordettes were asked, "Are you going to make any single records?" Their answer was, "We do not put out more solo records because our present contract is restricted in that direction." The next question was, "Do you look over music that is sent to you?" To which the Chordettes replied, "Yes, we always look over all music that is sent to us. However, again, there are restrictions by CBS that prohibit us from doing un-published music on the morning shows or the TV show."

One other interesting question was, "How long do you rehearse for the morning show and TV show?" The answer was, "We rehearse approximately twenty hours a week for the morning shows and sixteen hours a week for the TV show."

Also included in the journal was a letter from the Chordettes, dated May 7, 1952 and included news about an upcoming album. The letter went as follows:

"Hello Everybody:

It's been some time since we've written to you last, and so some of the things we have to tell should prove very interesting. The one thing that is most interesting and exciting right now, to us of course, is the new album we are about to make. This would be just routine except for the fact that we are going to have these arrangements published in book form at about the same time. For the longest time so many of you have been requesting some of our arrangements, but of course it was impossible to release them until this time. We just didn't have the right to release them, but now they will be published and many of you will be able to get the arrangements and also follow us on the records. We hope that this will prove helpful to those of you that are interested in starting a quartet and in singing out type of harmony. The album again will have four records, eight sides, and the book of arrangements will have about fourteen songs. Some of the songs will be, "Sentimental Journey" "S'posing" "Garden in the Rain" "Basin Street Blues." We will start recording May 16th, and we are looking forward to an early release date."

"By now you all probably know about the swimming show that we are going to do on the 30th of July, you probably know that we go swimming every Thursday afternoon at the Shelton Hotel, but did you know that Dottie doesn't swim at all? That is she didn't until we started our swimming, now she is doing fine. We're sure you will enjoy our swimming show as much as we'll enjoy doing it for you."

"So until next time."

CHORD-ially yours,

The Chordettes

Jinny, Dottie, Carol, & Jan

On August 23, 1952, The *Sheboygan Press* reported, Virginia Cole Osborn Weds Thomas Blake Lockard Jr." The article stated, "Mr. and Mrs. O.H. (King) Cole, 2733 Highland Ter., announce the marriage of their daughter, Virginia Cole Osborn, New York City, to Thomas Blake Lockard Jr., also of New York."

"The 6 o'clock ceremony was held Aug. 15 in the Lutheran Church of Sayville, Long Island. Rev. Mr. Martin was the officiant. Parents of the bridegroom are Mr. and Mrs. Thomas Blake Lockard Sr., Los Angeles, Calif."

"The bride attended Francis Shimer School in Mt. Carroll, Ill., and her husband is a graduate of Columbia University. He also attended the University of California, Los Angeles. For three years he was in the Coast Guard."

"Both persons are currently on the Arthur Godfrey show in New York. Mrs. Lockard is a member of the Chordettes. Her husband is also one of a quartet appearing on the Godfrey radio and television shows, the Mariners, in which he sings baritone."

The Mariners are shown in this publicity photo from 1952. Tom Lockard, Jinny's husband is shown in the upper left hand corner. Other members are in the front row, left to right, Nat Dickerson and James Lewis. On the right side of the back row is Martin Karl. (Photo courtesy of Dorothy Schwartz)

Lockard's group, the Mariner's was a quartet of four men. The thing that was very unusual and did cause problems for the group and Arthur Godfrey was that this group was made up of two white men (Martin Karl & Tom Lockard) and two African-American men (James Lewis & Nat Dickerson). The problems were due to the narrow mindedness of the times. These four men had started to sing together, as a group during World War II, when they were serving together in the U.S. Coast Guard.

In the southern U.S., the Mariners were not welcome and Georgia Governor Herman Talmadge wrote out against the Mariners and Arthur Godfrey for having them on the show, as it broke the South's segregation laws.

Godfrey sent his answer to the newspapers as follows, "I am sorry for Governor Talmedge, but as long as I'm on the show, the Mariners are going to stay with me."

The Mariners served together on a Coast Guard ship during the war. If they are good enough to serve together for Uncle Sam, they are good enough to sing for me."

"It's a pretty tough place where human beings can't sing together. In such a place, liberty is going to collapse."

"I'm sorry about the Governor's segregation laws. I don't know why he wants to separate one human being from another human being. It just doesn't make sense."

On November 7, 1952, the Chordettes appeared at a Parade of Quartets in Schenectady, New York. The next day, the local newspaper ran a lengthy article about the program, but only one paragraph out of 16 was about the Chordettes. That paragraph stated, "Taking no credit away from local barbershoppers, this reviewer found the tones of the Chordettes the easiest listening. The girls were coordinated smoothly in their broken or rolling chords, which in the case of 'For Me and My Gal,' one of their selections, more than faintly reminded listeners of a carillon." This was the only paragraph about the Chordettes, but at the top of the article was a large picture of the Chordettes with Doc Fendley, president of the Schenectady chapter of the Society for the Preservation and Encouragement of Barbershop Quartet Singing in America.

In 1952, Columbia Records released the third album by the Chordettes. This album was titled, "Chordettes Harmony Encores." The album was released as a 10 inch record with all of the songs on the same record. The other version was a two record set of 45s. In an odd way of numbering the 45s, the first record was numbered B 309-1 and the backside was B 309-4. The other record was numbered B 309-2 and B 309-3. On side 1, the songs were "Carolina Moon," "Basin Street Blues," and "I'm Drifting Back to Dreamland." Side 4 contained, "S'posin'," "In The Sweet Long Ago," "Garden In The Rain," and "Angry."

The second record contained on the 2 numbered side, "Drifting and Dreaming," "Sentimental Journey," "A Little Street Where Old Friends Meet," and "Floatin' Down To Cotton Town." The other side contained, "The Sweetheart Of Sigma Chi," "The Anniversary Waltz," and "Kentucky Babe."

Here is the 45 RPM version of the Chordettes third album for Columbia Records, titled Harmony Encores. The cover was printed a light green color. (From the author's collection)

In late 1952, the Chordettes knew, but not many other people knew, that Dorothy was pregnant and was going to leave the group. This meant that a replacement was needed.

In the Both Sides Now interview by Bob Callahan, with Jinny, she said, "In late '52, we had Dottie out on the road, and by that time she was expecting. She had announced that fact that she was leaving us, and we had auditioned girls in New York. We even had two people from Sid Caesar's show come in and audition, in fact, but nobody worked. When you start off with a barbershop background, it's really kind of tough to find someone, especially when you're running short on time. And on top of that, we wanted someone we liked, a nice girl."

In the same interview, Carol added, "Also, one of the requirements was that you couldn't be too short. We had auditioned one of the sisters from a well-known family singing group. Although she had a good voice, she was very short, and I refused to have a very short girl in the group. I'm very tall, and I didn't want it to look like a comedy routine. We had been seriously looking around, but it wasn't really widely known that we were looking."

———————————

In November 1952, the Chordettes appeared in Youngstown, Ohio for a barbershop show. Jinny said in the Both Sides Now interview, "In the afternoon, it's customary for the hosting chapter to entertain the visiting quartets. We were in the hotel hospitality room with some of the other quartets, the Sweet Adeline quartets, and Dottie was not feeling well and excused herself to go lay down. All the girls from the other quartets said, "Oh, sing us a song, sing us a song." But we said, "We can't, we don't have a lead. If you lend us a lead…" And one of the girls said, "Take Carolyn, she's our tenor, but she can sing lead." And Lynn said, "Oh, I'd love to." She was very enthusiastic. So we started singing, and three of us started thinking, "A-Ha!" She didn't realize she was auditioning. We spent quite a bit of time singing."

The above photo shows Lynn Evans with the Chordettes in November 1952, not realizing that the Chordettes were actually auditioning her to replace Dorothy. Left to right are Jinny, Lynn, Carol, and Janet. (Photo courtesy of Lynn Evans)

In an email Lynn explained to me how this came about. She said, "While attending church in Youngstown, Ohio, I became involved with a barbershop quartet which we called "Belles of Harmony". We sang around town and loved watching and hearing "The Chordettes" on the Arthur Godfrey Radio and TV show. The Chordettes had put out two albums of Barbershop harmony and our group learned most of the arrangements. A husband of one of the girls in our group was President of the local SPEBSQSA and thought we should invite "The Chordettes" to a barbershop show they were planning in Nov. '52. When "The Chordettes" accepted, we were all so excited."

"Our group met them at the airport. We went to the hotel where we all relaxed and sang in the hospitality room. Dottie did not join the group as she was pregnant (which no one knew) and wanted to rest before the show. I sang with them in the room, as I knew their arrangements from the books and album. It was not apparent to me that they were listening to me and after several songs, Jinny and Janet went into the other room of the suite and the next thing I knew, I was invited to go with them to NY the next morning."

Lynn added more information about this event in the Both Sides Now interview, in which she said, "I sang "Angry" and "S'Posin'." They asked, "Do you know 'Moonlight Bay?" I said, "Sure." We sang all their arrangements. They were looking at each other, but I was just having a great time. Two of them, Janet and Jinny went into the other room, and when they came back, Janet pointed a finger at me and said, "You're coming back to New York with us in the morning." That was pretty shocking, because I was married at the time, and we were living with my mother. I had to go home and change, then come back and take them to dinner, then go to the show, and then be ready to leave with them to go to New York at 8:30. This was completely out of the blue, not something I had aspired to. I sang with the barbershop quartet for sheer enjoyment."

In the same interview, Jinny added, "It took her (Lynn) all of about two or three minutes to say yes. The first time we went to New York, back in 1947, we had spent hours talking our first lead singer, Dottie, into quitting her job at the phone company. She said, "But, I can't. That's security." And then when we got Carol to join us, she wasn't working in Chicago any more, she had just come back to Sheboygan and was working for the phone company, too! We were rough on the phone company. But Lynn just dropped everything and came with us. So off we went."

In her email to me, Lynn continued, "I left with them the next A.M. Nov. 12, 1952. Archie Bleyer met us at the Airport and from then on I was immersed in recordings and arrangements to learn. I stayed at the Tudor Hotel in NY and needed to have all arrangements learned for the audition with Arthur Godfrey (which wasn't thrilling) and be ready for the Dec. 15th show on Wed. night which was live TV."

On November 23, 1952, the Youngstown (Ohio) Vindicator reported, "About 2,800 persons jammed Stambaugh Auditorium Saturday night for the annual concert sponsored by the Youngstown division of the Society for Preservation and Encouragement of Barbershop Quartet Singing in America."

"Among the groups drawing prolonged applause were The Chordettes, a "beauty parlor harmony quartet," who are featured on both the Arthur Godfrey radio and television shows."

One week later, on November 30, the same newspaper ran another article on the Chordettes. This article had the headline, "Mrs. Carolyn Evans Signs With Godfrey's "Chordettes" and the article started, "Carolyn Hargate Evans of 22 N. Richview Ave. has been signed as a member of "The Chordettes," the quartet that rose to fame on Arthur Godfrey's radio and television show."

"Carolyn, who in everyday life is Mrs. Robert B. Evans, got her opportunity through the Barber Shop Quartet Parade at Stambaugh Auditorium Nov. 22 sponsored by the Youngstown Chapter of SPEBSQSA ."

"It was just a quirk of fate," she says. This she explains, is what happened: Mrs. Evans was a member of the Belles of Harmony, a women's quartet that organized under the auspices of the SPEBSQSA, and became honorary members of the Youngstown Chapter."

"Saturday, when the Chordettes were expected here, she and the two other members of the quartet who reside in Youngstown, Jane Williams and Peggy Fuller, were asked to meet the singers at the airport and get them settled at the hotel."

"It was terrible," Mrs. Evans said. "I almost didn't get to go because I didn't find a baby sitter for Bobby, my three-year-old son, until the very last minute."

"When the Chordettes arrived, there were only three. The fourth, Mrs. Dottie Schwartz, had come in to Youngstown early with her husband to visit friends and had arranged to meet other members of the quartet at Stambaugh Auditorium."

"They told us then that she was expecting a baby in a few months," Mrs. Evans said."

"After the Chordettes arrived at the hotel, members of the Barber Shop Society invited them to a hospitality room that had been set up where members of visiting quartets could get acquainted and sing for each other."

"Everyone was so anxious to hear the girls sing," Mrs. Evans said, "and they couldn't because they didn't have anyone to sing lead. Then Jane Williams, (bless her) said 'Carolyn could sing with you."

"I almost went right through the couch," Mrs. Evans said. "But all the men insisted that I try and we had heard so many records of the Chordettes when we were practicing as the Belles of Harmony that I thought maybe I knew their style."

"Mrs. Evans says she got a "big thrill" singing with the celebrities, and although none of the members of the Chordettes complimented her, they didn't say she was bad either, for which she felt very grateful."

"Then just as we were on our way out to dinner, the girls asked me to come to New York with them at 11:20 a.m. the next day and audition for a place with the quartet. Imagine-it was 5 o'clock then!"

"The family talked it over that night and finally decided that Carolyn might as well go. The consensus was that it would be a nice vacation, but Mrs. Evans says, "I resolved to do my very best." After the girls got to New York, they sang together every time they had a chance. The audition was Friday."

"All the men sat behind the glass panel in the control room and after we had sung, we couldn't hear what they were saying," Mrs. Evans said. "Then they came out and threw their arms around me and everyone was hugging everyone so I knew I was in."

"She will return to New York Wednesday morning for more rehearsals but isn't sure when her first broadcast will be. She will sing under the name of Lynn Evans, because there already is another member of the Chordettes named Carol. Sponsors thought the two similar names would be confusing to the audience."

"This weekend she is shopping for ice skates and other paraphernalia she will need in New York. Besides rehearsals, her schedule also includes ice skating and swimming lessons in preparation for special scenes in Godfrey's shows. CBS will take care of costumes."

"A daughter of Mrs. George A. Hargate, who helps take care of Bobby. Mrs. Evans minored in music at Ohio Wesleyan University. She has been serving as music consultant of the church school of St. John's Episcopal Church and has also has sung in the church choir. She has done some solo work. She was married in 1949."

"Two brothers are rectors of large Episcopal churches in Ohio. Canon G. Russell Hargate, rector of St. Andrew's Episcopal Church in Elyria, will be honored Dec. 9 on his tenth anniversary at that church. Rev. Arthur W. Hargate is rector of Trinity Episcopal Church in Toledo."

Dorothy officially left the Chordettes on December 31, 1952 and Lynn officially became a member of the Chordettes on January 1, 1953. She became the first non-Sheboygan member of the Chordettes. She also had to change her name. She started going by the name of Lynn, to avoid confusion with Carol.

After Dorothy left the Chordettes, it did not take her and her husband long to move back to Sheboygan. On January 19, 1953, the *Sheboygan Press* reported that Mr. and Mrs. William Schwartz had arrived that day from New York and were now living with her parents at 1435 Superior Avenue.

On January 20, 1953, Dwight "Ike" Eisenhower was sworn in as the new President of the United States. Ten days later, the *Sheboygan Press* reported, "Chordettes Will Sing At Party In Honor of "Ike". The article went on to report, " The Chordettes are in Washington D.C., this week end and on Saturday evening will be singing at the dinner given by Vice President Richard M. Nixon in honor of President Dwight D. Eisenhower. It will be the first big social event in the nation's capital since the inauguration."

"Regularly each Tuesday, Wednesday and Thursday morning, the Chordettes sing on Arthur Godfrey's radio show, which is televised. They also are on a transcribed program on Saturday morning, the Robert Q. Lewis Show, for which they have been singing for over a year."

"Lynn Evans, lead, is replacing Dorothy Schwartz, who at present is at the home of her parents, Mr. and Mrs. Arthur Hummitzsch, 1435 Superior Avenue."

Unfortunately for the Chordettes, they had to cancel their appearance at the White House with President Eisenhower. The reason was given in an article in the February 16, 1953 edition of the *Milwaukee Sentinel* newspaper. Part of this article stated, "Laryngitis or hoarse throats prove a real threat for an organization like the Chordettes, which sings without any accompaniment that could cover or hide flaws. When that happens to any one of the girls, they just don't sing. Recently they missed out on a trip to Washington and a booking to sing for President Eisenhower at Vice-President Nixon's party because one of the girls got laryngitis the day of the trip."

On February 14, 1953, the *Press* printed an article titled, "Former Chordette Leaves Show Business To Have A Baby Expected In March." The *Press* also printed a photo of the Chordettes, titled, Sheboygan's Gift To Godfrey Before January 1" and showed a photo taken at the Sheboygan Armory in September 1951. The article, started, "There's no business like show business, but planning to have a baby is even more important, more wonderful."

"That's the attitude of Mrs. William Schwartz, formerly Miss Dorothy Hummitzsch of Arthur Godfrey's famous Chordettes. She and her husband are staying with her parents, Mr. and Mrs. Arthur Hummitzsch, 1435 Superior Ave., awaiting the event which is expected in March."

"Of course I miss my singing companions and all of the other wonderful friends I got to know on the Godfrey show, but this is more important," said Mrs. Schwartz." In conversations with Dorothy, more than 50 years after she left the group, she still says, "I made the right decision. All these years later, I still don't regret it."

The article continued, "You see, when Bill and I got married we had an agreement. I could stay in show business as long as I wanted to, but if we ever decided to have a family I was to quit. Well this is it." Her husband, who was present during the interview beamed." Later the article said, "The personnel has changed twice. Previous to the most recent replacement, Carol Hagedorn (now Mrs. Robert Buschman) took the place of Alice Buschman, her future sister-in-law. That leaves Virginia Cole Lockard, who is married to one of Godfrey's Mariners, and Janet Buschman Ertel as the two original members of the quartet who are still with it."

The rest of the article reported on how the Chordettes searched for a replacement and how they discovered Lynn Evans. Near the end of the article, the Press reported, "Back in New York, Mr. Godfrey also was highly pleased with the new addition and now-with a new schedule for the girls since the first of the year-everybody is happy. By alternating with the McGuire trio, the Chordettes can do all of their Godfrey shows on Tuesday, Wednesday and Thursday Mornings, with one evening show on Wednesday. So there's still plenty of time for recordings, other engagements, and frequent trips back home."

The following day, February 15, the Milwaukee Journal printed almost the same article in their newspaper. This was followed by the *Milwaukee Sentinel* running the article on February 16. Both newspapers also ran a photo of the Chordettes, taken in September 1951, during their last appearance in Sheboygan, as an all-Sheboygan quartet.

March of 1953 brought both pleasant and unpleasant news for the Chordettes. The unpleasant news was found in some newspapers on March 14. One of these newspapers was the Progress of Clearfield, Pennsylvania, which reported, "On the Arthur Godfrey Show, the Chordettes, Sheboygan, Wis., girls quartette which came from his talent scouts nearly three and a half years ago, have been replaced by the McGuire Sisters Trio, a recent addition also from the talent scouts. The sisters hail from Miamisburg, O. (Ohio)" It was later revealed that the Chordettes had been fired. Godfrey claimed that they didn't need him anymore and he didn't want to stand in their way.

The pleasant news was found in the *Sheboygan Press* of March 24, under births, "Mr. and Mrs. William Schwartz, 1435 Superior Ave., son, today. The baby's mother is the former Dorothy Hummitzsch, former member of the Chordettes."

In March 1953, the McGuire Sisters replaced the Chordettes on the Arthur Godfrey show. The card shown is card number 48 from the 1957 Topps Hit Stars set. The Chordettes were card number 52 in the same set.

In June of 1953, another fan of the Chordettes had this to say according to an email sent to me by Marjorie Latzko. Margie said, "I was a stewardess (as we were called then), flying out of Chicago, IL, while living at home in Berwyn, and I sang in a barbershop quartet just as a hobby with my mother. (I had some musical training as I had been a music major at DePaul University for two years). My mother and I used to go to a place called "The Ship's Café" on Rush Street in Chicago, where the barbershoppers hung out. The owner loved barbershop harmony, and didn't mind having people singing in all corners of his tavern. I learned many of the standard barbershop songs from several good friends named Bob Haeger, Buzz Haeger and Lyle Pilcher, all of whom were big names in the barbershop world."

"On a Wednesday in late June (June 26) 1953, I received a call from Bob Haeger who asked me, "How would you like to sing with the Chordettes?" I replied "Are you Kidding?" I was a big fan of the group. It seems he had the Chordettes on the other line calling from Pittsburgh where they were appearing in a nightclub. They were looking for a replacement (not just a temporary substitute as some uniformed people write) for their tenor and founder, Jinny Osborn Lockard, who was going to have a baby. I agreed to fly to Pittsburgh to audition on Thursday after my return flight from Mobile, IL."

"I went to the Chordettes' Pittsburgh hotel room. We chatted, and I sightread through a couple of songs with them. They invited me to join them and asked how soon I could begin rehearsing. I said that I had a flight to Los Angeles on Friday, would return on Sunday, and could join them on Monday in Cleveland, OH where they had a nightclub engagement. They said that would be fine. So I quit my job, packed my worldly belongings and on Monday, July 1, I joined the Chordettes, not knowing where I would be living, how much money I would make, or what performing I would be doing. In ten days, I learned sixteen songs and their nightclub act and was outfitted with the Chordettes' wardrobe (formal and informal). I made my debut with them at the Radisson Hotel in Minneapolis, MN."

"We were on the road for a month and arrived back in New York City the end of July. It was while we were rehearsing at CBS for the Robert Q. Lewis show that I was introduced to the Chordettes' arranger and coach, Walter Latzko. We fell in love, and Walter and I married in December 1953 with the three Chordettes and Arthur Godfrey's secretary as my bridesmaids. Tom Lockard of the Mariners and husband of Jinny sang at the ceremony."

On August 22, 1953, one month after Margie joined the Chordettes, the *Sheboygan Press* reported this change as part of an article, titled, "Chordettes Sing In Chicago Tonight At Music Festival." The short four paragraph article, reported, "The Chordettes, formerly featured on the Godfrey television and radio shows, will appear tonight at Soldier's Field in Chicago in the annual Chicagoland Music Festival on a program which also includes such stars as Victor Borge and Wilhel Silber, lyric tenor."

"The quartet will sing "Wait Til The Sun Shines Nellie" and "For Me And My Gal" in their first appearance on the program which is expected to attract 80,000 to Soldier's Field. They will also offer "I Believe," following announcement of vocal contest winners."

The article later added, "Lynn Evans of Youngstown, O., has replaced Dorothy Hummitzsch Schwartz and Margie Needham of Chicago, Ill., joined the quartet in July, replacing Virgina Cole Lockard."

The final paragraph stated, "The quartet has been signed by Robert Q. Lewis as regulars for his fall CBS television show. Lewis recently completed three months of replacement chores on radio for Arthur Godfrey."

This was actually the second Robert Q. Lewis Show on television. The first show debuted on CBS TV on July 16, 1950 and lasted only 14 weeks until January 7, 1951. The second Robert Q. Lewis Show, where the Chordettes were a part of, also on CBS, debuted on January 11, 1954 and lasted almost two and a half years until May 25, 1956.

The following day, on August 23, the *Chicago Tribune* reported that "75,000 Persons Cheer 24th Annual Chicago Music Festival in Soldier's Field." About the Chordettes, the Tribune said, "Four was a lucky number for the audience when the Chordettes were highlighted on a stand in the center of the field and harmonized in "Wait Til the Sun Shines Nellie" and "For Me and My Gal."

"Then the stadium darkened, and as from some corner of one's conscience came the voices of the Chordettes singing the declaration of faith, "I believe.""

The Chordettes fourth album cover for Columbia Records is shown here. It was titled, "The Chordettes Sing Your Requests." (From the author's collection)

In 1953, Columbia released the fourth album by the Chordettes, which was titled, "The Chordettes Sing Your Requests," which contained the three songs that the Chordettes sang at the Chicagoland Music Festival. Like the album in 1952, the album also came as a 10 inch 33 RPM record with all the songs on the same record, or a two-record set of 45s. The songs on this album were, "Wait 'till the sun shines, Nellie" and "They say it's wonderful" on side one. Side two included, "I wonder who's kissing her now," "For me and my gal" and "I believe." The third side contained, "Down among the sheltering palms" and "Hello! Ma baby." The final side included the final two songs, "Wonderful one" and "Darkness on the delta."

On Monday, October 19, 1953, Arthur Godfrey fired Julius LaRosa, live on the air during a radio program. Two days later, band director Archie Bleyer was fired. Archie Bleyer never said anything publicly about his firing.

The person that was hurt most by these firings was Arthur Godfrey. Some writers described how he fired LaRosa as "career suicide." In a PBS documentary in the early 2000s about "Pioneers of Television", the documentary said about the LaRosa firing, "With that, Godfrey's professional life was never the same. Godfrey went from loved icon to the penultimate example of the broadcast phony: someone who seemed common and pleasant on the air, but who really was cruel and paranoid." Another writer wrote about LaRosa's firing, "This action lowered the public's esteem of Godfrey, and his career soon afterwards went into decline."

The firing of LaRosa, and Bleyer made headlines across the country. The Wednesday, October 21, 1953 edition of the *Evening Journal* of Lubbock, Texas, reported under the headline, "Romances On Godfrey Show Claimed Back Of Dismissals."

The article reported, "NEW YORK, Oct. 21, 53 – The *New York Journal American* said today two romances inside the Arthur Godfrey group really were the start of singer Julius LaRosa's and band leader Archie Bleyer's dismissal from the Godfrey shows on CBS TV and radio. The Journal-American story said:" "The decision finally of LaRosa to hire a personal agent was only the straw that broke the boss' intention never to bust up the Godfrey gang."

"The first straw was piled on when testimony to a torrid love affair between Archie Bleyer and a member of Godfrey's feminine singing quartet, the Chordettes, was thrown into the public prints by Bleyer's wife, Kitty…in supreme court."

"The final straw before the thundering final coast-to-coast announcement by Godfrey himself Monday that Julius was through, was a growing romance between LaRosa and …a member of the singing trio which replaced the Chordettes." (The Chordettes were replaced by the McGuire Sisters.)

"The newspaper said LaRosa has not discussed marriage with the girl because she is still married, though separated for some time, from a soldier."

"The Journal-American quoted a personal friend of LaRosa as saying "nothing can happen between them for at least a year. At this point, it's just a nice boy and girl thing, sweetheart stuff. Not even they know yet if it will end in marriage."

Godfrey's answer to the above article was also printed in the same edition of the newspaper. Godfrey said, "I warned the boy (LaRosa) when he came in two years ago that so long as he maintained his 'God-given humility, that indefinable something' he could remain on the show."

"He deliberately avoided a ballet lesson for the whole staff and on top of that he hired an agent." "As for the firing of Bleyer, Godfrey declared: "I loved Bleyer. Ever since he formed a record company he just did nothing but wave a stick around here."

Over the next few days, papers across the country were reporting on the Julius LaRosa and

Archie Bleyer firings. It even knocked off, as most important entertainment story, the fact that John Wayne had gotten a Mexican divorce on the same day that LaRosa was fired.

The *Chicago Daily News* of October 22, went into great detail about the firings. They said, "If you want to keep a job with Arthur Godfrey, you'd better not be late for ballet class. This is one of the reasons why Julius LaRosa, the popular baritone on the Godfrey radio and television shows, got his walking papers."

"It was a Godfrey command that all the 'Little Godfreys' should take ballet lessons, but Julie came in late last Thursday. Whether it was because he was attending to personal family business, or just thought it was a silly idea, is something that no one seems sure about at this point. Anyway, when Julie showed up on time Friday, he was handed a memo from Godfrey which read, "We got along pretty well without you yesterday and can do without you today.""

"On Monday, Godfrey told Julie, while a dumbfounded coast to coast audience listened in, that he had sung his swan song. Julie said that the news hit him, "like a bolt out of the blue." But being late to ballet class is only one of several reasons behind the firing of Julius Larosa."

"Julius' friend, Archie Bleyer, musical director for the Godfrey shows, has also been fired from all but one of the Godfrey programs."

"The two of them offended their red-haired, husky boss, according to Columbia broadcasting sources, because:

1. Their backstage romances did not meet with his approval.

2. They would not play the game according to his rules."

"In an unprecedented press conference yesterday, Godfrey said he had released the two stars because they had lost their sense of humility and, accordingly, their usefulness to him."

"But network insiders insist that the trouble began first with Archie Bleyer's romance and then Julie's. Archie's wife, Kitty, went into court and gave testimony linking his name with a member of the Chordettes, who subsequently got a Mexican divorce. The Chordettes, a girls' quartet, were replaced by a trio and one of them, a pretty girl named Dorothy McGuire, has become the apple of Julie LaRosa's eye. Dorothy likes Julie, too. But she already has a husband, a soldier, from whom, however, she is separated."

"The insiders say that these backstage romances which the boss frowned on have been a source of friction between him and the two stars. The friction turned into big trouble when the stars began to show a little independence and strike out for themselves. Archie made a recording featuring Don McNeill, star of the rival ABC network. Julie himself hired a personal manager, breaking an unspoken agreement among the Godfrey gang that they would not hire managers or compete with each other for publicity."

Other newspapers on the same day, also reported that the romances were part of the reason for the firings. *The San Mateo Times* newspaper added, "As far as the Bleyer affair was concerned, Godfrey shed some interesting light on why the popular Chordettes were suddenly dropped. It seems that Bleyer's wife got a divorce early this year. She named a member of the quartet in her testimony."

"Bleyer went to Chicago last week to record Don McNeill. Apparently, Godfrey had been informed that Archie was on vacation. Godfrey found out that the boy was actually recording McNeill, ABC competition for the big red-head. "I called him about it last Monday and asked him to explain. He had a 'what the hell attitude," Godfrey related to newsmen. "I told Archie that I had just fired Julie, and it was like tearing my eyes out, but that I guessed he was next.""

"Bleyer will stay on the Talent Scouts shows until I can't stand him any more," Godfrey explained. He added, however, that he hoped he could patch up the misunderstanding."

While the Chordettes were on the Arthur Godfrey Show, Arthur Godfrey recorded, "Jingle Bells" and "'Twas the Night Before Christmas" with the Mariners and The Chordettes.

CHAPTER 5

HIT AFTER HIT
1954 TO 1959

Shown here is the first Chordettes record released by Cadence Records, titled, "True Love Goes On and On." This was also the only Chordettes record to use the solid red Cadence label. Future Chordettes records would have a red and silver label. Notice how the Cadence name is at the bottom of label and easily overlooked. (From the author's collection)

The beginning of 1954 saw the Chordettes release their first record for Cadence Records. The record was Cadence #1239 and contained the songs, "True Love Goes On and On"/"It's You, It's You I Love." The record did not sell very well and failed to make the top 100 charts of most popular records.

Shortly after 1954 started, the Chordettes also released their first album for Cadence Records and it was only the second album released by Cadence for any of their recording artists. The album was titled, "The Chordettes, Close Harmony." The album was only available as a 10 inch, 33RPM record. Songs on the album included, Oh Baby Mine , I Get So Lonely, A Good man Is Hard To Find, Careless Hands, It Looks Like Rain In Cherry Blossom lane, Makin' Love Ukulele Style, Oh How I Miss You Tonight, San, Sweet and Low, Watermelon Weather, and We Three." The cover of the album contained a group photo of the Chordettes and a photo of Chordettes' arranger, Walter Latzko, on the back. A song book with arrangements for the songs on the album was also sold for $1.00. The song book used the same photo on the cover as the album.

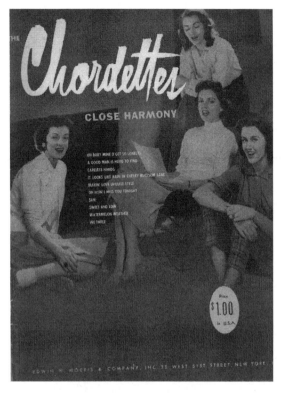

Shown here is the song book that was sold for $1.00 that contained the same songs as the Chordettes album with the same name. The same photo was also used on the album cover. (From the author's collection)

According to the *Ames Daily Tribune* fromAmes, Iowa, of January 8, 1954, "Robert Q. Lewis Finally Gets Own TV, Radio Shows." The article started, "The name's the same, but Robert Q. Lewis now has his own store."

"After seven years of being the frequent replacement for Arthur Godfrey, Lewis, who also has done practically everything at the Columbia Broadcasting System but declare dividends, is being launched this month as his own man in both radio and TV."

The radio program started last week. It is an hour-long show on the CBS network starting at 11 a.m. every Saturday. The TV show, 4:30 to 5 p.m. Mondays through Fridays, begins next Monday on CBS."

"Naturally, it's a great feeling to get on the air with my own spots and with a supporting cast of my own choice," the be-spectacled humorist said. "At the same time, I want to say that filling in for Godfrey was the greatest training in the world."

Three days after the above article appeared, on January 11, 1954, the Robert Q. Lewis Show premiered on CBS TV. The show was a 30-minute show that featured Robert Q. Lewis as the star of his own show. Prior to this show, Lewis was known mainly as a game-show host and substitute emcee for other stars.

Shown here is part of the cover from the Robert Q. Lewis record album. The photo shows Robert Q. Lewis Show cast members, left to right, front row, Betty Clooney, Lois Hunt, Robert Q. Lewis and Chordettes' Lynn, Carol, and Margie. Back row, left to right shows, Don Liberto, Earl Wrightson, Ray Bloch, and Janet from the Chordettes.

I'll use the same people on both radio and TV," Lewis said. "I've got Earl Wrightson, Lois Hunt, Jan Arden and Jaye P. Morgan as my vocalists and Don Liberto is the dancer and choreographer. I'll have the Chordettes, the girl singers who used to be with Godfrey, on the Wednesday TV shows. Ray Block handles the orchestra."

The Robert Q. Lewis show lasted until May 25, 1956, almost two and a half years. Among the stars of the show, in addition to Robert Q. Lewis, were the Chordettes, Jaye P. Morgan, Jan Arden, Betty Clooney (Sister of Rosemary Clooney), Jane Wilson, Lois Hunt and Earl Wrightson, Merv Griffin, Julann Wright (who later married Merv Griffin), and dancer-choreographer Don Liberto. The announcer for the show was Lee Vines.

Shown here is a photo showing the Chordettes on the Robert Q. Lewis show (Photo courtesy of Carol Buschmann)

With the success of the Robert Q. Lewis show, an album was released in 1955, titled, Robert Q. Lewis and His Gang. One of the songs Lewis did on the album was "Mention My Name in Sheboygan." As you know by now, Sheboygan was the hometown of the Chordettes.

On the album, the Chordettes sang, "Dixie Danny." The back of the album said about the Chordettes, "THE CHORDTTES (Courtesy of Cadence Records) need no introduction to record fans. Their *Mr. Sandman* topped the million mark. The girls, Janet, Carol, Lynn, and Margie, work out their own unique arrangements and are one of the few quartets who can sing without musical accompaniment. In 1949, these young ladies from Sheboygan were given a regular spot on the *Arthur Godfrey Show* and they've been going strong ever since. Between recording dates, regular chores on the *Robert Q. Lewis Show* and nightclub engagements, the Chordettes have earned themselves a top name. Their recording of *Dixie Danny* in this album is typical of their wonderful harmony and musicianship."

The end of summer 1954, saw the 2nd Chordettes record released by Cadence and within a very short time, it was the most popular record in the U.S. "Mr. Sandman (Cadence record #1247) hit the number one spot on the charts in October 1954 and remained in the top 100, for most popular records for 20 weeks (five months). "Mr. Sandman" sold over two million copies. One unusual thing is that on the record, the title was "Mr. Sandman" but on sheet music that was sold, it was "Mister Sandman" with Mr. spelled out. The back side of the record was, "I Don't Wanna See You Cryin'."

Mr. Sandman was the first Chordettes' record for Cadence to feature the maroon and silver label found on most Cadence records. Notice the part of the label that reads, "Knees played by Archie Bleyer." (From the author's collection)

Radio station disc jockeys would get samples (Promos) of new records to play to build interest in new songs. Shown above is a disc jockey version of Mr. Sandman. Cadence promo records used a white label with a black top, instead of red with a silver top used on versions to be sold to the public. This record shows a lot of wear on both the record and label, due to it being played so often, as it was the most popular song in the U.S. for 20 weeks. (From the author's collection)

Mr. Sandman was also issued as a 78 RPM record as shown above. 78 RPM records had been popular for over 50 years, but by 1954, were going the way of the dinosaur. Production of 78 RPM records would end in the late 1950s. (From the author's collection)

On November 9, 1954, in the *Sheboygan Press* and many other newspapers, an article appeared with the headline, "Janet Buschmann Ertel Will Wed Archie Bleyer." The article reported, "Weehawken, N.J., Two former members of the Arthur Godfrey cast plan to be married here Nov. 15."

"Composer - arranger Archie Bleyer, of New York, and singer Janet Buschmann Ertel, Freeport, N.Y., applied for a marriage license yesterday.

"Bleyer, 45-year-old owner of Cadence Record Co., left Godfrey after a seven year association in December, 1953. Miss Ertel, 41, is a member of the Chordettes, originally of Sheboygan."

"Both have been married before. Bleyer was divorced in Mexico in 1952 and Miss Ertel was divorced in Mexico last year."

But, in an article written before "Mr. Sandman" reached number one, but published after it hit number one, the Milwaukee Journal newspaper of Sunday, November 21, 1954, in their entertainment section, reported, "After eight years of trying, the Chordettes have finally hit the jackpot. The girls' barbershop quartet that was born in Sheboygan, Wis., is riding high on a Cadence record, "Mr. Sandman." It's No. 4 on Variety's hit parade and No. 11 on Billboard's honor roll of hits. And it's just getting up a head of steam.

"This must be sweet music indeed to the two original Chordettes still with the group—bass Janet Ertel and baritone Carol Buschmann." (Actually Carol was not an original Chordette.) "For them "Mr. Sandman" is a dream come true."

"The other originals have long since retired to raise babies. They are Virginia Osborn, organizer of the group and wife of one of the Mariners, and Dorothy Schwartz, wife of Bill Schwartz."

"That's the occupational hazard of a girls' quartet," says Janet. Incidentally, Janet and Archie Bleyer were married at Weehawken, N.J., last Sunday."

"People said we wouldn't be able to replace the girls," adds Carol. "They said we couldn't keep the same sound. But we were very lucky. Thanks to Margie and Lynn we still sound the same." (Margie Needham, tenor, Berwyn, Ill., and Lynn Evans, lead, Youngstown, Ohio)."

"The Chordettes began by singing accappella because they really were a girls' barbershop quartet. Now they usually have a band behind them. But they still sing genuine four part harmony. Janet the bass, gets down to low D. "On a bad morning I can hit A, but I wouldn't want to count on it," she adds. There are other girls' quartets, but none with a bass like that."

"The girls hit the big time in 1949 on the Arthur Godfrey show, where they were fixtures for the next four years. Suddenly, without any explanation, they disappeared from the show."

The article later ended, "The record ("Mr. Sandman") also is a triumph for another former "little Godfrey"—Archie Bleyer, head of Cadence Records. His first hit was "Eh, Cumpari," recorded by still another "little Godfrey," Julius La Rosa. Then Bleyer hit the jackpot with "Hernando's Hideaway."

"Mr. Sandman" was written by Pat Ballard. To show what a tough business writing songs is, Pat recently took an advertisement in Variety, headed: "Two Hits in a Row." (The other one was "I Get So Lonely.") Underneath he wrote:

"Also writer of 248 lousy songs."

According to his obituary in the New York Times, Francis Drake Ballard (Pat Ballard was his professional name) was born in Troy, Pennsylvania on June 19, 1899, and was still living in Troy when he died at the young age of 61 on October 26, 1960. He suffered a heart attack while on a business trip to New York City and died at the Medical Arts Center Hospital. .

Ballard started writing songs and radio scripts in the 1920s. In addition to "Mr. Sandman" Ballard also wrote "So Beats My Heart For You," "Say That You're Sorry," and "Just A Faded Rose." He was also author of articles and magazine stories on songs and music. For two years, he was editor of College Humor. When Fred Waring, the bandleader, was first starting his career (Remember, the Chordettes appeared on the Fred Waring show when they were just starting out), Ballard became associated with him and wrote many of his early shows.

Ballard was also interested in violins. He owned up to 50 violins at a time. He also wrote two books on violins, The Old Violin Market Survey and The Appreciation of Rare Violins.

The only survivor in his obituary was his wife, the former Hilda Gramlic.

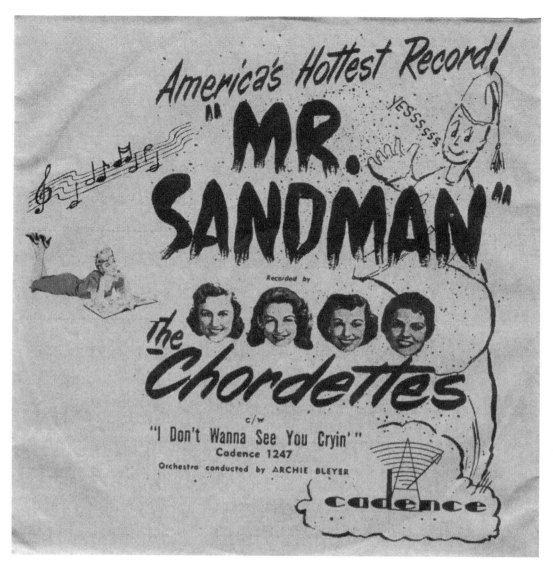

When Mr. Sandman became the number one song in the country, a special paper sleeve was issued for the record, with the name in large letters and small headshots of each of the Chordettes and advertising it as "America's Hottest Record." Today this sleeve is very hard to find. (From the author's collection.)

About "Mr. Sandman" Ballard said that he sent the song to his publisher, but nothing happened. "Mr. Sandman" was on the back side of a record by Vaughn Monroe, titled, "Mombo." Nobody paid any attention to "Mr. Sandman" because everybody wanted to Mombo.

"But suddenly," Pat recalled in November of that year (1954), "Archie Bleyer decided to make the record with the Chordettes." The song was an overnight smash and a hit in sales at the music counters."

THE CASH BOX

VOLUME XVI   NOVEMBER 27, 1954   NUMBER 10

The Chordettes and Archie Bleyer, president of the hot Cadence label, pose with another hot item, the new Rock-Ola 120 selection phonograph model 1446. Since forming the label, Bleyer has come up with several top hits. Currently, The Chordettes have one of the best selling records in the country in "Mr. Sandman" and Archie himself has a big hit in "The Naughty Lady Of Shady Lane".

Shown here is the cover of The Cash Box from November 27, 1954 with the Chordettes and Archie Bleyer. Left to right are Janet, Lynn, Archie, Carol, and Margie. The caption in the box at the bottom reads, "The Chordettes and Archie Bleyer, president of the hot Cadence label, pose with another hot item, the new Rock-Ola 120 Selection Phonograph model 1446. Since forming the label, Bleyer has come up with several top hits. Currently, The Chordettes have one of the best-selling records in the country in "Mr. Sandman" and Archie Bleyer has a big hit in "The Naughty Lady Of Shady Lane".

December 9, 1954, saw newspaper articles about the Chordettes in various newspapers across the country. The article was always the same, but had different headlines. Among the headlines used, were: "Chordettes Score With Mr. Sandman," "Chordettes High in Popularity," "Chordettes Hit New High," and "Chordettes Conquer New Fields."

The same article which appeared under these headlines reported, "The Chordettes of radio and television are riding a crest of popularity in another field--phonograph records."

"The Chordettes, once a fixture on the Arthur Godfrey programs, are leading most record popularity polls with their 'Mr. Sandman.' It has sold close to 800,000 copies in 12 weeks and seems to be a good bet for the charmed one million mark."

"Another ex-Godfreyite, Archie Bleyer, who left the Godfrey shows in the same blowup that brought Julius La Rosa's exit, figures in the story. Bleyer, married to Janet Ertel of the Chordettes, picked the tune as a likely one for his Cadence Records and assigned the girls to do it."

"It was the third major hit record for Bleyer's fledgling company. 'Mr. Sandman' is the biggest record hit yet for the Chordettes but they have been keeping fully and profitably occupied with TV, radio and personal appearances."

"Of the present Chordettes, Miss Ertel and Carol Buschmann are original members of the quartet organized back in Sheboygan, Wis."

When Mr. Sandman was moving up the charts, the Chordettes were doing a nightclub act at the Thunderbird Hotel in Las Vegas, shown here. (From the author's collection

The Ed Sullivan Show is today know as the TV show that introduced America to stars such as Elvis Presley and the Beatles. But on December 19, 1954, the Chordettes made their first appearance on Ed Sullivan's Toast Of The Town TV show. On this show, the Chordettes performed, "Mr. Sandman." Another guest on the same show was Julius La Rosa.

118

The Hotel Thunderbird used the above ad to promote the Chordettes engagement at their hotel. This ad first appeared before "Mr. Sandman" was released. Just above the word, "Thunderbird" the ad reads, "Latest Cadence Recordings, "True Love Goes On And On" and "It's You, It's You I Love." These were the two songs on their first Cadence record. "Mr. Sandman" was their second record for Cadence. (Photo courtesy of Lynn Evans Mand)

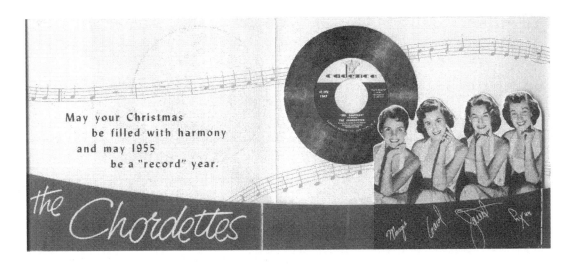

For people who were lucky enough to be on the Chordettes' Christmas card list in 1954, the Chordettes sent the card shown above, telling people, "May your Christmas be filled with harmony and may 1955 be a "record" year." The record shown is Mr. Sandman. (Photo courtesy of Lynn Evans Mand)

119

C.E. Broughton, president and editor of the *Sheboygan Press* read an editorial over WHBL radio in Sheboygan on December 29, 1954. Broughton said, "The Chordettes, who brought fame to Sheboygan, are still as popular as they were in the days when the girls left Sheboygan for a try at fame via the Arthur Godfrey Talent Scout Show."

"When they won the opportunity to appear on the Arthur Godfrey show on a temporary basis, they had no indication of the brilliant future laying before them. They returned to Sheboygan for a brief vacation, and then went on to new heights."

"In the original Chordettes were Virginia Cole, Carol Hagedorn, Dorothy Hummitsch and Janet Ertel." (Author's note, note that Alice May Buschmann was left out) "They practiced here at home, spending many an evening at the home of Mr. and Mrs. King Cole, whose daughter was more or less the 'spark plug' of the enterprise."

"Following their brief appearance on Godfrey's morning show, they signed a contract with him and for three and a half years were regular daily attractions."

"While there have been some changes in the make-up of the Chordettes, the name has been retained, and over the period of their lifetime, this musical organization has created and sold more records than any other. Today their records are tops in the nation so far as sales are concerned. 'Mr. Sandman' has sold over 800,000 copies so far, and no one can tell what the exact number will be."

"In the last few years, Virginia Cole and Dorothy Schwartz have retired, and Lynn Evans and Margie Needham have taken their places. Sheboygan will always get the credit for producing one of the country's most outstanding popular musical groups, and we are proud to claim them as our own."

One interesting story relating to Mr. Sandman occurred at New York City radio station WNEW. One of their disc jockeys, Al "Jazzbeaux" Collins, late one night, played "Mr. Sandman." After the record was done playing, he said something like, "That was nice, I'll play it again." He locked the door to the studio and played "Mr. Sandman" again and again, and again. Police were even called to investigate because people thought something had happened to the disc jockey. At the end of his shift, Jazzbeaux was fired for playing "Mr. Sandman" 55 times in a row! A little more than 10 years later, he was rehired by the radio station. The first song he played was, "Mr. Sandman." But only once.

In February 1955, the Chordettes took some time off, but not willingly. A headline in the Saturday, February 19, 1955 issue of the Long Island Daily Press reported, "Temporarily Out of Commission." The article started out by saying, "The singing Chordettes are temporarily out of commission because of a couple of bad breaks. A case of chicken pox and a broken leg, to be exact."

The article continued, "Last Sunday Chordette Lynn Evans of Rockville Centre, came down with chicken pox, contracted from her 5-year-old son, Bobby."

"The rest of the quartette decided to go on vacation until next Monday, when they were schedules to resume their stint on Robert Q Lewis' CBS radio and TV show."

"Yesterday Chordette Carol Buschmann of Oceanside broke her leg skiing at Morrisville, Vt., leaving only two girls, Marjorie Needham of White Plains and Janet Ertel of Freeport, healthy and kicking."

Carol's in Copley Hospital in Morrisville and the quartette's manager estimates they'll be out of action for at least three weeks. The group's manager said the enforced idleness will cost the Chordettes $50,000 in advance bookings."

On February 18, 1955, Carol broke her leg while skiing in Vermont. The above photo of Carol shows her reading fan mail with her leg in a cast. (Photo courtesy of Carol Buschmann)

A very short article about Carol and her broken leg was printed in the May 18, 1955, *New York Journal-American* newspaper. The newspaper reported, "The cast on Chordettes' Carol Buschmann's busted gam comes off any day. She'll frame its 500 celebrity autographs."

Another sign that the Chordettes had hit the big time was found in the February 1955 issue of Song Hits magazine, where the Chordettes were the subject of an article that covered two-thirds of a page and included a photo of the "Barbershop Beauties." The article started out by saying, "The Chordettes, four young female singers who are stars of the Robert Q. Lewis radio and television shows and formerly were headlined on the Arthur Godfrey programs for three years, have suddenly blossomed into the hottest item in the music field today. They owe it all to a ditty called, "Mr. Sandman", a tune that's been around for years, but is now whistled, hummed and sung by millions of Americans. Archie Bleyer, Musical Director of Cadence Records, took the song, gave it a catchy arrangement, threw in phrases about Pagliacci and Liberace, added tones remindful of the "dum de dum, dum" of "Dragnet", and the Chordettes took it from there. The record has already sold 750,000 copies in three months."

The above photo of the Chordettes was used in the February 1955
issue of Song Hits magazine. (From the author's collection)

"As a result of their dreamboat, 'Mister Sandman", the Chordettes' manager Jack Bartell, has been deluged with requests for the girls for personal appearances at television and radio shows, theaters, newspaper interviews, night clubs, and the like."

"However, even prior to this, the Chordettes-Janet Ertel, Carol Buschmann, Lynn Evans, and Margie Needham-were busy girls. Besides staring on the Robert Q. Lewis radio and TV shows, they stage many one-nighters, schedule permitting. Most people probably remember the Chordettes when they were official members of Arthur Godfrey's "little family". They were with Godfrey for three years."

"The girls organized their group in Sheboygan, Wisconsin (their home town), but only two of the original four are still left. Five years ago, on a quiet Sunday afternoon, the young ladies decided to while away idle hours by singing, and that impromptu songfest was to change their lives. Pleased by their harmonies, they stuck together, and dubbed the Chordettes and launched a career, which several years later, made them permanent members of Arthur Godfrey's family, after they copped top honors on his "Talent Scouts" show."

"They feel like four Cinderellas now, but success and recognition came only after hard work in perfecting their own style of barber-shop harmony. Decision to adopt that particular style was prompted by their manager, Jack Bartell, plus the fact that Sheboygan, their home town, is the accepted home of barber-shop singing."

"When Archie Bleyer, whom the girls met while he was with Godfrey, formed Cadence records, he quickly signed the Chordettes to a recording contract. He met "Mr. Sandman", liked him and introduced him to the girls. Now the girls are introducing the "Sandman" to the world."

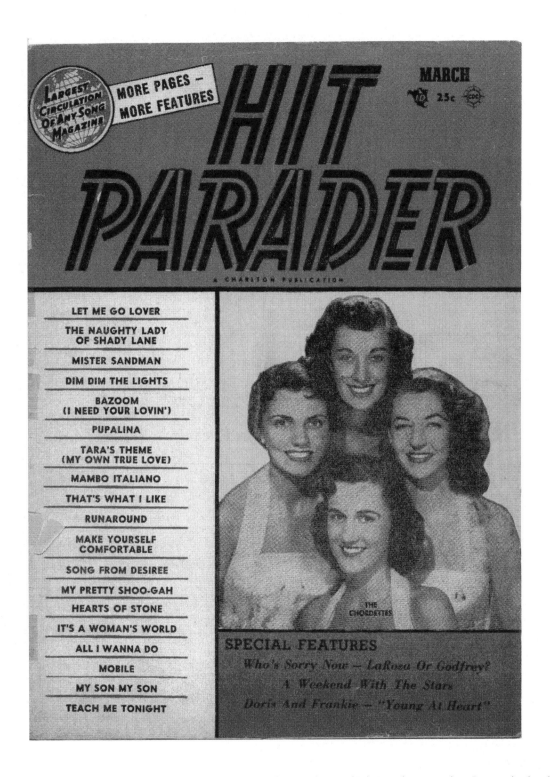

The Chordettes were featured on the cover of the March 1955 issue of Hit Parader magazine. Interestingly, the Chordettes appeared on the cover, but there was no article inside about them. (From the author's collection)

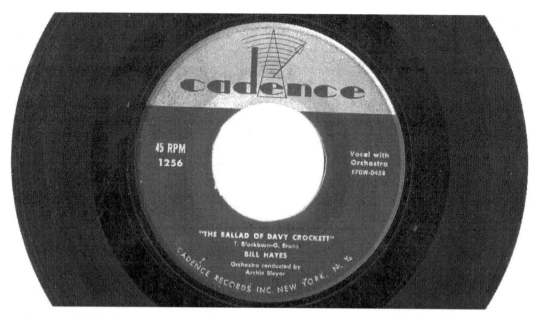

It was this record, "The Ballad of Davy Crockett" by fellow Cadence recording artist, Bill Hayes that knocked "Mr. Sandman" out of the number one spot as most popular record after 20 weeks. (From the author's collection)

In April 1955, The Chordettes were featured in an article in that month's "TV Radio Mirror" magazine. The article was titled, "Four Girls And A Dream." A sub-headline said, "Mr. Sandman" has been so good to the Chordettes, they don't want to wake up for anything, except the Robert Q. Lewis shows."

The article was seven pages long, and also included four pages of pictures of the Chordettes, with three pages of black and white individual pictures of the Chordettes showing what they liked to do when they weren't working. Archie and Janet were shown in the record shop they owned. Carol was shown in two photos, one of her golfing and one with her husband Bob and one of the parakeets they enjoyed raising. Lynn was also shown in two pictures with her son Bobby and one with her husband. Margie was shown in two photos with her husband Walter Latzko, including one playing scrabble. The final photo was a full color group photo.

The article by Jack Mahon started, "As far back as Dad can remember, the mention of a barber-shop quartet brings back memories of four mustached dandies in checkered suits gathered around the village bar or barber shop. There'd be sawdust on the floor, gaslights on the wall and songs like, "Moonlight Bay," "Wait Till the Sun Shines Nelly," "My Gal Sal," and other bits of nostalgia to fill the air."

"Well that was long ago. This is the story of another barber-shop quartet Daddy would certainly never recognize. It's the tale of four highly intelligent and provocative young ladies from out of the Midwest who'd look ridiculous indeed with mustaches. Their search for a dream came true and, in the short space of six months, the girls have shot into the spotlight of national TV and recording fame."

"They are the Chordettes, an all-girl barber-shop quartet formed a few years ago in Sheboygan, Wisconsin--cradle of many barber-shop combinations--and today are the stars of the Robert Q. Lewis TV and radio shows. They recorded a song written by Pat Ballard, "Mr. Sandman, Send Me a Dream," last August, and this one number--given a tricky arrangement by Archie Bleyer, former musical director of the Arthur Godfrey shows--has made them the talk of the TV and recording industry. In less than two months, the record sold more than half a million copies, and Bing Crosby and Guy Lombardo complimented them on it."

"The story of the Chordettes is something of a Cinderella story, too, for it was the tricky arrangement of the melody by Bleyer, combining some of the "*dum*-da-*da*-dum" tones of the *Dragnet* theme with timely references to Pagliacci and Liberace that had much to do with the success of the danceable ditty."

After a few paragraphs about winning and being hired for the Godfrey shows, the article continued, "Archie says: "I was always stuck on these kids, the Chordettes, too, and was convinced they could sing pop songs if they'd only try. They insisted they wanted to stick with barber-shop harmony because the popular field was too jammed with all-girl combinations. I went after them as soon as they left Godfrey. You can see now just where they're going. They're being swamped with offers from every big night club and theatrical office in the country. It's surely great how just one song can do all that for you."

"The 'Sandman' was only the second popular record cut by the Chordettes. Their first, 'It's You, It's You I Love' and 'True Love Goes On,' attracted but scant attention. 'Mr. Sandman,' in addition to hitting the million mark in sales, held its own for a good while as the nation's number one song."

Archie and Janet Bleyer are shown inside their music store in this photo from the April 1955
TV Radio Mirror magazine.

Shown here are two more photos from the April 1955 TV Radio Mirror. Above are Carol and Bob Buschmann with one of the parakeets that they raised. Below is a photo of Carol golfing.

"The Cinderella story of the Chordettes began quite by accident. They were formed as a "Sunday afternoon hobby," out in Sheboygan. The current quartet contains only two of the original foursome, Janet Ertel Bleyer-she married Archie last November-and Carol Buschmann. The founder of the group was Virginia Cole and the other Chordette was Dorothy Schwartz. The visits of Sir Stork put Virginia and Dottie out of the act and brought in Lynn Evans and Margie Needham as substitutes." Notice they referred to Carol as an original Chordette, even though she had actually taken over for Alice Mae Buschman.

"At this point, let's turn the mike over to Janet, the oldest of the four. Only Margie, the 'baby' of the group would admit her age (21), for the background of the happy little harmonizers."

"Virginia Cole's dad, O.H. 'King' Cole, was the president of the National Organization for the Society for Encouragement and Preservation of Barber Shop Quartet Singing in America," Janet explains, "and Jinny naturally heard plenty of same, and joined in with her dad and his friends at home and at parties at which the local Sheboygan Barber Shoppers appeared. She was actually raised on barber-shop harmony."

"Things were usually dull around town on Sunday afternoons, so Virginia decided to call a couple of us kids together and form our own quartet. That's all there was to it. Carol, Dottie Schwartz and I would drop over to the Cole household every Sunday and bone up on new arrangements of all the old-timers."

"There were all-girl groups in the process of organizing all over the country and, when 'King' Cole decided we were ready, he spotted us on a Saturday night 'Parade of Barber Shop Quartets' show in which many groups from neighboring cities and villages took part."

Bob and Bobby, Lynn's family

Lynn Evans
April 1955 TV Radio Mirror magazine

"That was our start. We went over big and, from then on, we were in constant demand for private parties, club affairs, benefits, and what not. We did it just for 'kicks,' but the word spread and soon we were accepting invitations to guest on other 'barber shop' shows in other cities. In January of 1947, we came east to do a show in Jersey City and, when it was over, we came to New York and visited the Fred Waring show. He had heard of us and asked us to do a number for him on his morning radio show. It was the biggest thrill of our lives. We did "I'd Love to Live in Loveland with a Girl Like You.' Fred was very pleased and told us to keep at it, for he thought we had what it took to make good professionally. He promised to look us up when he came to Sheboygan later in the year. He did, and we appeared with him before our home folks. If that didn't cause quite a ruffle of excitement in dear old Sheboygan."

"The girls did considerable banquet work for General Motors Corporation, and it was an executive of that organization, Wendell Anderson, who inadvertently started them on their way to their big break. Mr. Anderson retained the girls to entertain at his niece's wedding party at Watch Hill, Rhode Island. While there, an advertising executive from the Ruthrauf and Ryan Agency of New York heard them and urged them to try out for the Arthur Godfrey Talent Scouts program."

"We didn't feel good enough," Janet continues, "and it took a lot of persuading, particularly by Ted Rau, a member of the Hasbrouck Heights, New Jersey, Barber Shop Quartet, which won the International Championship in 46, to make us apply."

"We appeared on the Godfrey show, September 26, 1949, did "Balling the Jack, and won. Arthur signed us for his regular show the very next day and we were with him, and very successful too, until we decided to go out on our own in March of '53." (Author's note: Actually the Chordettes were fired in March 53.)

"That winter of 1952-53 proved to be quite a hectic season. For one thing, a change in personnel had become vital when Dorothy Schwartz announced she was going to have a baby. The hunt began for a replacement."

"After listening carefully to all the various quartets they met on their inter-city visits, the group wound up one night on a courtesy call in Youngstown, Ohio. "Lynn Evans was on the local reception committee," Janet recalls, "and at each town you visit there is what is known as a hospitality room in the hotel. We were asked to sing a few songs, but Dottie was pretty tired, Lynn filled in her place. The girls sang a couple of numbers and we knew we had our replacement for Dottie."

"Lynn had a little boy, now five years old, and it took some tall talking to convince her we really wanted her to join us. Her husband, Bob, told her to go right ahead, that it might be her big chance. She came back to New York with us and has been our 'lead' ever since. This was in November 1952."

"In July of the following year, it was Virginia's time to call off barber-shop singing in favor of lullabies, and we picked up Margie in Berwyn, Illinois, a suburb of Chicago."

"Incidentally, it should be pointed out at this time that, while all the girls are peppy and individually attractive, Margie is the beauty of the foursome. She won the "Miss Community Chest" title of Berwyn in 1947 and was Miss Berwyn-Cicero on 1951."

"Margie had done considerable barbershop singing as a hobby. She was working as a stewardess with United Air Lines at the time the Chordettes found her, and her brunette beauty and pleasing 'tenor' voice proved just what the girls were looking for in a substitute Choredtte. So Margie quit the airlines for the airwaves and has never regretted the choice. Besides, she met Walter Latzko, the Chordettes' musical arranger, and married him last year."

"Though they seldom give it a thought, Janet says she guesses you'd call Lynn the 'lead,' Margie the 'tenor,' Carol the 'baritone,' and herself the 'bass' in the harmony team. In line with these masculine-sounding titles, the girls are all tall, somewhat above average feminine height."

"Carol, five-feet, nine and a half inches, and with dark hair and big brown eyes, is the comedienne of the group. She plays a 'Dumb Dora' type on the Robert Q. Lewis show, reading letters from an equally nit-witted sister back in 'Snalflax,' Ohio. I'll give you an example," she says. "For example, sister might write: 'Uncle Homer ran for mayor here and he won. He got 34 votes. This surprised a lot of people because Snalflax only has 27 people.' You know, real yak-yak stuff," Carol laughs."

"Lynn is five-feet, eight inches, is fair. Margie, the 'baby' is five feet seven, with jet-black hair, bright blue eyes and a very fetching figure. Janet who looks taller, is five-feet six, and acts more or less as the business manager and spokeswoman for the group."

"The girls really started on their way, however, when Archie Bleyer, his record company now on solid footing, signed them in January of 1954. 'Archie always insisted that we do popular numbers,' says Janet, "but the girls, myself included, were agreed that 'barber shop' was more to our liking, and there were too many girl combinations."

"He kept pestering us to try a couple of new songs, and pointed out that even the fans had agreed it was impossible to reach a mass audience with barber-shop *acapella* harmony (without musical accompaniment)."

"We had been signed to do the Robert Q. Lewis radio show late in '52, after a sponsor had heard us down in Jackson, Mississippi, but had been featuring ninety percent old-time numbers, with only an occasional popular song thrown in for variety."

"We decided to take a chance. After all, what did we have to lose? Thank heavens, we took the gamble! As I said, our first two sides didn't attract very much attention. Then Archie heard 'Mr. Sandman' and decided to dress it up a bit, and, well, the rest you know."

"Vaughn Monroe had also made a recording of the number, and we were quite understandably swept off our feet when word reached us in Las Vegas, last September, that our record had virtually exploded on the industry and that disc jockeys all over the country were wiring for our pictures and background material."

"It was like a dream come true. Not quite the dream we had asked 'Mr. Sandman' to bring us -but a mighty happy substitute just the same."

"The 'Sandman' also proved a godfather of sorts for Pat Ballard, who wrote it. Ballard, a veteran songwriter, had not had a solid 'hit,' except for 'I Get So Lonely,' in almost twenty years, since his 'So Beats My Heart for You' clicked almost two decades ago. All in all, the months of August and September, 1954, won't soon be soon forgotten by Messrs. Bleyer and Ballard and the four young ladies from Sheboygan, Wisconsin." Actually only two of the young ladies (Carol and Janet) were from Sheboygan.

"The Chordettes are managed by Jack Bertell. They decided to have Bertell handle them again, rather than a larger outfit where they might have gotten lost in the shuffle. It proved a happy choice. They like to work with Bertell, who has been around a long time and who knows he's working with a friendly and grateful group of girls who won't let success turn their pretty little heads."

"The Chordettes' fan mail has tripled in the past few months and fan clubs have sprung up in New York, Chicago, Milwaukee, Dallas, Los Angeles, San Francisco and virtually every other major city in the country. Their favorite fan letter, however, is the one from Bing Crosby."

"Bing heard us do 'Alice Blue Gown' on a Godfrey show," Janet recalls. "He heard it while vacationing at his ranch in Elko, Nevada, and he wrote how much he enjoyed it. He said he knew the value and importance of a 'boost' on a job well done and wanted us to know how much he enjoyed us. He urged us to keep up the good work and said we couldn't miss."

"We were never so thrilled at anything in our lives! It just shows you what nice people there are in show business, and you can bet we wrote him right back, thanking him and telling him how happy he had made us."

"That's true of most big people," Carol chimes in. "Why, the other night I had dinner at Guy Lombardo's beautiful restaurant in Freeport, Long Island. Guy came over and paid us all a wonderful compliment. He said he thought 'Mr. Sandman' was the greatest recording he'd heard in the last ten years."

"Speaking of mail," puts in Margie, "why don't you tell about all the mail we're received about the 'mystery voice' and the 'knee business' on 'Mr. Sandman'?"

"Janet hastens to explain: "You hear the patter of tapping on the knees with open palms at the opening of the record." she explains, "and then, later on, in the second chorus, there is a male voice who answers 'Yes' when we croon 'Mr. Sandman.' These two bits had listeners mystified and I'll bet we've received almost a thousand inquiries asking who the 'mystery voice' is. I won't keep you in suspense. It's Archie Bleyer."

The favorite fan letter The Chordettes got was from Bing Crosby. When I first met with Carol Buschmann, to get information for this book, one of the first things she showed me was a copy of the letter from Bing Crosby. Lynn and Margie also asked me if I had seen the letter. (From the author's collection)

"The future? The girls are a little too breathless, after all that's happened so quickly, to know for sure just what they'll do this year. One thing they will do, definitely, is to continue to search for 'pop' songs which fit their style. They will not desert 'barber shop' by any means and have recently completed another album of old-timers, along with a music book of their individual arrangements for study and use by embryo all-girl quartets-in high schools and colleges-who might like to follow in their footsteps."

"Their income has doubled, of course, in the past six months and their night-club and theatrical dates are being carefully spotted by manager Jack Bertell. It looks like a golden year for the Cadence Record Corporation and all concerned."

The lengthy magazine article ended, "A happy year because of one happy little song. The 'Sandman' acted in reverse when he awakened the entire entertainment world to the real talents of these four fine girls. And if all this is the 'dream' they asked him to send them, the Chordettes hope the 'Sandman' never wakes them up. They like it very much indeed in dreamland."

––––

The Chordettes spent the 4th of July 1955, holiday in New York City. On the evening before the holiday, the Chordettes appeared on Ed Sullivan's Toast of the Town TV show. This was the Chordettes second appearance on Sullivan's show. It was an unusual show in that the show was not done in a studio, but on the deck of the aircraft carrier U.S.S. Antietam. The Antietam was in New York undergoing major alterations.

Shown here is the United States aircraft Carrier, U.S.S. Antietam (CV-36) in 1953. The Chordettes performed on the deck of this ship, as part of the Ed Sullivan show, "Toast of the Town" on July 3, 195.5

This was the second Antietam (V-36) and was launched on August 20, 1944. After further work, she was ready for her first battle mission and left Pearl Harbor on August 12, 1945 for the western Pacific. But, three days later, the ship received word that Japan had surrendered. The Antietam later served in the Korean War. In September 1953, she entered the New York Naval Shipyard for major alterations. Upon completion of the work, the Antitiem emerged from the shipyard as the United States' first angled-deck aircraft carrier. The Antitem served until she was decommissioned on May 8, 1963. In February 1974, she was sold for scrap.

On August 26, 1955 some newspapers reported, "Archie Bleyer, former band leader for television star Arthur Godfrey, announced today that he has signed Godfrey's former quartet, the Mariners, to a contract with Cadence Records."

"Bleyer, who is president of Cadence, already had signed a number of Godfrey alumni, including Julius LaRosa, Marian Marlowe, and the Chordettes."

"He said the Mariners' first record would be released Aug. 28, to coincide with the group's appearance on Ed Sullivan's 'Toast of the Town' television program."

The end of August saw the Chordettes performing at the Ohio State Fair in Columbus, Ohio. The Fair was held from Friday, August 26, through Friday, September 2, 1955. Even though the Chordettes were coming off the success of "Mr. Sandman" they did not receive top billing at the Fair. The top headliner for the Fair was the star of the TV show, "Lassie" a golden retriever, named Lassie. But, a brochure for the fair, showed individual photos of the Chordettes on the top of the page and Lassie at the bottom of the page.

The Chordettes were actually part of the "Parade of Stars" grandstand show. The brochure stated for this act, "PARADE OF STARS-featuring The Chordettes, Snooky Lanson, Peggy King, Eddie Peabody, Bill "Davy Crockett" Hayes, The Billy May Orchestra with Sam Donahue and vocalist Sherry Kaye-plus six other attractions. (7:30 p.m., Sunday, August 28 through Wednesday, August 31, Grandstand.) Reserved seats for this show were $2.50 and $2.00. General admission was $1.50 for adults and 75 cents for children under 12.

Before the State Fair, one Ohio newspaper reported, "It isn't every housewife that can take a week's vacation and come home money ahead. But that's what The Chordettes, four lanky, lovely songbirds, plan to do."

"The four, Margie, Janet, Lynn, and Carol, arrived in Columbus Sunday to rehearse for a four day stand at the Ohio State Fairgrounds. From Columbus, they go to Lake Geneva, Wis., for another round of performances, then home again. All at someone else's expense."

"Of course the girls' week off from their weekly Robert Q. Lewis show is what you might call a busman's holiday, but the Chordettes don't mind. Singing to them has never been a chore. Their main job is keeping house."

"All four Chordettes are married. Two have children. Each likes to cook and sew, but none would admit to too much liking for the dust mop. "I like to refinish furniture, though," piped Lynn Evans. "I have to take care of eight parakeets," lamented Carol Buschmann."

"Carol is one of the original two Chordettes. She is married to Bob Buschmann, a photographer. And Bob is brother to Janet Ertel, the other original Chordette. Janet was recently married to Archie Bleyer. The two new Chordettes are Lynn Evans, married to a businessman, and Margie Needham, married is to Walter Laztko, arranger for the Chordettes."

A couple of weeks after the Ohio State Fair, it was reported in various newspapers, "Robert Q. Lewis, quietly but firmly, let the Chordettes go. Betty Clooney is next in line, though Q. is still very friendly with everyone. A change of program policy, and Q. was smart enough not to make enemies doing it."

The final news for 1955 about the Chordettes was found in newspapers on December 3, when it was reported, "Archie and Janet Bleyer, celebrating their first wedding anniversary, are planning a vacation in Puerto Rico. Mrs. Bleyer is a member of the singing group, "The Chordettes."

The Chordettes had released only three 45's in 1955 and none of the songs did very well. The first 45 was Lonely Lips/The Dudelsack Song. It failed to chart. The Chordettes' second record release, Hummingbird/I Told A Lie also failed to chart. The final release for 1955, The Wedding/ I Don't Know, I Don't Care did the best of the three records for the year, as it did make the chart of 100 most popular songs, but it barely charted, at #91 and only for one week.

But, Janet of the Chordettes also released a solo record late in the year. Cadence released a 45 RPM record (Cadence #1279) with Archie Bleyer singing "Nothing To Do" on the "A" side and Janet singing, "Cause You're My Lover" on the "B" side. Janet was the only member of the Chordettes that would have a record released as a solo singer.

The first four months of 1956 was very quiet for Chordettes news, as nothing was found. In March 1956, The Chordettes recording of "Eddie My Love" was moving up the charts and gained some attention in the music industry for the Chordettes. "Eddie My Love" reached a high of #14 on the charts in March of 1956. This was the best a Chordettes' record had done on the charts in over a year.

The Chordettes also released two other singles in 1956. "Born to be with You/Love Never Changes, was released in May. In June, "Born to be with You" hit number 5 on the charts, making it the second Chordettes record to make it into the top five spots of most popular records. The final record released for 1956 was, Lay Down Your Arms/Teenage Goodnight. "Lay Down Your Arms" reached number 16 on the charts in September and "Teenage Goodnight" reached the number 45 spot on the charts, the following month.

In May and June 1956, the Playdium in Sheboygan was running a series of ads announcing that they now had new entertainment. One part of this new entertainment was the Roy Stephens Orchestra. This orchestra was advertised as having "8 Outstanding artists featuring Alice May, former member of the famous Chordettes."

On June 27, 1956, various newspapers reported another change on the Arthur Godfrey shows and they were not kind to Godfrey. The article said, "Arthur Godfrey, who chopped down his TV family tree with his little hatchet, buries it officially at the end of this week."

"The redhead and what are left of his friends will go separate contractual ways from midnight, June 30 on. Performers such as Jan Davis and the McGuire Sisters will float in and out of Godfrey's shows, but they won't be bound to him by contracts. No one will anymore, says Godfrey."

"The ax that Godfrey wielded was perhaps the strangest in the history of show business. It was a blade of gold, it brought money and fame to almost everyone it touched. It also brought love and occasional appearances on the Ed Sullivan Show."

"Perhaps the most fortunate of the Godfrey small fry has been Julius LaRosa. A crooner with a pleasant, but undistinguished voice. LaRosa got an allowance of about $900 a week while he was with Godfrey."

"Godfrey put Julius' head on the block on Oct. 19, 1953, for cultivating one of the McGuire sisters instead of humility. It was a surprise stroke, but a rewarding one. Julius, say those close to him, earned $300,000 that first year away from Godfrey."

"Romance came to the Chordettes who were let out by Godfrey in March, 1953. One of the girls, Janet Ertel, married bandleader Archie Bleyer, who was fired the same day as LaRosa."

"Another Chordette, Virginia Osborn married Tom Lockard, one of the Mariners, a male quartet fired in April 1955. The Chordettes, who were making about $50,000 annually with Godfrey, more than tripled that after getting the heave-ho. They record for Archie Bleyer's record firm. The Mariners earnings have doubled since Godfrey sped them on their way, says their manager."

"Singer Marion Marlow is another romantic and financial success. She was fired in April 1955, after toiling five years for Godfrey. She married Larry Puck, former producer of Godfrey's 'Talent Scouts," he was ousted in Oct., 1955, and is now her manager. She draws down as much as $5,000 for a single shot, hot money in any league. Oh yes, she has appeared nine times on Ed Sullivan's show."

Janet Bleyer of the Chordettes did this solo record for Cadence late in 1955. The other side of the record was her husband singing, "Nothing To Do." (From the author's collection)

The final person mentioned, "Singer Lu Ann Simms earned about $50,000 her first six months away from Godfrey, about double her TV salary. She got her walking papers last October after taking maternity leave. The baby, incidentally, was a girl, Cynthia Leigh."

The Chordettes again had a one page article about themselves in the September 1956 issue of Hit Parader magazine. The article repeated their history and mentioned that their current record, "Born To Be With You" was moving up the charts.

At the end of November, ads appeared in the *Sheboygan Press*, advertising that the Chordettes would be appearing in Milwaukee at Devine's Million Dollar Ballroom on Saturday, November 24. On November 23, the Press included a photo of the Chordettes.

Cadence Record #1324, A Change of Heart by the Bobbsey Twins is shown here.
The back-side contained the song, Part Time Gal. (From the author's collection)

Early in 1957, Cadence released a record by the Bobbsey Twins (Cadence #1324). This was actually something that Archie Bleyer had thought up as a way to attract interest in Cadence Records, as it was actually a contest for disc jockeys to see if they could guess who the Bobbsey Twins really were.

In an interview for "Both Sides Now," Carol and Lynn talked about this recording by the Bobbsey Twins. Carol said, "Janet was my sister-in-law, and we were over there at Janet and Archie's every once in a while. We were just fooling around, and ended up recording a single, just the two of us, as the Bobbsey Twins. Nobody was supposed to know who was on that. Archie had some kind of a contest to see if disc jockeys could figure out who the Bobbsey Twins were. Somebody thought one of us was Gisele MacKenzie. Nobody did figure it out." (Gisele MacKenzie was a popular singer and TV star in the 1950's, and was most know for her performances on the popular, "Your Hit Parade" TV show. Previous to appearing on "Your Hit Parade" she appeared on the Jack Benny Program and the Ed Sullivan Show.)

In the same interview, Lynn said, "Janet and Carol did a single as the Bobbsey Twins. What was funny about that, was even we didn't know about that single. They did that on the sly. We found out afterwards. Nothing happened with the single, and we were wondering, "Who did it?' And when we found out, we felt like saying, "Well!" With this record, Janet became the only member of the Chordettes to record a record as a solo artist, part of a duo, and part of a quartet.

The 45RPM record by the Bobbsey Twins contained the songs, "A Change of Heart" and "Part Time Gal." It appears that this record had a very small distribution and even Carol thought that it had not been released. The only way to find these two recordings by the Bobbsey Twins is to search for the 45 record.

In the April 2010 issue of Times Lines, a newsletter put out by the Sheboygan County Historical Society and Museum, they felt this record was so special they wrote a short article about it. The headline was, "New to the Collection." The article started, "Ask any Sheboyganite which renowned recording artists have called Sheboygan home, and they're bound to be familiar with the singing group, The Chordettes. But what about the Bobbsey Twins? This female duo released one 45 RPM record in 1957, containing the songs 'A Change of Heart' and 'Part Time Gal' (Cadence #1324). The recording was the centerpiece of a contest dreamed up by Cadence Records founder Archie Bleyer to attract interest in the label. The prize for the winning disc jockey was to be a 21" color television set. However, no one guessed who the Bobbsey Twins really were, not even the other two members of their usual singing group - The Chordettes!"

"Chordette member Carol Buschmann recounted the story: "Janet [Bleyer] was my sister-in-law, and we were over there at Janet and Archie's every once in a while. We were just fooling around, and ended up recording a single, just the two of us, as the Bobbsey Twins." The other two members of the quartette had no idea the recording had been created until much later."

"This recording, which had such a small distribution, even Carol thought that it had not been released, is now part of the museum's collection, thanks to a donation by Scott Lewandoske."

The Chordettes themselves released four 45 RPM singles in 1957. The first was Cadence #1307, "Come Home to My Arms/(Fifi's) Walkin' the Poodle." Next was Cadence #1319. "Echo of Love/Like A Baby." The third Cadence 45 of the year was #1330, "Just Between You and Me/Soft Sands." The final record released for the year was #1341, "Photographs/Baby of Mine."

Shown here is part of an ad that appeared in the Cash Box magazine of July 20, 1957. The remainder of the ad was for other Cadence acts, including The Kirby Stone Four and Ocie Smith. (From the author's collection)

The 45 containing "Just Between You and Me/Soft Sands was the most successful record of the year for the Chordettes. Just Between You and Me became the Chordettes third record to reach the top 10, making it to number eight in September 1957. That same month, the "B" side of the record, Soft Sands made the top 100 chart for most popular songs, making it to number 73.

The Chordettes song "Just Between You and Me" also became a part of music history. On Monday, August 5, 1957, a local Philadelphia, Pennsylvania TV show, called "Bandstand" became a National TV show on the new ABC network, and the name was changed to "American Bandstand" with Dick Clark as Host. American Bandstand would become one of the most popular and longest running shows in TV History, running for 30 years, making it the longest-running variety show in the history of television. The first act to appear in person on American Bandstand, were the Chordettes singing, "Just Between You and Me."

The other act to appear on this first show, was Billy Williams who sang, ""I'm Gonna Sit Right Down and Write Myself A Letter (and pretend it came from you.) The first song on the show was actually a record. That record was Buddy Holly's, "That I'll Be The Day."

The December 1957 issue of the Hit Parader magazine contained a one page article about the Chordettes and their new song, "Just Between You And Me." The magazine probably came out around October with the article written even earlier. The picture that appeared with the article showed Lynn, Janet, Carol, and Margie, even though Margie had left the group in 1956 and was replaced by Jinny.

The Hit Parader article stated, "In this day and age, speed seems to be one of the main topics of conversation, and when we talk of speed, we naturally think of the jet plane and the 'records' that are being set every day. However, one of the newest 'records' to come on the national scene is 'Just Between You And Me'. That's the latest hit done up by four charming gals known to all as the Chordettes. They have made the headlines by breaking the 'sound' barrier, this barrier being that for the past several months, it has been a man's world when it comes to close harmony hits. All we have to do is to look at the recent top tunes, and we find that there hasn't been a real winner on the female side of things for quite some time. The ever popular McGuire Sisters haven't scored recently with a topper, The Fontanes haven't been in the winner's circle, and, although Patience and Prudence have had a fairly successful run with 'Tonight You Belong To Me" and "Got Along Without You", there is no doubt that the gals have not been up there and folks in the trade were wondering why."

"Nevertheless, with 'Just Between You And Me' critics feel that the Chordettes have broken the trend that has existed, and in all probability, the female vocal groups are on the way back up."

"It is not surprising that The Chordettes have come into the national spotlight, for they have been singing their way to fame for quite some time. These four lovely lasses set the music world afire with their 'Mr. Sandman', and from the time they were singing with Arthur Godfrey, their popularity has been constantly on the rise. Archie Bleyer, of Cadence Records, is another Godfrey graduate who has made the grade, as he is the arranger for the group, and is also married to one of the Chordettes, Janet Ertel."

"Needless to say, there are still many fine female vocal combines. The DeJohn Sisters, the Bobettes with their hit, 'Mr. Lee", and the DeMarcos with, 'This Love Of Mine' are but a few, and with the Chordettes paving the way, there is no reason why the music world shouldn't soon be enjoying the female groups once again."

The article ended, "HIT PARADER, with its many readers across the country, is anxiously awaiting the day when it will once again be able to say, 'It's a woman's world.' Welcome back, Chordettes!"

The Chordettes most popular record for 1957 was "Just Between You and Me" shown above. This record became the Chordettes third record to crack The Top 10 most popular records, reaching a high of number eight in September 1957. (From the author's collection)

A sign of just how popular the Chordettes were occurred near the end of 1957, when Topps Chewing Gum Company, issued an 88 card set of "Hit Stars." These cards were available in 1-cent or 5-cent packages and featured hit stars from music, TV, and movies. The Chordettes were number 52 in the set. Cards 51 and 53 featured The Crickets (with Buddy Holly) and Jerry Lee Lewis.

Today, this is a rather expensive set to collect, due to condition and the stars in the set. This Hit Stars set, as with the 1957 Topps baseball card set, had many cards printed off center, with some cards missing the entire border on at least one side. This set also had many stars that made it popular then and now. Some of the stars in the set included four different cards of James Dean, two different cards of Jerry Lewis, Tony Curtis, and Debbie Reynolds. Some of the other stars with one card included Elvis Presley, Nat King Cole, Johnny Mathis, The Diamonds, Little Richard, Fats Domino, Andy Williams, Burt Lancaster, Bob Hope, Gene Kelly, Sammy Davis Jr., Elizabeth Taylor, Kirk Douglass, and Steve Allen. Another card featured the McGuire Sisters who had replaced the Chordettes on the Arthur Godfrey show.

The back of the Chordettes card said, "The Chordettes formed their famous singing group in Sheboygan, Wisconsin just to fill up a couple of idle hours. But when they appeared on the Arthur Godfrey Talent Scout Show and waltzed off with first place honors, they were in show business "for real." Their record, "Mr. Sandman" swept the nation and they sang the song at a Dinner at the President's (Eisenhower) request."

Shown here is the front of the Chordettes card in the
1957 Topps Hit Stars set. (Photo from the author's
collection)

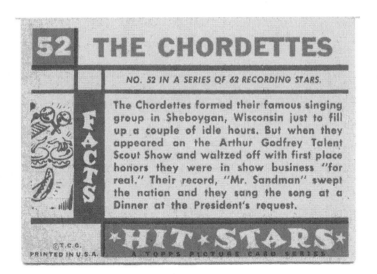

The back of the Chordettes "Hit Stars" card is shown here.
This card measured 2 ½ inches by 3 ½ inches.
(Photo from the author's collection)

Shown here is the cover of the Chordettes 1957 album, titled "The Chordettes." The album even mentioned their hometown of Sheboygan on the front. From left to right are Janet, Carol, Lynn, and Jinny. Archie Bleyer is the person driving the car, which is a 1957 Mercury convertible. (From the author's collection)

"When they sing, The Chordettes think and act as one, but down deep they're four rugged individuals."

"There's Janet Ertel (She's far left in the picture)." (This refers to the picture shown on the album cover.) "Janet was one of the original organizers of the quartet when it started in Sheboygan, Wisconsin. She's married to Archie Bleyer."

"Right next to Janet sits Carol Bushman. Her husband is Bob Bushman, restaurateur and brother to Janet Ertel."

1957 also saw the Chordettes release their second album for Cadence Records. The album was titled simply, "The Chordettes." The album cover also stated in bold lettering, "They loved them in Sheboygan." The album number was Cadence CLP-3001.

The back of the album contained the following information. "Mr. Sandman, please send me a dream" was the plaintive plea that echoed and re-echoed around the land in 1954. The radio stations and the jukeboxes made it one of the most popular phrases of the day and the Chordettes became one of the country's most popular singing groups. For, it was their recording of "Mr. Sandman" that sent the tune to the top of the nation's song-pile"

"The mythical "Mr. Sandman", in return for services rendered perhaps, sent the Chordettes much more than the dream requested in the song. Along with the enviable gold record for selling more than 1,000,000 records of this tune, they received fame, fortune, and an established position in our musical history."

"That it was all deserved is attested by the fact that the Chordettes were able to come back time and time again with the new records that would keep the citizens humming and the turntables spinning."

"This then, is what the album is all about. It is a sort of recorded documentary in song of the Chordettes. Here, of course, is "Mr. Sandman" and eleven other tunes popularized by the Chordettes. They are presented here as they were originally released with all the bounce, zest, and lively harmonizing that makes the Chordettes a standout attraction."

"There is no better proof of how good the Chordettes really are than their recordings. Listen to them do "Eddie My Love", "Born To Be With You", "Soft Sands", "Come Home To My Arms", "Echo Of Love", "Just Between You And Me", "Teen Age Goodnight", "Humming Bird", "Like A Baby", "Lay Down Your Arms", "Love Never Changes", and "Sandman". You'll see what we mean."

"When they sing, The Chordettes think and act as one, but down deep they're four rugged individuals."

"There's Janet Ertel (She's far left in the picture)." (This refers to the picture shown on the album cover.) "Janet was one of the original organizers of the quartet when it started in Sheboygan, Wisconsin. She's married to Archie Bleyer."

"Right next to Janet sits Carol Bushman. Her husband is Bob Bushman, restaurateur and brother to Janet Ertel."

"Next comes Lynn Evans. She joined the group five years ago and is married to Bob Evans, manager of a credit corporation."

"And, last but not least is Jinny Lockard. Her husband, Tom Lockard, now an insurance broker, was at one time a "Mariner". They met when both the Chordettes and Mariners were appearing on the Arthur Godfrey television show."

"As you can see, these are four girls who live separate lives with different purposes. But when they get together as the Chordettes they react as one with only one purpose. And that's to get the best out of a song."

"The Chordettes, as evidenced here, operate on a simple musical theory: If you put the best of yourself in a song, only the best can come out."

Also, on the back of the album were three small photos of albums by Andy Williams and the Everly Brothers.

Late in 1957, the Chordettes were voted the leading female recording group in a nationwide vote by teenagers. 1958 would turn out to be a very interesting year for the Chordettes, with one new member joining the group and one of their songs flirting with being the number one song on the charts.

At the beginning of February 1958, Cadence Records released a new Chordettes' single. By the end of the month, it was so successful that it was in the top 10 on the charts. It eventually made it all the way to number two.

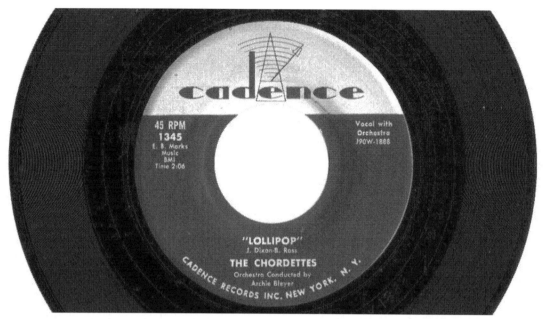

The first single for the Chordettes in 1958 was Lollipop (Cadence 1345). It sold over a million copies and reached number two on the charts for most popular record. The backside of the 45 contained the song, "Baby Come-A, (Author's Collection)

On May 4, 1958, newspapers were reporting that the Chordettes would be performing their hit song "Lollipop" on the Ed Sullivan Show that evening. Newspapers were also reporting on the same date, "Some are saying the Chordettes' new tune, "Zorro", will be another "Davy Crockett."

This was followed by a mention in Bob Foster's music column, one week later. Foster wrote, "Walt Disney he's "done it again" a couple of times recently. First of all he gambled on an adventure series based on a fictitious character of old Los Angeles, "Zorro." This program not only has developed quite a following among the moppets, but has caused both NBC and CBS a lot of pain, rating wise."

"Now four girls, The Chordettes, have recorded the theme song of the "Zorro" show and it looks like it may smash right into the fading "rock 'n' roll" tunes and climb to the top, just as "Davy Crockett" did several years back." Zorro didn't do as well as expected, but did make it into the top 20 on the charts, reaching number 17 at the end of May. The TV show, Zorro started Guy Williams as Zorro. In the 1960s, Williams would star in the TV show, "Lost In Space."

April of 1958 saw the appearance of a new member of the Chordettes, Nancy Overton. Janet had decided that she no longer wanted to go on the road and do tours, so Nancy was hired to be a "Road Chordette" and perform on the road. Janet remained in New York and still did the recording for records.

Nancy Overton was born Anna Swain on February 6, 1926, in Port Washington (Nassau County) New York. Prior to joining the Chordettes, according to information supplied by Nancy in an email to me, she said, "My sister, Jean Swain, and I formed a vocal quartet with two of our college friends in 1946 and auditioned for Tommy Tucker's Orchestra. That took us on the road with him as "The Two-Timers" for six months until we decided we could go it alone." While touring with that orchestra, she met Hall Overton, whom she married in 1951.

In 1958, the Chordettes welcomed Nancy Overton, as a new member of the group. Nancy became known as a "Road Chordette" because she joined the Chordettes on the road for tours, but did not do any recording for the group.

Continuing from Nancy's email, "There were some lean years until we landed a featured spot on "The Bert Parks Show." By then we were the "Heathertones." (Having sung with Ray Heatherton's Orchestra.) It was a live coast-to-coast TV, first with NBC and then with CBS. It aired three times a week for two years, and we were required to do the opening and closing themes, skits, our own production numbers including staging, commercials, and cast numbers. And we wrote all our own vocal arrangements and band lead sheets. We were fortunate in having Bobby Sherwood as the band leader, and Bert was a wonderful man to work for."

"During that same time period we were also singing on "The Frank Sinatra Show." That too, was a live network TV program. On this show we also did our own vocal arrangements, even those we sang with Frank. Once we asked him how he'd like to phrase a certain passage and he said, "It's your arrangement, I'll follow you girls." Talk about the ultimate compliment! Too bad the show was so short lived. Jackie Gleason appeared on the show several times, and would corner us for a private singing of "I Get a Kick Out of You." And the tears would stream down his face. (And I'm pretty sure these were tears of joy—at least I hope so!)

"My husband, Hall Overton, finally put his foot down about my being away from home so much, so the group disbanded in 1953." (Hall, who died in 1972, was a classical composer, jazz pianist, teacher and arranger. He taught at Juilliard, The New School and the Yale School of music.")

When asked about joining the Chordettes, Nancy said, "The paths of the Heathertones and the Chordettes had crossed at a benefit we were both singing for. Jinny had remembered this and contacted me to come and audition for them in 1958 as a "road" member. Janet no longer wanted to travel with the group, but continued recording with them. Hall agreed to let me join since "everybody was married and we wouldn't be on the road that much. But my four years with the group involved a great deal of travel, and many wonderful experiences."

Nancy Overton
From the author's collection

143

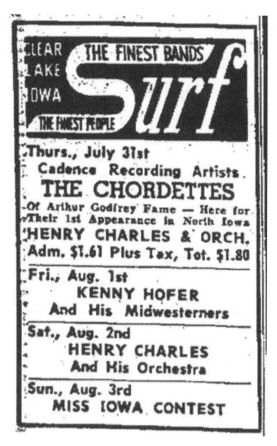

The ad at left for the Chordettes appearance at the Surf Ballroom in Clear Lake, Iowa appeared in the Mason City Gazette of July 31, 1958. Six months and two days later, Buddy Holly, Ritchie Valens, and the Big Bopper (J.P. Richardson) appeared on the same stage. A couple hours after their show ended, the three of them died in a plane crash. (From the author's collection)

On July 31, 1958, the Chordettes appeared at a Rotary Club meeting at the All Veterans Social Center in Clear Lake, Iowa. Among the guests for this meeting was Iowa Governor Herschel Loveless. According to the Mason City Iowa Gazette the following day, "THE CHORDETTES, recording artists, introduced by Carroll Anderson, set the tempo of the meeting with their two selections, Wait "Til the Sun Shines, Nelly" and "Wonderful One."

The evening of July 31st, The Chordettes performed at the Surf Ballroom, also in Clear Lake, Iowa. Ads for the show stated, "The Chordettes Of Arthur Godfrey Fame – Here for their 1st Appearance in North Iowa." Also appearing with the Chordettes was Henry Charles and his Orchestra. Admission to the show was $1.61 plus tax, for a total of $1.80.

Six months and two days later, on February 2, 1959, Buddy Holly, Ritchie Valens, and the Big Bopper (J.P. Richardson) would perform on the same stage. Shortly after these three performers finished their show, they would die in a plane crash.

Because of the Chordettes popularity and the addition of a new member, a new press release about the Chordettes was issued. The four page release said, "Four comely girls are currently at the pinnacle of show business popularity due to their haunting voices which blend into the world's finest harmony. The nation's teenagers have just voted them the leading female recording group for 1957, and their barbershop albums are collectors' items as they include incomparable arrangements of the old songs that will never die."

"These girls are called the Chordettes, stars of radio, television, nightclubs and records. The personable quartet first aroused the music world with their record of 'Mr. Sandman' and they have been the hottest property in the entertainment industry ever since 'Mr. Sandman' sold two million copies and marked only the second time in the Hit Parade's history that a tune remained in first place for twenty-one weeks."

"Swarmed by hundreds of requests for personal appearances, The Chordettes have been extremely busy filling the various engagements. Some of the high spots in their personal appearance schedule include the Annual TV & Radio Correspondents Dinner in Washington, D.C. where President Eisenhower thrilled to their barbershop arrangement of 'Wait 'til The Sun Shines Nellie' plus 'Mr. Sandman'. They co-starred with Victor Borge at the Chicagoland Music Festival where they sang for over 75,000 people. They broke all records at the Radisson Hotel in Minneapolis where they appeared for one week in the exclusive Flame Room; also headlined the show at the Thunderbird Hotel in Las Vegas where they drew sensational crowds for two weeks. The girls have appeared as special guests entertaining for the Mrs. America contest in Florida for the past three years; for two consecutive years were requested to appear at private parties in Boca Raton, Florida for the Oldsmobile Division of General Motors, and a host of other noteworthy appearances."

"Among the Chordettes recent credits are the Robert Q. Lewis television and radio shows, Ed Sullivan, Perry Como, Eddie Fisher, Vaughn Monroe, Russ Morgan, Sammy Kaye and Jonathan Winters Shows, plus the Jack Paar Tonight Show."

"The Chordettes are especially unique in that their barbershop harmony is a refreshing change in their well-rounded club act. They are equally talented in singing modern or "pop" songs. Launching their career in the popular record field was their smash record, 'Mr. Sandman', which sold two million copies and was the second tune to remain in first place on the Hit Parade for twenty one weeks. This spectacular beginning founded what was to be one of the most successful combinations in the record industry…Archie Bleyer and the Chordettes. Mr. Bleyer's creative genius and the Chordettes infallible harmony produced such hits as 'Humming Bird', 'Born To Be With You', 'Lay Down Your Arms', 'Teenage Goodnight' and most recently, 'Lollipop' and 'Zorro."

"The Chordettes originally organized their group about 10 years ago, on a Sunday afternoon in Sheboygan, Wisconsin. They decided to while away idle hours by singing, but that impromptu songfest was to change their lives. Mr. Cole, the father of one of the girls, who was then the President of the Society for the Preservation and Encouragement of Barbershop Quartet Singing in America, Inc., was very pleased with their harmonies. He boosted and encouraged them until they were ready to sing on the local barbershop show. From there they were on their way…they continued to sing at shows all over the country. The organization calls the girls 'Sweethearts of the society' as they have done much to encourage the youth of the country to form a quartets and sing. A year or two later they were encouraged by friends to try out on the Arthur Godfrey's Talent Scouts and the rest is fairly well known…Arthur took the girls to his heart and 'family' where they remained for four years."

"Jinny Lockard is the originator of the group and sings the lovely lilting tenor, which floats above the medley or 'lead' as it is termed in barbershop circles. She majored in dramatics and music at Downer Seminary and Frances Shimer College, little knowing then that she would later be involved professionally in the music business. Jinny is married to Tom Lockard one of the Godfrey Mariners and you can guess that they have quite a record collection at their house."

"Carol Bushman is the baritone of the group and sings the harmony part below the lead or melody. Carol is probably the more versatile of the group as she can sing any part with ease. She sang with a group while in school and majored in dramatics and speech in Chicago. She is married to Bob Bushman who is the owner of a local restaurant."

"Nancy Overton, has a long record of professional singing, having sung as bass voice in 'Heathertones' a group well-known on television. She has appeared with Frank Sinatra on his own television show, on the Bert Parks Show and many others. Her husband, Hall Overton, is a jazz musician, a teacher and composer, and is well-known in the jazz field."

The press release ended, "Lynn Evans, whose radiant smile and endless energy endears her to her fans, is the lead and sings the melody. When attending Ohio Wesleyan University, Lynn majored in Sociology, only minoring in music…although it was always a great love. She sang with her own barbershop quartet before joining the group and is married to Bob Evans, who is in the credit business."

The year 1959 saw the Chordettes make music history by doing something that no one else had ever done before in the music industry.

There was also other news for the Chordettes in 1959. Archie Bleyer had arranged a tour of Europe to promote a few of his recording artists. Among the artists that went to Europe, in addition to the Chordettes, were, Andy Williams and the Everly Brothers. Unfortunately, Carol was pregnant and couldn't go on the tour. So, a replacement was needed, and Margie Needham Latzko re-joined the group. Margie had been a member of the Chordettes from 1953 to 1956.

Cadence Record Company European Tour members in 1959

When the European tour was over, Carol had to quickly rejoin the Chordettes before she had planned. The reason for this, was that Margie and her husband decided to stay in Europe after the tour ended.

In 1959, the Chordettes released two 45's. The first one was "No Other Arms, No Other Lips/We Should be Together." No Other Arms did make it into the top 30 chart, reaching #27 in March. The second 45 for the year was "A Girl's Work is Never Done/No Wheels." The 45-cover sleeve featured Janet's daughter, Jackie Ertel, who was also Archie's step-daughter. The "No Wheels" side of the sleeve also featured, Jeff Kron. The sleeve was released in both black & white versions and rare color versions.

"No Wheels" was the sad song about a teen-age boy who didn't have a car. Kron happened to be in the right spot at the right time. In a phone conversation with Jackie (Ertel) Everly, she said that one day after school, she was walking home with Kron, who was a high school class-

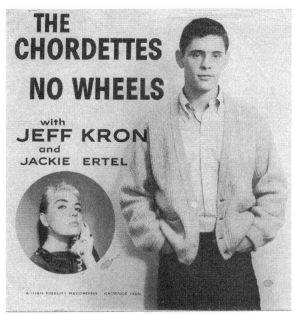

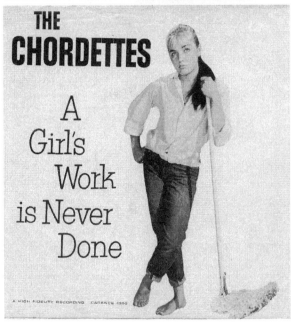

mate of hers and they decided to stop at the Cadence Records studio. Archie enlisted Kron to help with the song "No Wheels." A film clip of the song shows Kron sitting on some porch steps, lamenting the problems with not having a car, while the Chordettes are singing behind him. Also featured in the film, is Jackie Ertel who is shown in a split screen talking on the phone with Kron. Jackie is saying, "no, no, no," when Kron asks her out, because he doesn't have a car. This film clip was like every other song that was sung on TV, at the time, in that the singer would be standing or sitting, while doing the song.

But, for the song on the other side of the record, "A Girl's Work is Never Done," Archie Bleyer would try something different and the Chordettes would make music history. Bleyer had the idea of filming the Chordettes acting out the song. The plan was to show this film version of the song at drive-in movies both before the movie started and during intermissions.

The song featured the Chordettes, singing the song, while sweeping the floor, mopping the floor, vacuuming the carpet, chasing after a child running through the house leaving muddy footprints on the carpet, making the bed, ironing, washing dishes, peeling potatoes, and cooking.

This was the first song that was acted out while it was being sung. Music historians now consider the Chordettes doing "A Girl's Work is Never Done" to be the first ever music video.

After the Chordettes toured Europe in 1960, this card was issued in a set of cards printed in Holland. The Chordettes were card #14 in the set. The card shows, left to right, Janet, Margie, Lynn and Jinny. (From the author's collection)

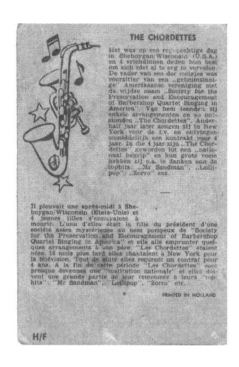

There were two versions on the reverse of the Chordettes card printed in Holland. The version on the left was printed in red ink and the writing was in Dutch (top) and French (bottom). The version on the right was printed in black ink and the writing was in English (top) and French (bottom) (From the author's collection)

In 1959, The Chordettes and a few other stars from Cadence Records went on a promotional of Europe. Shown here is a photo from the tour. Left to right around the piano are Don, one of the Everly Brothers, Jinny and Lynn from the Chordettes, Andy Williams, Margie from the Chordettes (Margie filled in on the European tour while Carol stayed in the U.S. to have a baby), Janet from the Chordettes, and Phil of the Everly Brothers. The person with his back to the camera playing the piano is Archie Bleyer.

(Photo courtesy of Carol Bushmann)

This photo shows the Chordettes acting out the song from, "A Girl's Work is Never Done." Left to right are Jinny, Lynn, Carol, and Janet. Notice that Carol is barefoot as a way to make her look shorter compared to the other Chordettes. The Chordettes film version acting out this song while singing it, is now considered to be the first ever music video. (Photo courtesy of Carol Buschmann.)

There was one Chordettes album released in 1959, but it was not issued by Cadence. Instead it was released by Harmony and was titled "Drifting and Dreaming and contained the Chordettes singing barbershop songs.

The second Chordettes EP (Extended play) record was also released in 1959. This record contained four songs, all covers of songs done by other recording artists. The songs were, Pink Shoe Laces; Tall Paul; Charlie Brown; and I Cried a Tear. The record cover for this record was also unusual, as it featured a group photo of the Chordettes in color. But, the unusual thing about the photo is that the Chordettes were all wearing different colored blouses. Lynn wore a red blouse, Carol a light green blouse, Janet a yellow blouse, and Jinny was wearing a dark green blouse. Most photos of the Chordettes show them all wearing the same type and color clothes.

In 1959, the United States Army used the song, "Mr. Sandman" in an effort to get women to enlist in the United States Army. The label contained red and blue printing on a white background. The backside of the record contained the song, "Racing with the Moon" by Vaughn Monroe. (From the author's collection.)

There was also one other 45 RPM record for the Chordettes in 1959. The U.S. Army Recruiting Service issued a record to recruit women into the U.S. Army. For some unknown reason, they used the song, "Mr. Sandman" which at this point was five years old.

Before and after the song was a message for women to join the Army. The reverse side of the record contained the song, "Racing with the Moon" by Vaughn Monroe.

Before the song started, the following message was given, "Hi there. This is Martin Block again with another all time hit, only I'm almost afraid to play this one, for you know what happens when the sandman comes around. People go to sleep."

"There's one sandman I think we could listen to that might keep us all awake and that's the sandman presented by the Chordettes with Archie Bleyer and the Orchestra. Mr. Sandman sold well over a million copies for Cadence Records. Archie Bleyer and the Chordettes are standing by to do it for us in just a moment."

"Young lady, are you graduating from high school soon? Well, if so, there is a valuable career waiting for you with the Women's Army Corp. A career that offers the finest technical training, good pay and foreign travel too, and what's more, you can choose how you will serve before you enlist. See your nearest United States Army recruiter. He has the information and there is no obligation. You get choice, not chance from your Army recruiter. And now, Chordettes, Archie, what's say we sprinkle a little of that stardust as we sing, Mr. Sandman."

After the song, Block came back with the following, "Mr. Sandman, thank you very much, Chordettes, and Archie Bleyer. The band was presented by the United States Army Recruiting Publicity Center with the cooperation of the United Federation of Musicians, James C. Petrillo, president. Now, this is Martin Block saying so long to you and you, and especially to you.

On Tuesday, July 7, 1959, *The Progress* newspaper of Clearfield, Penn. announced in their paper, that the featured attraction at the 1959 Clearfield County Fair would be the Chordettes. The Progress went on to say, "The Chordettes, four pretty girls who were voted by the nation's teen-agers as the leading female recording group for 1957, have been secured for the two Saturday night shows." Later, the article said, there would be no increase in price for the Chordettes show. Prices would be "Box seats, $1.50; reserved seats, $1.25; and general admission, 75 cents."

On Thursday, July 16, 1959, the Big Spring Daily Herald, of Big Spring, Texas, ran an article under the headline, "Jerry Lewis Show Scheduled in Area." Accompanying the article were photos of Jerry Lewis and the Chordettes.

To promote the Jerry Lewis Show, Furr's Supermarkets issued a souvenir brochure. When opened, it featured, (top), information about Jerry Lewis and other stars of the show. When folded, the right side of the bottom photo was the front cover. The Chordettes (bottom) were shown on the back cover. (Folder courtesy of Carol Buschmann)

The article went on to say, "Jerry Lewis, that delirious, energetic and zany clown of show business will make several West Texas personal appearances in a special series of Furr's Super Market presentations."

"With a number of other entertainers, he will be in Midland, September 25 at the Highland High School auditorium; in Lubbock, September 19-20-21, at the Coliseum; and in Abliene, September 24, at the Rose Field House. Lewis will top a two-hour variety show playing a 15-day tour through the Furr's Super Market trade area-West Texas, New Mexico, and Colorado-September 14 through 28. Some 300,000 persons are expected to see the show. It opens in Colorado Springs and plays these towns in order: Denver, Albuquerque, Amarillo, Roswell, Hobbs, Abilene, Midland, Odessa, and El Paso."

Tickets for these shows were not sold. Instead to get tickets, people had to save their Furr's store cash register receipts and for every $25.00 worth of cash register receipts, a person received one free ticket.

The last paragraph reported, "Along with him (Lewis) in the show will be the Chordettes, girl quartet of Arthur Godfrey fame." This was the only mention of the Chordettes in the article, but their picture with the article was just as large as Jerry Lewis' picture.

One Texas newspaper reported on Jerry Lewis' show and the Chordettes segment of it. This unknown newspaper stated, "Supporting Jerry Lewis are the Chordettes, a talented girl foursome that has soared the recording heights with releases such as "Mr. Sandman," and a host of others. Expertly disciplined and beautifully gowned in white and rhinestones, the girls provided a knockout few minutes with their turn."

But, before the Chordettes joined Jerry Lewis on his tour, they performed at the Clearfield County Fair in Pennsylvania on August 8. One person that they met after a few years was Ted Rau, who introduced the Chordettes on their first appearance on the Arthur Godfrey show. The next day, the Progress newspaper of Clearfield ran a 30 paragraph article about the Chordettes with a photo.

Most of the article was about their history. But two interesting items were reported on. The newspaper reported, "When it comes to graciousness and talent, the Chordettes can hold their own with any performers. Backstage visitors Saturday night were impressed with their friendly personalities and their complete lack of temperament. They signed autographs with the same eagerness that their admirers requested them."

The second interesting item started, "But the Chordettes are old hands when it comes to playing fairs and other outdoor engagements and even the drizzle in which they sang Saturday night, didn't faze them. They've experienced much worse."

"In fact, Lynn says nothing will probably ever match the weather conditions of an appearance they made at the opening of a drive-in theatre in Chicago."

"While we were appearing, it snowed, sleeted, rained, and hailed. The musicians' chairs were blown away by the gales of wind and you couldn't open your mouth or the hail stones would hit your teeth. Then lightning struck nearby and every time I would start to touch the microphone, some one would say, 'Don't touch it or you'll be electrocuted."

"They laugh when they recall that under such conditions, they hadn't looked forward to singing, but the theatre manager encouraged them with the words, "Don't worry about it, girls, we have nice yellow slickers (raincoats) for you to wear."

"They also remember it was the only time their applause was in the form of honking car horns."

Rock & Roll 12. CHORDETTES consists of Jinny Lochard, Carol Bushman, Nancy Overton and Lynn. Won an Arthur Godfrey Talents Scout Contest.   Printed in U.S.A.

As mentioned earlier, in 1957, the Chordettes were part of a Topps Hit Stars set. In 1959, the Chordettes appeared in another set of cards, this time a set put out by Nu-Cards, titled, "Rock & Roll Recording Stars." The set contained 64 cards and came in packs of three cards for five cents and it was possible to see what the top and bottom cards were in each pack. Each card measured 3 ¼ inches by 5 3/16 inches and the backs were blank. Photos on all of the cards were black and white.

The 1959 Nu-Card of the Chordettes is shown above. The Chordettes were card number 12 of 64 in the set. Notice that Lynn was identified only by her first name. Going clockwise from the bottom are, Jinny, Nancy, Carol, and Lynn. (From the author's collection)

The Chordettes were card number 12 in the set. Some of the other stars in the set included, Johnny Cash, Connie Francis, Ricky Nelson, Patti Page, Andy Williams, Frankie Avalon, Pat Boone, Bobby Darin, Everly Brothers, Elvis Presley, Frank Sinatra, Annette Funicello, Chuck Berry, Nat King Cole, Perry Como, Dion and the Belmonts, Fabian, Dean Martin, Johnny Mathis, Fats Domino, and Frankie Lyman and the Teenagers.

The final big event for the Chordettes in 1959 occurred on October 18, at State College in Pennsylvania, when they did a concert as part of a celebration and fund raiser for the United Nations. Tickets for the Chordettes concert were $1.25 each and over 1,000 people attended.

A motorcade ushered Mary Alice Fox down Eighth Street to her alma mater, Central High School, and then to the old Hotel Foeste on Eighth Street, where she was received in the Parkside Room and interviewed and photographed there. Only five months earlier, presidential candidate John F. Kennedy addressed a lunch gathering in the same room.

Mary Alice Fox, Miss Wisconsin - 1959, was first runner up for the 1960 Miss America Pageant. She was also Sheboygan's Bratwurst Queen of 1957.

CHAPTER 6
THE CHORDETTES FINAL YEARS
1960 TO 1963

The Chordettes started out the year 1960 performing in the Washington D.C. area. They even included a performance at the Walter Reed Army Medical Center in Washington. According to the Stars and Stripes newspaper of January 15, 1960, "Patients on Ward 31 and at the NP recreation on Friday got a close-up view of the famous 'Chordettes,' a quartet whose recordings have sold in the millions."

"Through facilities of the hospital radio station, the program was also broadcast throughout the entire hospital. Sgt. Alex Smith, a pianist with the U.S. Army Band, accompanied the Chordettes."

The Chordettes were featured in a photo found in the *Stars and Stripes Newspaper* of January 15, 1960, for Walter Reed Medical Center. The original caption said, "SING FOR PATIENTS- The Chordettes, who sang on Ward 51 last week and WRGH radio, visit with patients after the show.

The article continued, "The Chordettes took time off from their busy schedule in Washington last week when they were appearing in the blue Room of the Shoreham Hotel to entertain the patients here."

"The well-known quartette appeared on the Arthur Godfrey and Robert Q. Lewis shows and are presently recording artists for Cadence records. The Chordettes have been in show business for 10 years. Like other groups, they are not related. All are married, have children and live in New York City."

On May 16, the Chordettes appeared on the Kate Smith TV show. Some newspapers for TV listings said, "Kate Smith Show, The Chordettes, one of the nation's leading female vocal quartets will be Miss Smith's guests. The Chordettes, Jinny Lockard, Carol Bushman, Nancy Overton and Lynn Evans, are especially known for the barbershop harmony which has brought them success in radio, television, night clubs and recordings."

Other newspapers reported, "The Kate Smith Show. The Chordettes combine their usual barbershop style for 'Wait Till the Sun Shines, Nellie,' with the unusual (for them) 'A Summer Place.'"

On May 23, 1960, comedian George Burns opened a two-week engagement at Harrah's in Lake Tahoe, Nevada. On May 28, 1960, the Nevada State Journal of Reno, Nevada gave a review of this show. The article's headline was, "George Burns 'Smash Hit' In New Show at Harrah's" The newspaper article which followed, stated, "There's a big smile on his face today, and comedian George Burns has a very good reason for wearing it. His new nightclub act at Tahoe Harrah's is a smash hit."

"In addition to his own inimitable comedy styling, five good reasons for the new hit are: Molly Bee, pert young singer; the harmonizing and pretty Chordettes; the talented tapping teenage Steiner Brothers; the Dorothy Dorben Singers and Dancers; and the superb music of the Leighton Noble Orchestra."

Later the article continued, "For his wind-up act in his new presentation, Burns introduces the Chordettes-Jinny, Lynn, Carol, and Nancy-who he describes as the "prettiest and best harmony group in the world," South Shore Room patrons back up his words with warm and generous applause for their efforts. Among the songs sung by the Chordettes were "Alabama Jubilee" and a blues melody including "I get the Blues When it Rains," "Mood Indigo," and "Birth of the Blues," "Mr. Sandman" and "Lollipop, Lollipop."

"The Chordettes' "Mr. Sandman" brought spontaneous applause and also fond memories of the hit recording made not too long ago by the songstresses. Burns joins the Chordettes in a closing bit before bringing the entire company back on stage again for introductions and a final hand."

The last information about the Chordettes that was found for 1960, was information about the Iowa State Fair, held in Des Moines, Iowa from August 27 thru September 2. The Iowa State Fair had big names as the headliners all seven days of the fair. The first two days was Johnny Carson. The middle three days, the headliner was Johnny Cash, and for the final two days, the headliners were The Chordettes. Reserved tickets for the shows were $2.00 and box seats were $2.50.

The Chordettes did not have any records that charted in 1960.

From March 7 through March 11, 1961, the Winnipeg (Canada) Motor Dealer's Association held their annual new car show at the Winnipeg Arena. For an admission price of 75 cents, a person could attend the car show and a stage show. The stage show featured ventriloquist Edgar Bergen and Charlie McCarthy and for music, the Chordettes. Shows were held daily at 3:15, 7:15, and 10:15 p.m. Ads for the show, showed small individual photos of each of the Chordettes.

In an article from the *Winnipeg* (Manitoba, Canada) *Free Press* on March 6, 1961, the newspaper said about the Chordettes, "Winnipeggers attending this year's auto show will have an opportunity to see four pretty girls who rank as one of North America's top female vocal groups."

"The girls are called the Chordettes and they are stars of radio, television, nightclubs and records. The personable quartet first aroused the music world with their record of "Mr. Sandman" which sold two million copies. They followed up their initial success by selling a million copies of the record, "Lollipop." Their popularity reached a peak in 1957 when they were chosen America's leading female recording group."

"In recent years, the Chordettes have been extremely busy fulfilling personal appearances. Specialists in barbershop as well as modern style singing, they gave their rendition of "wait Till The Shines Nellie" for former President Eisenhower at a banquet in Washington D.C."

The end of the article gave a short history of their beginning, "The group was originally organized on a Sunday afternoon in Sheboygan, Wisconsin. After vocalizing at a number of Sheboygan barbershop shows, they got their big break on Arthur Godfrey's Talent Scouts and the rest is history."

One month later, on April 24, 1961, the *Sheboygan Press* announced, "Sheboygan is about to lose the leader of one of the most popular dance bands around."

The rest of the article reported, "Roy Spielvogel, conductor of the Roy Stephen's Band is pulling up stakes after many years of providing some of the best live music available to Sheboygan. Roy already has accepted a new job in Chicago and expects to move his wife, Alice, and three children down to the Windy City after school ends in June."

Shown here is a photo of the Roy Stephens Orchestra about 1960. The woman sitting on the far right side of the photo is Alice Mae Spielvogel, one of the original Chordettes, who left the group in 1947.
(Photo courtesy of the Sheboygan County Museum)

"Alice as all recall is a former Buschmann girl – one of the original Chordettes. And Roy, in addition to directing his own band, also has been the conductor of the Sheboygan Municipal Concert Band since November, 1958."

"The Roy Stephens Orchestra will continue here under new direction and ownership – but it and Sheboygan will be the losers. However, as the story goes, brighter things beckon down the Windy City way for Roy – and our very best."

In the 1961 Sheboygan City Directory, Roy and Alice were still listed as living at 812 North 5th Street. But, Roy's job listing was, "Customer Relations, Continental Can Co., Chicago."

The Chordettes had two records that charted in 1961. The first one was "Never On Sunday" which reached #13 on the charts and was on the charts for 12 weeks. The second record to chart was "Faraway Star," which was on the charts for only one week at number 90. It turned out that "Faraway Star' would be the last Chordettes record to chart.

On August 11, the Chordettes were the stars of the opening night grandstand show for the Illinois State Fair. Newspaper articles about the fair said, "Attraction for the opening night of the grandstand show will be outstanding. On the program will be the Chordettes, well known for appearances on the Arthur Godfrey and Perry Como shows. They appear on the same billing with Anita Bryant, Huckelberry Hound, Yogi Bear and the Three Stooges."

The *Sheboygan Press* ran a short, two paragraph article in their newspaper on July 17, 1961. The article reported, "A CELEBRITY- Mrs. Archie Bleyer, wife of the famous bandleader, was a guest in Sheboygan over the weekend, visiting relatives."

"She will be better remembered here as the former Janet Buschmann, one of the Chordettes. She now lives on Long Island, N.Y. The Chordettes are still going strong and at present have another big record in 'Never on Sunday.'"

From September 1 thru the 4, the Chordettes were the headliners at the New York State Fair. On the first two days, they did three shows both days, with the times being at 2:00, 5:00 and 7:00 p.m. On the last two days, they did only two shows each day, at 4:00 and 7:30.

The Sept.-Oct. issue of Song Hits magazine included a one page article on the Chordettes, titled, "The Chordettes, It Happened on a Sunday." A reference to their hit song, "Never On A Sunday." Most of the article repeated what had been said about them in other articles over the years. But two paragraphs did include some new information, which was, "They had hits with 'Born To Be With You,' 'Lollipop,' and now, with 'Never On Sunday,' the prospects look bright for another top ten winner. This effort may very well be their greatest to date. The song has been picked by the top deejays across the country as a sure bet for the top and, judging from the first reaction, it looks like they're right! Out of five versions, theirs is the 'best bet' pick."

"The girls still do personal appearances, night club dates, TV and radio, and, somehow have time for their private lives. Over the years, they've matured into one of the great night club acts by incorporating comedy routines into their act along with that wonderful harmony they do so well."

September 1961, saw George Burns open a new show at Harrah's in Lake Tahoe, Nevada. The Chordettes were again part of the show.

The Chordettes last known appearance for 1961 was reported in the NCO NEWS newspaper for the U.S. Air Force base in Laon, France. The front page included a photo of the Chordettes and under the photo, it said, "The Chordettes are coming to Laon AB, Wed. Dec. 13, to entertain the Airmen Club at 8 p.m. and NCO Club at 10:30 p.m. These stars from television… Arthur Godfrey show, Perry Como show, Ed Sullivan show and Eddie Fisher show; will be singing their hit records, Mr. Sandman, Lollipop, Never on Sunday and many others. This is the BIG SHOW of the month, so come early; you can't afford to miss this one."

The December 1961 and Jan.-Feb. issues of Rooster Tales, a small magazine published for the Rooster Tail Supper Club in Detroit, Michigan contained articles and pictures about the Chordettes. The December issue promoted the Chordettes' appearance at the Supper Club starting on January 1, and running for two weeks until January 13, 1962. The Jan.-Feb. issue contained a photo showing the Chordettes appearance.

On Tuesday, January 16, 1962, Jinny's father, King Cole announced his retirement as president of Kingsbury. In an article found in the *Sheboygan Press* on that day, the newspaper reported, "O.H. King Cole today announced his retirement as president and general manager of Kingsbury Breweries Co. at Sheboygan and Manitowoc." Cole had been with Kingsbury for 32 years and had been president of the company for 32 years, since 1948.

The *Press* reported, "Cole said he purchased a home in Palm Springs, Calif., last spring in anticipation of his retirement at age 65. He and Mrs. Cole plan to leave shortly for their new home on the west coast. Cole said he will continue as chairman of the board of Kingsbury Breweries and will look over sales in western states for both Kingsbury and G. Heilemann Brewing Co. Heileman has acquired ownership of the majority of Kingsbury stock."

Later the article added, "Cole's No. 1 hobby was singing—barbershop style. Organizer and first president of the Sheboygan chapter of the Society for the Preservation and Encouragement of Barbershop Quartet Singing in America, he served as master of ceremonies at numerous song festivals put on by Sheboygan and Manitowoc chapters throughout the years."

"In 1948, he was elected national president of the SPEBSQSA at its convention in Oklahoma City."

"He also took a lively interest in amateur baseball, sponsoring the local diamond entry in the Land O' Lakes League, along with backing Manitowoc area teams for many years. During his years in Sheboygan, Cole was active in the Elks Lodge and served as director of the Association of Commerce."

"Elect Schwartz To Head National Advertising Guild" was a headline found in the March 1, 1962 edition of the *Sheboygan Press*. The article started, "William W. Schwartz of Sheboygan was elected president of the Advertising Specialty Guild International during the organization's convention this week in Chicago. Schwartz owns and operates William W. Schwartz Associates, a Sheboygan specialty advertising firm."

The last paragraph of the article said, Schwartz and his wife, the former Dorothy Hummitzch have two children. "Mrs. Schwartz was an original member of the Chordettes, the well-known singing quartet of radio and television fame."

Starting in the middle of April 1962, ads appeared in the *Sheboygan Press*, saying, "It All Started in Sheboygan, The Nationally Famous Chordettes. Appearing at Milwaukee's Most Famous Supper Club, April 27 thru May 5, The Holiday House." The ad also included a photo of the Chordettes.

The *Milwaukee Sentinel* of April 29, gave a review of the Chordettes show at the Holiday House. The review said, "The only thing closer and smoother than a barber shop shave is a good barber shop quartet and the Chordettes are acknowledged to be among the best practition-

The Chordettes are shown in this photo found in the Stars and Stripes Newspaper of January 15, 1960, for Walter Reed Medical Center. The original caption said, "SING FOR PATIENTS- The Chordettes, who sang on Ward 51 last week and WRGH radio, visit with patients after the show. From left are Lynn, Pfc. Gent Gromulski, Nancy, Jinny, Pfc. Phil Grime, and Carol." (Photo courtesy of Carol Buschmann)

ers of this vocal art. The talented female foursome, which originated in Sheboygan, is caroling and cavorting nightly at the Holiday House. Their act is a nice blend of vintage song and finger-popping currently popular music. Even the Twist swivels into their performance."

"Current members of the quartet are Carol Bushmann and Jinny Lockard, original members, and Joyce Weston and Lynn Evans, who have supplanted charter members called way by matrimony and mother hood."

They are attractive ladies, varied in size and hair color, but identically clad in aqua gowns embroidered with pearl white palettes. In addition to their admirable vocal and physical attributes, they have a sense of humor about themselves. They kid each other about secret fantasies, becoming a ballet dancer, for example, or an operatic diva, a Monroesque sexpot or a gold digger."

"The singers repeated many of their recording successes - "Mr. Sandman," "Summer Place" and "Never On Sunday" among them. They added a barbershop medley and some newly recorded tunes. All of it was pleasant and all of it will be available at the Holiday House through May 5."

The above review mentioned Joyce Weston as a member of the group. Joyce had replaced Nancy Overton, one month earlier in March, as a Chordette. Joyce was born in McKeesport, Pennsylvania. Her birth name was Joyce Wasson, but went by the stage name Joyce Weston. When she was a teenager, she formed her own group, the Bon-Bons and also performed on a Saturday morning radio show on Pittsburgh radio station. In 1954, the Bon-Bons signed a record contract with London Records, a British Record company. Chordettes records would also later be sold in England on the London label. Joyce left the Bon-Bons in 1958 and got a job with the G.A.C. booking agency, where her accounts included Frankie Avalon and Fabian. She later left G.A.C. in order to work for Chancellor Records, where she became press agent for Avalon and Fabian. She was working for Chancellor records when she heard about an audition to replace Nancy of the Chordettes.

While the Chordettes were performing in Milwaukee, the Milwaukee Journal of May 3, 1962 in their Green Sheet section printed an article about the Chordettes that was totally different than the usual articles about them. The headline was, "Three Chordettes Are Mothers Who Show the Children Around." The article that followed started out, "It must be nice for a youngster to have a mother who is also a singing Chordettes. They tag along when their mothers sing at Miami Beach or in Bermuda. Maybe they'll go to Italy this summer. Three of the four Chordettes, appearing at the Holiday House this week, are mothers. Among them they have five children."

"The 8, the 5, and the 3 year old were with us just a short time ago when we played the Forty Thieves, a night Club in Bermuda," said Jinny Lockard, a pretty blond who is the only one of the original Chordettes still singing."

"Mrs. Lockard, the former Jinny Osborn, has two children, a boy, 16, and a girl, 8. Carol Buschman, also originally from Sheboygan, has a daughter, Janet 3. Lynn Evans has a boy, 12, and a girl, 5. "We try to hold our traveling down as much as possible because of the children," Mrs. Lockard said. "We're all working at singing because we dearly love it, but it's not a career in the sense that we'd throw everything to the four winds and say, 'This is it!' forgetting everything else."

"The Chordettes made their name a number of years ago as four young Sheboygan girls who won an Arthur Godfrey talent scout contest. They were barbershop harmonizers in those days, and they appeared with Godfrey for nearly four years on his radio and TV shows, making popular such bouncy tunes as "Dance Me Loose."

"Nowadays, they still harmonize in a barbershop sort of way, but most of their tunes are arranged for orchestra, and they do some dancing. They also get around quite a bit, in spite of efforts to stay home (in the New York city area)."

"We were going to Aruba, in the Dutch West Indies, in July," Mrs. Lockard said. "When the job first came up, we thought it would come in December, and it would be a Christmas vacation for the kids, but then they moved the date up. So actually, we're delighted it's in mid-July, because the children will be on vacation then, too."

"Even though the Aruba engagement was postponed, the Chordettes had an overseas job in December. They went to Europe where they did 23 shows in 11 days at army and air force bases in Germany and France. They drove 2,500 miles in a small car in that time, with a chauffeur who was a former German army officer with a limited grasp of English. He had an itinerary, though, and followed it with German thoroughness. This summer, after Aruba jaunt, the Chordettes probably will make a similar tour of service bases in Italy."

"The fourth Chordette, the bachelor girl, is Joyce Weston, from Pittsburgh. She used to sing with a group called the Bon-Bons. When she left them, she got into public relations and did work for singers Frankie Avalon and Fabian."

"What about "Mr. Sandman?" they're always asked, and they always sing it as part of their night club act. "We were so young then," said Carol Buschmann, "It was in late 1954, and we had just left the Godfrey show. We were doing a date in Las Vegas, just after recording 'Sandman."

"While we were there, we got a wire from Archie Bleyer, composer and arranger, who married Janet Ertel, one of the original Chordettes. 'You've got a hit,' he said, and our response was something like, 'Oh, isn't that nice.' We really didn't know much about taking advantage of a hit record."

"Mr. Sandman" was a record industry sensation. It sold two million copies. It was such a catchy tune that disc jockeys all over the country played it over and over. One liked it so much he played it 42 times - in a row - and got fired."

The article ended, "The Chordettes of course, would like to record another hit. They came close recently with "Never on Sunday," and made another one, "The White Rose of Athens," which never caught on in this country, but approached hit proportions in Europe."

The *Indianapolis Times* of Tuesday, July 10, 1962, gave a review of the Chordettes show in that city. It said, If all the dreams 'Mr. Sandman' has brought the Chordettes were laid pillow to pillow, they'd make a feather bed halfway around the globe. The four pretty singers at the B & B have included this bouncy melody in every show since they made it a top click a decade ago, and sometimes have to do a repeat for a request encore."

Shown here is a photo of the Chordettes and some of their children at an airport. Left to right is Carol with her daughter, Janet; Lynn with her daughter, Carolyn, Jinny with her daughter, Kaye; and Nancy. This photo was taken shortly before Nancy left the group. (Photo courtesy of Carol Buschmann)

"Two of the girls, Carol Bushman and Jinny Lockard, are half of the original Chordettes, Arthur Godfrey made prominent on his TV show in 1949. All from Sheboygan, Wis., the quartet had won a national contest for barber shop harmony when they made the big time on radio and television."

"Little blonde Jinny is the tenor of this group too, and willowy Carol sings baritone or the feminine equivalent. The melody is taken by 'newcomer' sparkling Lynn Evans, and the pert one, Joyce Weston, a group member since April, does the lady-bass honors, and most of the wonky turns."

"Sweetly Glamorous in gold brocade with chiffon bodices and short, crisp white gloves got Friday's opening show warmed with 'Alabama Jubilee' then slipped into 'Getting to Know You,' backed by Billy Moore and Orchestra."

"Never on Sunday' and 'Lollipop,' featuring a torrid Twist session by Joyce were a couple of live ones, and a good preface to the barber shop style favorite 'Wait Til the Sun Shines Nelly.' 'I Enjoy Being a Girl,' from 'Flower Drum Song,' with Jinny taking the lead and the girls' encore, 'Personalities,' both got double checks in the notebook."

"After the B & B, the Chordettes head for an island off the coast of Venezuela - not for vacation, to play a date there. They're not sure what they'll find, but Carol summed it up, "It'll be a captive audience.""

The last item for 1962 relating to the Chordettes was found in various newspaper of September 18. In the TV listing, it was announced that SPEBSQSA would be the subject of a one hour special on CBS-TV. The show would feature three different national champions of the SPEBSQSA plus the Chordettes.

The *Sheboygan Press* on January 12, 1963 carried a wedding photo from New York. The first part of the caption, in bold under the photo stated, "Daughter Of A Chordette, Miss Jacqualine Alice Ertel, 22, is shown with her bridegroom, Phillip Everly, 23, one of the singing Everly Brothers, following their marriage Saturday in New York. The bride is the daughter of the former Janet Buschmann Ertel of Sheboygan, original "bass" in the feminine barbershop quartet that gained national attention. Jacqueline's mother is now Mrs. Archie Bleyer of Long Island and her father is John Ertel of Peoria, Ill., formerly of this city. The bride's grandfather is Albert Buschmann, 1415 Mehrtens Ave."

The photo at left entitled the "Daughter of a Chordette" appeared in the *Sheboygan Press* of January 12, 1963.
(From the author's collection)

Phil and Jackie Everly were divorced in March 1970. They had one son, Jason Everly, who lives in Los Angeles, where he is a successful singer and songwriter.

On March 28, 1963, the Chordettes were the subject of an article in the *Rochester (Minnesota) Post-Bulletin*. The Chordettes were appearing in Rochester for the 11th annual Rochester Home Fair. That evening, they were scheduled to do a show at 9:00 p.m. with the fair opening its doors at 6:00. The next two days, Friday and Saturday, the Chordettes were scheduled to give shows at 3:00 and 9:00 p.m.

The article started, "With a maidenly flurry of spray net, lipstick and scramble for coats, the

Chordettes made ready-not for the stage-but for morning coffee."

"The four girls of the internationally starring Chordettes remain anonymous except for given names, Jinny (blonde, blue eyed and business-like), Joyce (shortest of the group with fluffy brown hair and blue eyes), Lynn (statuesque and red-haired) and Carol (tall, willowy, brunette, brown eyed)."

"This morning, having found spray net, lipstick and coats, they headed for the Zumbro Hotel Coffee Shop. There they chatted about their joint career, past, present, and future, over coffee between flashing smiles for the popping flashbulbs."

Following the usual history about Sheboygan, Arthur Godfrey and Mr. Sandman, the article continued, "Among top records for the group have been "Lollipop," a gingerly approach into the world of rock and roll. 'It sold a million copies,' said Jinny, 'but you can't count the foreign sales, so we never got a gold record."

"Working from New York, the girls meanwhile beat a path coast to coast through the United States appearing with stars like Jerry Lewis and George Burns. "We were with George Burns for over two years,' said Jinny. 'He's a doll. One night he set Lynn's dress on fire with his cigar.' It seems Burns was flicking ashes from his famous cigar on stage and there were live ashes. 'He really does smoke cigars, they aren't just a prop,' Lynn said, "About 50 a day or something."

For the immediate future, the article ended, "The current tour takes the Chordettes from Rochester to Hot Springs (Arkansas) to Reno where they open April 25 with Dennis Day." The article also included a photo of the Chordettes having coffee at the Zumbro Coffee shop that morning.

From April 25 thru May 8, the Chordettes were in Reno, Nevada for shows with Dennis Day, one of the stars of the Jack Benny show, at the Nugget Sparks in East Reno. Show times were a 8:15 and Midnight, Sunday thru Friday and at 8:15 p.m., 11:30 p.m., and 1:45 a.m. on Saturdays.

Near the end of July 1963, the Chordettes appeared in Regina, Saskatchewan, Canada, and there were a couple of problems with their visit. The exact headline in the *Regina Leader-Post* of July 30, was, "They sang THAT song and the crowd loved it."

The first part of the article reported, "The Chordettes sang "Never on Sunday" at the grandstand show, Monday evening and received nothing more dangerous than a hearty round of applause from the audience. The four-woman group, featured vocalists in the show had been requested to omit the song from their performance by several women's groups who found the song objectionable."

The remaining part of the article added, "Other than this, the quartet suffered only the handicap suffered by all performers in the show, a poor sound system. A speaking voice was, for the most part, unintelligible, jokes fell on deaf ears, and some songs, even from the 14-member Freedom Chorus faded away before they reached the first row."

The article ended, "The Chordettes didn't stop at "Sunday" but sang everything from Dixieland to barbershop in a well-rounded and highly appreciated performance."

In what could be called unusual, the same newspaper, the *Leader-Post*, on the same date, July 30, 1963, also had a second article about the Chordettes, under the headline, "Singers' varied interests" and gave some interesting background info on the four ladies. Also included with the article was a photo, taken the night before at the fair.

The article started, "A day in New York is as big a thrill for people who live there as for visitors. At least that is the impression one gathers from talking to the four attractive members of the Chordettes singing group, featured performers at the grandstand show at this year's Provincial Exhibition in Regina."

"Tourists see a lot, after all it's a concentrated thing with them, but we put it off thinking we'll do it next time and we never do," said Jinny Lockard who sings tenor with the group."

"Jinny, Carol Bushmann, baritone, Lynn Evans, lead and Joyce Weston, bass were interviewed Monday at Hotel Saskatchewan."

"Lynn's idea of a day on the town is to get dressed up and go out to dinner and the theatre. "I love live theatre. All types from heavy drama to musicals." As far as music is concerned, she admits a liking for Dixieland jazz and the romantic ballads. "And I love to cook, especially preparing and serving a meal, but not the cleaning up after it," she admitted with a grin."

"Pulling on a sweat shirt and a pair of old pants and spending the day water skiing is Jinny Lockard's idea of fun."

Carol pointed out that "I have more free time on the road. I have obligations at home and I like to spend my time with the family. (She has a daughter.)

"Joyce's taste in music extends to the music of the 40s, the big band era. She enjoys the pretty ballads, "compared to the music of today."

"The girls admitted they never have enough time to do the things they enjoy. When they're together on the road, they spend their time seeing movies or playing bridge. "We really don't play much bridge, but we talk about it a lot," Carol quipped."

The article continued, "The girls rehearse if they are breaking in a new number, but not otherwise. When they're at home, they spend little time together. Joyce lives in Manhattan, an hour -and-a-half, from the other girls who make their home on Long Island."

"In the group's repertoire are Broadway tunes, a medley of their hit parade tunes, as well as a group of barbershop numbers. Originally, the girls sang barbershop selections entirely, but over the years, they have branched out to include a more varied program. In the winter, they perform in clubs and as Lynn pointed out, "people won't hold still for barbershop alone. It isn't commercial enough."

"I enjoy singing barbershop, but I guess I get a bigger kick out of being a participant, and taking part," said Jinny."

"Regina is the first stop on the fair circuit which will take them to Watertown, N.Y. after a two day rest. They will also be in Detroit and London, Ont. (Ontario, Canada) for appearances."

The next part of the article contained comments on how kind the people of Canada were. "The courtesy of Regina cab drivers made an impression on Jinny, who flew in from Palm Springs, Calif. via Vancouver and Calgary. "In New York, the cab driver never opens a door. They never even get out of the cab unless they have luggage in the trunk. In that case, they just set your bags on the street or perhaps on the curb." To see a cab driver carry luggage right into a house or apartment amazed her."

Later, the article ended, "The girls, all prepared for 90 degree temperatures, arrived without coats. The early morning chill caught them unprepared. When assured the temperature would probably be at least 75 during the day, Carol commented, "Well I guess we'll just stay in, in the morning."

The last article relating to the Chordettes in 1963 was also a sad article. It was an obituary in the *Manitowoc Herald* newspaper of October 1. The obituary started, "Funeral services for Mrs. Katherine Cole, 68, wife of O.H. King Cole, who died Friday at Palm Springs, Calif., were held at 9:30 Tuesday."

Later, the obit said, "Survivors are the husband, a daughter, Mrs. Tom Lockard, the former Virginia Cole, who was one of the Sheboygan girls in the nationally-known singing group, the Chordettes."

CHAPTER 7
CADENCE RECORDS

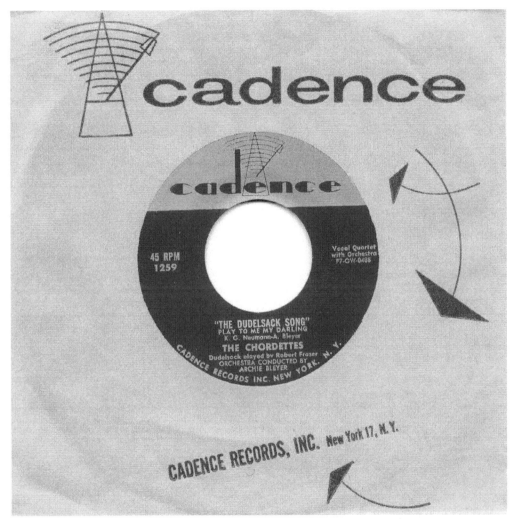

Shown in the above photo is a Cadence 45 RPM record in it original sleeve. The sleeve had printing in maroon to match the maroon on the record label. For most of their years in business, Cadence used maroon and silver as the colors on their record labels. Some special rec-

Archie Bleyer who at the time was bandleader for Arthur Godfrey and his various Radio and TV shows, founded Cadence Records in December 1952. The original location was on 49th Street in Manhattan, New York City. Cadence was never a very large company and had very few artists over the years, but it was a successful company.

A young Archie Bleyer is shown here in an autographed photo from 1952. The photo was signed to Dottie Schwartz in December 1952, when she left the Chordettes and the Arthur Godfrey Show. (Photo courtesy of Dorothy Schwartz)

Bleyer was born in the Corona section of Queens, New York on June 12, 1909. By the age of seven, he was already playing the piano. Following his graduation from high school in 1927, he went to Columbia College, planning on becoming an electrical engineer, but during his sophomore year, switched to a music major. He left Columbia without graduating to become a music arranger. In 1934, Bleyer had his own band, which was playing at Earl Carroll's club in Hollywood, California. Bleyer's band recorded for Brunswick Records. One other member of the band was Johnny Mercer, who would become well known as a songwriter and as co-founder of Capital Records.

Shown here is a Conqueror 78 RPM record from the 1930's recorded by "Archie Bleyer and his Orchestra." The label was printed in gold on a dark brown background. (From the author's collection.)

In 1946, Archie Bleyer was hired to be musical director for Arthur Godfrey's radio shows. When Godfrey added a TV show, Bleyer also became the musical director of the TV show in addition to the radio shows.

Bleyer founded Cadence Records in late 1952. In 1953, Archie Bleyer released five records on the Cadence label, all sung by Julius LaRosa. The first record was "Anywhere I Wander" (Cadence #1230) which did pretty well on the record charts, becoming the fourth most popular song in the country in February 1953. In September of 1953, another LaRosa record, "Eh Cumpari" (Cadence #1232) did even better, reaching the number two spot on the charts.

Following Bleyer's firing in October 1953, he was able to devote all of his time to his record company. He started out by signing new artists to record for his new company. One of the first artists he signed, were the Chordettes, later followed by Marion Marlowe, both of whom he worked with on the Arthur Godfrey shows.

In 1954, 20 singles were released on the Cadence label with eight of them again by LaRosa, including the first three of the year. This meant that the first eight records released by Cadence were all by Julius LaRosa. The first non-LaRosa record released by Cadence was "The Happy Wanderer" by Alfred Drake (Cadence #1238) followed by the Chordettes' first record, "True Love Goes On And On (Cadence #1239)

The next two released by Cadence both did well with Julius LaRosa's "Three Coins In A Fountain" (Cadence #1240) reaching #21 on the charts, followed by another #2 hit, "Hernando's Hideaway" (Cadence #1241) sung by Archie Bleyer himself. Both records charted in May of 1954.

Shown here is the label that was used on early Cadence records. The colors were light red with silver lettering. The drawing on the top center is Julius LaRosa who was the only artist signed for Cadence Records as of early 1953.

The next five singles by Cadence did not chart. But, then the Chordettes released a record which became the first Cadence number one hit in October 1954, "Mr. Sandman" (Cadence #1247).

The final record released by Cadence in 1954, was again by Archie Bleyer and reached #17 on the charts in December 1954. This record was "The Naughty Lady Of Shady Lane" (Cadence #1254)

In February 1955, Bill Hayes' "The Ballad Of Davy Crockett" (Cadence #1256) based on a TV show became the second number one hit for Cadence Records, knocking Mr. Sandman out of the top spot. To show how popular the Davy Crockett TV show was, for a while, there were four different singers, whose versions of "The Ballad of Davy Crockett" were all in the top 100 most popular songs.

In October 1955, Julius LaRosa's recording of "Suddenly There's A Valley" (Cadence #1270) reached number 20 on the charts. This was to be LaRosa's last record that he recorded for Cadence Records.

Near the end of 1955, Cadence released an unusual record, with Archie Bleyer doing one side, "Nothing To Do" and his wife, Janet (of the Chordettes) doing the back side, which was "Because You're My Lover" (Cadence #1279). The record failed to chart.

As you may recall, on October 19, 1953, Arthur Godfrey fired Julius LaRosa at the end of his live radio show. The next day, Archie Bleyer was fired as musical director of the Arthur Godfrey shows.

In the book, *Arthur Godfrey* by Arthur Singer, Singer wrote, "Bleyer never discussed his dismissal publicly. It was left to the press and to Godfrey to explain it. They agreed on one thing: the precipitating event was a trip by Bleyer to Chicago to record a series of poems with Don McNeil. McNeil, the long-time host of ABC's "The Breakfast Club" was fairly popular, but he was hardly a threat to Godfrey's popularity. Yet for whatever reasons, Godfrey considered him a competitor."

It took over two years, but McNeil's first and only Cadence Record (Cadence #1285) was released in January 1956. The record was titled, "Make America Proud Of You." Today, this record is extremely hard to find. In watching Ebay for over five years, this record has appeared only once and sold for over $100.00.

Don McNeil is shown here in this 1953 photo. McNeil was born in Illinois, but grew up in Sheboygan and graduated from the Sheboygan High School. Back in November 1946, the Chordettes made their first radio appearance on McNeil's daily radio show. (From the author's collection)

Cadence released 22 records in 1956 and four of these songs charted in the top 20 most popular songs at some point during the year. One of these songs was "Canadian Sunset" by Andy Williams (Cadence #1297). Williams' song reached number seven in August. The other three songs from Cadence to make it into the top 20, were all by the Chordettes. The Chordettes' songs were "Eddie My Love" (Cadence #1284) which reached #14 in March, "Born To Be With You" (Cadence #1291) which made it to #5 in June, and "Lay Down Your Arms" (Cadence #1299) which made it to #16 in September.

1957 saw Cadence Records release 37 singles with five of these reaching the top 10 on the charts. Three of these songs hit number one. The three number one songs were Andy Williams' "Butterfly" (Cadence 1308) which reached the top spot on the pop charts in February. This was followed by the Everly Brothers with "Bye, Bye Love" (Cadence 1315) which reached number one on the country charts in May. "Bye, Bye Love" also reached number two on the pop charts, and number five on the R&B charts. The final number one song for Cadence in 1957 was again by the Everly Brothers, "Wake Up Little Susie" (Cadence #1337) which was number one on the pop charts, country charts, and R &B charts in September.

The other two songs to reach the top 10, both finished as high as number eight. They were "I Like Your Kind Of Love" by Andy Williams and Peggy Powers (Cadence #1323) and "Just Between You And Me" (Cadence #1330) by The Chordettes.

The year 1958 was also successful for Cadence Records, with two records hitting the #2 position on the charts and two others hitting the #1 top spot. The two #2 records were "Lollipop" (Cadence #1345) by The Chordettes and "Problems" (Cadence #1355) by the Everly Brothers. The two number one hits were both by the Everly Brothers. "All I Have To Do Is Dream" (Cadence #1348) which reached the top of the pop, country, and R&B charts in April. The other Everly Brothers record, "Bird Dog" (Cadence 1350) hit number one on the pop and country charts, but only number two on the R&B charts in August.

Only 16 singles were released by Cadence in 1959, but nine of the records made the top 100. The highest a Cadence Record reached on the charts for 1959 was #4 and it was the Everly Brothers, "Til I Kissed You (Cadence #1369) in August.

1960 saw Cadence release only 15 singles and the best selling record made it to #2 on the charts. The record was "Poetry In Motion" by Johnny Tillison (Cadence #1384).

In 1961, Cadence Records released only 18 singles. But, only one reached the top 10 and that was Johnny Tillison again with "Without You" (Cadence #1404) which reached #7 in August.

Cadence released 20 singles in 1962, but only four charted and none charted in the top 10. Cadence was reaching the end of the line in 1963 and released only nine singles and one of these was a previously unreleased song by Julius LaRosa. The only Cadence record to chart in the top 20 for 1963 was Lenny Welch's "Since I Feel For You" (Cadence #1439) which reached number four in October.

1964 was the final year for any singles by Cadence with only five. One of these was again a previously unreleased song by Julius LaRosa. Only one song hit the charts and that was barely hitting the charts, with Lenny Welch's "If You See My Love" (Cadence #1446) which reached #92.

While most Cadence records used silver and maroon as colors, EP (Extended Play) mini albums that contained songs from more than one Cadence artist, used a silver and blue label as shown here. This particular record (Cadence EP-4058) contained the songs, "Mr. Sandman" by the Chordettes, "Let Me Go Lover" by Mary Del, "Naughty Lady Of Shady Lane" by Archie Bleyer, and "Hearts of Stone" by the Chordettes. A second EP mini album (Cadence EP-4059) also came with the blue and silver label. Songs on that EP mini album, were "Melody of Love" by Archie Bleyer, "Make Yourself Comfortable" by Maddy Russell, "Dim Dim The Lights" by the Four Tophatters, and "Sincerely" by the Chordettes." (From the author's collection)

Over the years, Cadence used many different styles of record labels for promos. A black and white version of their regular label is shown here. Notice the "Not for sale" printed on the label. On later promos, this would be missing and replaced by "Advanced Pressing." (From the author's collection)

All Cadence promos had black and white labels. Two more versions of Cadence promos, which now contain the phrase, "Advance Pressing" or "Advance Pressings" (From the author's collection)

Still two more versions of Cadence promos are shown on this page. The reason for the different label styles on Cadence records is not known.

This version of a Cadence promo is a black and white version of the normal Cadence label, which was red with a black border around the edge. Promo records were sent out to radio disc jockeys to get them to play the songs on their radio stations. Promo records like this are also known as "Advance Pressings" and "Disc Jockey versions." (From the author's collection)

In late 1962, Cadence released an album, titled, "The First Family" spoofing President Kennedy and his family. Wikinedia, the internet encyclopedia said this about the album. "*The First Family* is a comedy album recorded on October 22, 1962, as a good-natured parody of President John F. Kennedy, both as Commander-in-Chief and as a member of a large, well-known political family. Issued by Cadence Records, it was honored as the 'largest and fastest selling record in the history of the record industry' selling more than a million copies per week for the first six and one-half weeks in distribution, by January 1963 it had sold more than 7 million copies. Cadence president Archie Bleyer credited the album's success to radio airplay. By the time of the release of *The First Family Volume Two*, the sequel, it had sold 7.5 million copies - unprecedented for any album at the time, let alone a comedy album."

"*The First Family* starred stand-up comedian and impersonator Vaughn Meader as Kennedy and Naomi Brossart as the first lady. Meader's skill at impersonating Kennedy was honed on the stand-up circuit-with his New England accent naturally close to Kennedy's familiar (and often parodied) Harvard accent, he needed to adjust his voice only slightly to sound almost exactly like the President. Bossart was a theatre actress and model making her recording debut.

"Effect on popular culture. Although the comedy album boom was mushrooming by 1962, production of a record imitating the presidential voice met stiff opposition. James Hagerty, a top executive for ABC-Paramount Records and President Dwight D. Eisenhower's former press secretary, called the proposed album "degrading to the presidency" and proclaimed that "every communist country in the world would love this record." After other rejections, Cadence Records agreed to take on the project, and within a month the record was appearing on, and just as quickly, disappearing from store shelves. Within two weeks, it had sold more than 1 million copies, pushing past the debut album by Peter, Paul and Mary."

"Within weeks, many Americans could recite favorite lines from the record (including "the rubber Schwan [swan] is mine," and "move ahead…with great vigah [vigor]," the latter lampooning the President's own words). The album poked fun at Kennedy's PT-109 history; the rocking chairs he used for his painful back; the Kennedy clan's well known athleticism; football games and family togetherness; children in the White House; and Jackie Kennedy's soft-spoken nature and her redecoration of the White House; and many other bits of knowledge that the public was eager to consume. Kennedy himself was said to have given copies of the album as Christmas gifts, and once greeted a Democratic National Committee group by saying, "Vaugh Meader was busy tonight, so I came myself."

"The First Family album won the Grammy Award for Album of the Year in 1963. That March, most of the same cast recorded a follow-up album, The First Family Volume Two, a combination of spoken-word comedy and songs. The sequel was released in the spring of 1963."

"Immediately upon hearing of Kennedy's assassination, producers Bob Booker, and Earle Doud (along with Cadence president Archie Bleyer) pulled both albums from sales, and had all unsold copies destroyed, so as not to seemingly "cash in" on the Presidents death. Both albums remained out of print for many years, until they were finally issued on CD together in 1999."

No new records were released by Cadence in 1964, and Archie Bleyer sold Cadence Records and retired.

Andy Williams wanted to buy the rights to his songs, but Bleyer made him buy all of the Cadence recordings, including the rights to The Chordettes songs. Williams bought all of the Cadence records and re-released many of the songs on his Barnaby Records label.

When Andy Williams died in 2012, he was still signing the royalty checks sent to the Chordettes for their recordings.

CHAPTER 8
LIFE AFTER THE CHORDETTES

During the first half of 1963, the Chordettes decided to stop accepting additional show dates, but would still do shows that were already scheduled. There were a number of reasons for reaching this decision. One was that Jinny's mother was sick and she wanted to spend more time with her mother, who lived in Palm Springs, California. Another was that Carol had a four-year-old daughter and preferred to spend time at home. Lynn also said in a 2002 interview, "When Jinny left, we decided that we didn't want to get another tenor to replace her. Once you've worked hard to perfect a sound, it's hard to be satisfied with anything less."

In a 2002 interview, Jinny said, "I arrived in Palm Springs (California) on the 4th of July 1963. Up until that time, my father hadn't been able to tell me what was wrong with (my) Mother, but when I got there, the doctor said it was cancer. We buried her on her birthday, October 1, 1963."

According to the *Sheboygan Press* of September 28, 1963, Jinny's mother, Mrs. Katherine Cole had died the day before in Palm Springs at the age of 66. "Mrs. Cole was the former Katherine Flack, born in Sisterville, West Virginia, a daughter of Ernest and Adele Flack, both of whom were Sheboygan County natives."

Later the obituary added, Mrs. Cole was an officer for many years in the wives organization affiliated with the S.P.E.B.S.Q.S.A. an international men's barbershop singing society of which her husband was president. She was instrumental in helping her daughter Virginia, and three other Sheboygan girls form the nationally-known singing group, The Chordettes."

Before she died, Mrs. Cole said to her daughter, Jinny, "You're here to take care of your Dad. You've got to stay. He can't even fix a peanut butter sandwich." Jinny added, "Which was sad, because I don't fix peanut butter sandwiches either."

Jinny continued in the interview, "I moved in with my father and took care of him, and the widows starting showing up at the front door with casseroles. I slammed the door in some cases, hid some casseroles under the doormat, but eventually my Dad found one and married her."

Even though Jinny was living in California in 1964, and the other members of the Chordettes were living in the New York City area, they still did a few shows. One of the final shows the Chordettes did was in Superior, Wisconsin for the Tri-State Fair, which was held from August 4 through August 9. The Chordettes were the main act for the grandstand show, which started at 8:15 each evening. Admission to the fair was 25 cents with free parking. Cost for the grandstand show with the Chordettes was $1.10 for adults and 50 cents for children.

On the Sunday (August 2) before the fair opening, the *Duluth, Minnesota News-Tribune* featured a full-page photo on of the Chordettes on the front page of their entertainment section of their newspaper. Inside was an article about the fair, which started, "The singing Chordettes, stars of TV, radio, and recordings will head the nightly grandstand show at the Tri-State Fair in Superior, Tuesday through next Sunday."

"Appearing with them will be the Appletons, a comedy Apache dance trio who performed in the movie "Can-Can"; Bobby Clark and his marionettes; Doug Hart, celebrated circus wire acrobat; and a Dixieland jazz band, the South Rampart Street Paraders."

Later the article continued, "The Chordettes got their start years ago in Sheboygan, Wis., their home town, where they first organized as a barbershop quartet. Their path led next to the Arthur Godfrey Show, on which they appeared for four years, and from there to other TV variety shows, recordings, world tours and coast-to-coast engagements with other top stars."

Shown here is the front page of the *Duluth (Minnesota) News-Tribune* Cosmopolitan section from Sunday, August 3, 1964. The Chordettes were listed as the headliners for the Tri-State Fair's Grandstand show. This appears to have been the Chordettes final public performance of their career. (From the author's collection)

"Their first hit recording was "Mr. Sandman" which has sold two million copies. Some of their other hit tunes they have recorded with Archie Bleyer include "Hummingbird", "Teenage Goodnight", "Lollipop" and "Never on Sunday"."

"The Chordettes are comprised of Jinny Lockard, Carol Buschmann, Joyce Weston, and

Lynn Evans. So called barbershop harmony remains a distinctive part of their style, but they have broadened it to include musical accompaniment and have also added dance routines to their act."

Also, in 1964, Archie Bleyer sold Cadence Records and retired. Lynn Evans had gone back to school to be a teacher.

Nothing was found about the Chordettes until 1970. In 1970, the *Green Bay* (Wisconsin) *Press Gazette* ran an article in their Sunday, August 16, Close Up section, titled "Two Chordettes Revisited. After Years in the Limelight, the Running is over." The front cover featured a color photo of Dorothy and Carol playing golf. The article that followed started, "Late in September of 1949, four young ladies from Sheboygan sang their way to national prominence by winning first place on an Arthur Godfrey Talent Scout program. With their unique barbershop harmony, the Chordettes were an instant hit."

"When the Chordettes finally disbanded, the group had made numerous personal appearances all over the United States, sung for royalty in Europe and participated in command performances at the White House. During the years, there have been varied combinations of Chordettes. But, what happened to the original group, the four young ladies who burst so suddenly into the big time?"

"The original group consisted not of four sisters, as many people believed, but Dorothy Hummitzsch, lead; Virginia Cole Osborn, tenor; Carol Hagedorn, baritone; and Janet Buschmann Ertel, bass. Actually Alice Buschmann was an "original" Chordette, but she was replaced by Carol two years before the group gained nationwide fame."

"Janet married Archie Bleyer, former owner of Cadence Records, retired from the group in 1959 and is now residing in New York. Her daughter, Jacqualine Ertel, is married to Phillip Everly of the popular Everly Brothers. Virginia, at one time married to Tom Lockard of the Mariners, believed to be one of the first integrated quartets on television, has since remarried and is residing in Palm Springs."

"Back in Sheboygan and happy to be there are Dorothy and Carol. It was Dorothy who was the first to break up "the old gang." Married to William Schwartz, a Green Bay native, Dorothy left in December of 1952 to await the birth of her first child, Jeff, now 17. She now also has a daughter, Sandi, 12."

"Although Dorothy thoroughly enjoyed her years as a celebrity, she didn't care for it as a steady diet. She and Bill had agreed that when they started a family, Dorothy would quit and she was delighted to return to Sheboygan and help her husband in his career."

"Carol, now Mrs. Robert Buschmann, has been back "home" (in Sheboygan) for only two years. She stuck with the Chordettes until the end and confesses, "I think I stayed with the business too long. During the last couple of years, when I got a phone call about a job, I would actually get sick to my stomach. I didn't want to go out on the road again, I had just gotten back."

"Reminiscing about their days in "show biz" on a recent afternoon in Sheboygan, Carol talked about the time they signed the seven-year contract "with options" with Godfrey. (With options, meant it could be terminated at any time.)"

"I remember thinking at the time," said Carol, "if we can last for 13 weeks, that's plenty. With the contract signing, the Chordettes were off and running, and running and running. Besides the Godfrey shows, they had to honor all their weekend barbershop commitments. Scripts for the Wednesday television shows were not handed out until Monday and then there were costumes to be found and fitted, movement, songs and dialogue to learn and rehearsals until the last minute. Finding identical outfits for the four girls was not always easy, but the group finally decided if it looked good on Carol, the tallest, it would suit them all."

"In their "spare time," (from 11 p.m. to 1 a.m.) the girls were taking swimming, dancing or skating lessons, depending on the format of the upcoming show. This was a snap for Dorothy, who was always athletically inclined and, interposed Carol, "our one-time star female baseball player."

"Everyone helped everybody else, Dorothy said. "If you were in the wrong place, someone would shove you to the proper spot." These were also the days before taping of shows, so "we went on before God and the whole country," and did it."

"Their years with the Godfrey people were marvelous, both agree, recalling how wonderfully they were treated. At the time of their singing, the Mariners and Marion Marlowe actually took a cut in pay to make room for the Chordettes in the budget until it could be revamped."

"Carol observed, "I enjoyed barbershop singing so much before the Godfrey era. It was like going to a party every weekend. But with Godfrey it became a job."

"But there were compensations," interjected Dorothy , and Carol concurred. "We were those four gals from Sheboygan," said Dorothy, "and had never traveled in that circle before. It certainly opened our eyes." "they used to tease us about our accents," recalled Carol, "and that brought about one of our record hits, "Down on Thirty Third and Third."

"All their albums were barbershop, and more were made from the originals. They did make several records with accompaniment, including two with Godfrey, "Candy and Cake" and "Dance Me Loose," which were big hits. But the Chordettes didn't make any money on those, they were paid scale for recording them and that was that."

"Their first recording with accompaniment was "True Love Goes On and On," which was "a lovely song and did well enough so that Archie (Bleyer) thought we should do another." That one, was of course, "Mr. Sandman."

"One of the group's biggest problems was laryngitis. Singing without accompaniment, everyone had to be in perfect voice - or forget it. Although they finally had to edge their way into the popular song field. "We never did get the same kick out of singing with a band that we did by ourselves. When we hit a chord with our voices, we knew we were creating music."

"Dorothy had already left the group by the time of the "famous" firings of the Little Godfreys, including the Chordettes. At least they were spared the public firing: "a network executive was sent to tell us we were no longer needed." The Chordettes never did have much to say about that incident and still are reluctant to talk about it. "We still think Mr. Godfrey is a remarkable man. He gave us our big start and after leaving the show, we did very well, so we have no complaints."

"It was then, recalls Carol, that things really got hectic, as the group left New York and embarked on numerous personal appearances tours. During that time, there was always "an extra Chordette around," explained Carol. The personnel changed while members took vacations, had babies, retired and then returned when needed."

"Dorothy, the quiet, but take-charge type, is today a typical housewife and mother. She is extremely proud of her husband, who started "from scratch in the den of our home" with Dorothy helping with the book work. He now heads William Schwartz Associates, selective promotional advertising, with his own office building in Sheboygan."

"They reside in a comfortable modern home on Sheboygan's northwest side and spend the summer months at a cottage at Crystal Lake, some 23 miles away. Every holiday season the family vacations at a warm weather fun spot, last year Hawaii, prior to that Florida and California."

"During winter months, Dorothy keeps busy with PTA (president of Cooper School PTA for two years), Red Cross, blood bank and church work and helps her children with projects."

"The field of entertaining is a very demanding life," says Dorothy. "A happy marriage to a wonderful man and a family meant more to me than show business with its travel and fame."

"The experience was great and it's fun to look back, but the happiness of seeing your children growing up, being with them and sharing this with Bill - this is real contentment."

"Carol is just starting the 'helpmate route,' assisting her husband in his new sporting goods store, Toro, on North Eighth Street in Sheboygan and caring for her 11-year-old daughter, Janet."

"Previously, Carol and Bob ran a restaurant and cocktail lounge in a small community in Long Island. 'We seldom went into the city,' reports Carol. 'We had had enough of night life and eating out."

"So moving back to a smaller community required no serious adjustments, 'although now people here tease my daughter about their Eastern accent."

"The Buschmans are residing in the Black River area and are remodeling a cottage. 'Actually the way things are now I still feel like I'm on a vacation. My friends warn me not to be to eager to get the carpeting in because it will change the whole atmosphere."

"Carol, one described as the comedian of the quartet, has retained her out-going personality. She gleefully reports learning all about Coho salmon fishing from the customers in her husband's store and is amazed at the interest in skiing."

"We did a fabulous business last winter, and I could hardly wait for Christmas and what I thought would be blessed relief. But the next day it started all over again, but I love it."

"As is usually the case, Carol and Dorothy, although living in the same town, rarely get to see one another. They were happy to get together recently to reminisce about 'those days' that affected their lives so much."

On October 4, 1974, the *Sheboygan Press* ran an article about the Chordettes in honor of the 25th anniversary of their winning the Arthur Godfrey Talent Scouts Show. The headline was titled, "Chordettes: Afterglow 1974." Two pictures accompanied the article including one of Dorothy and Carol Reminiscing in Sheboygan.

Most of the article recounted how the Chordettes won and were hired to be on the Arthur Godfrey shows and mentioned Dorothy's scrapbooks from the time. Near the end of the article, after discussing what Carol and Dorothy were now doing in Sheboygan, it stated, "Carol's sister -in-law, Janet Buschmann Ertel, left the group in 1959. She is married to Archie Bleyer, who was Godfrey's musical director during the Chordettes' heyday. The Bleyers live in the New York City area and return to Sheboygan regularly to visit with relatives."

"The original tenor in the group, Virginia Cole Osborn, married another of Godfrey's regulars, Tom Lockard, who sang with the Mariners quartet. Jinny resides in Palm Springs, Calif."

"When Dorothy and Carol discuss their time in the limelight, they admit it was fun - but frantic. The excitement of the world of entertainment was great, but they both feel they are too busy to miss it now."

The article ended, "These days, about the only time they get together is when Dorothy drops in on Carol at the sporting goods store."

The beginning of 1978 saw some sad news related to the Chordettes. On January 9, the *Sheboygan Press* reported, "Former Kingsbury President 'King' Cole Dies at 82." Part of the obituary said, "His interest in music found a fresh outlet during the 1950s when he helped the Chordettes, a singing group from Sheboygan, on their way to nationwide fame. His daughter, Virginia, was a member of the quartet."

In 1978, the city of Sheboygan celebrated 125 years as a city. To help celebrate this event, the *Sheboygan Press* on August 1, 1978, published a special section on the history of Sheboygan. One of the articles was, "From the Fabulous Fifties...Chordettes Helped Spread The Name Of Sheboygan Everywhere." The article written by Marion Stewart started, "The Chordettes could still be Sheboygan's greatest claim to fame. But Carol Hagedorn Buschmann and Dorothy Hummitzsch Schwartz, the two members of the famous singing group of the 50s and early 60s who still live in Sheboygan, definitely don't live in the past, exciting though it was."

"A recent visit to Carol proved that point. She was painting trophy bases in the family trophy shop, Toro Trophy Supplies, 502 N. Eighth St., and graciously capped her paint and sat down to reminisce about the Chordettes."

After a few paragraphs about the Arthur Godfrey days and barbershop singing, the article continued, "Though dedicated to the barbershop style of singing, they did do some numbers with instrumental backing. 'Mr. Sandman' was one of these. The record sold more than 2 million copies and is still played today, sometimes referred to as 'a hit of the Fabulous Fifties."

"How does it feel to hear those voices coming over the radio? 'It's fun,' says Carol. 'Every once in a while I hear one of our recordings over the radio here in the shop turn it up loud and say to the customers, 'Hey, that's us!' I probably get more of a kick out of it now than I did then."

"Both Carol and Dorothy remember with delight the welcome the city of Sheboygan gave them when they returned briefly in the winter of 1949, after their initial success on the Godfrey show."

"Many of the people who were so good to us are gone now,' Dorothy said, 'but it's a fond memory."

"They met us at the Sheboygan railroad depot and escorted us in a caravan all the way down Eighth Street,' Carol recalled. 'We were very excited."

"The girls rode in a convertible driven by Edward Klozotsky, then local manager of the Wisconsin Telephone Co., who figured in anecdotes the women told about the early days of their career."

"Dorothy was working for Mr. Klozotsky when we first began making appearances, and he was very kind about letting her have time off,' say Carol. 'Later, I worked there, too, and it seemed as though I was out more than in as our schedule picked up."

"Finally, Mr. Klozotsky said there was only one thing he would ask of job applicants in the future and that was 'Are you a singer?"

"Both women lamented the fact the four of them are living so far apart. Virginia Cole Osborn, now Mrs. Sam Janis, lives in Palm Springs, and Janet Buschmann Ertel, now Mrs. Archie Bleyer, lives in New York."

"We were very close,' said Carol "All in all, we got along fantastically well together.' She mentioned a get-together in New York about five years ago. 'Of course we had to try a few songs. It was amazing how it came back,' she said. 'It actually brought tears to my eyes.''

"The Buschmanns' daughter, Janet works in the family shop. She and Carol's husband, Robert, teased her lightly about appearing in the *Sheboygan Press*'s 125th Anniversary issue. 'You're not old enough to be 'history,' a customer protested to the still youthful looking Mrs. Buschmann."

"But she just laughed. 'Oh yes we are,' she said, before getting back to the busy life around her. 'We're part of Sheboygan's history.

On February 13, 1979, an obituary appeared in the *Sheboygan Press* for Otis B. Osborn, 54, a former Sheboygan resident and president of the Dillingham Manufacturing Company. Near the bottom of the obit, it said, "On May 19, 1945, he was married to Virginia Cole of Sheboygan, who later became a member of the Chordettes, a woman's barbershop quartet from Sheboygan that won fame on radio and television. That marriage ended in divorce in 1950."

The *Sheboygan Press* on Tuesday, January 6, 1981, reported, "Alice Mae Spielvogel, Former Chordette Dies." The article that followed stated, "Alice Mae Spielvogel, 55, an original member of the Chordettes, a popular singing quartet of the 1950s, died Sunday (January 4) at North Little Rock, Ark."

"The former Alice Mae Buschmann was a member of the group at the time of its formation in the late 1940s."

"In 1947, just eight months after formation, the quartet had appeared twice with Fred Waring and had also done a stint with Sheboygan native, Don McNeill, on his popular "Breakfast Club." The quartet was also a success on the Morris B. Sachs "Amateur Hour.""

"Mrs. Spielvogel was no longer singing with the Chordettes when they joined the Arthur Godfrey Show in 1949."

"She was born July 31, 1925, in Sheboygan, a daughter of Albert and Alice Buschmann. She attended Sheboygan schools and was a 1945 graduate of Central High School. She married Roy Spielvogel."

"Survivors are two sons, Terry of Omaha, Neb., and Roy Jr. of Kansas City; a daughter, Ruth Baker of Russelville, Ark.; three grandchildren; a brother, Robert Buschmann of Sheboygan; and a sister, Janet Bleyer of New York, who was also a member of the singing group."

"Mr. Buschmann's wife, the former Carol Hagedorn, replaced Alice Mae in the group in 1947."

"Funeral services will be held at 2 p.m. Wednesday at Owens Funeral Home, North Little Rock, Ark. Burial will be in National Cemetery, North Little Rock."

Just over two years after Alice Mae died, the Chordettes were the subject of another article in the *Sheboygan Press* dealing with an obituary, on Thursday, March 17, 1983. The headline read, "Sheboygan's 'Chordettes' Remember Godfrey As A Charming Perfectionist." Sheboygan's two Chordettes, Carol and Dorothy were again interviewed for the article.

The article reported, "He demanded perfection from his performers and he wanted them to be dependent on him…yet he was charming and generous, and in the early years of his television shows, the entire cast was 'one big, happy family.'"

"Those are the reminiscences of Arthur Godfrey by two Sheboygan members of the

Chordettes, the women barbershoppers who skyrocketed to national popularity on Godfrey's TV show."

"Godfrey died Wednesday in New York at the age of 79."

The article continued, "I didn't know he was that ill,' said Mrs. William Schwartz, the former Dorothy Hummitzsch of the Chordettes. But Mrs. Robert Buschmann, the former Carol Hagedorn, said she'd had an inkling that the man who'd propelled her group to success more than 30 years ago was not well."

"We'd been at the International Barbershoppers Show in Pittsburgh last summer and I'd talked to Arthur's brother, who said then that he was very sick,' she told the Press. Nevertheless, the news of Godfrey's death 'came as quite a shock,' Buschmann said."

"Carol, Dorothy, Janet Ertel (now Mrs. Archie Bleyer of New York) and Virginia Cole (now Mrs. Sam Janis of Palm Springs, Calif.) reached the big time after being discovered on Godfrey's Talent Scouts Show - the same showcase that put the national spotlight on Pat Boone, Vic Damone, the McGuire Sisters and Shari Lewis."

"Sheboygan's Chordettes were immediately signed as regulars for Godfrey's prime time hour-long variety show, 'Godfrey and His Friends," which week after week was watched by 82 million back in the early 1950s, the pioneer days of national television." (Author's note, at this time the population of the United States was around 150 million people, meaning over half the population was watching Arthur Godfrey on a weekly basis.)

"Schwartz recalled today that the immense popularity of Godfrey's show was due to the variety of the show, and the fact that it was something the whole family could enjoy. 'For us, it was a wonderful experience; his show people were super,' she said."

"Buschmann agreed: 'We had a marvelous time on the show, especially in the beginning. Arthur was charming. It was one of those real friendly atmospheres…one big, happy family. There were trips to Florida for the entire cast, lovely gifts,' she said."

"But, as the show continued to produce high ratings year in and year out, she added, the fun sort of wore out."

"Arthur changed. He became less friendly. He'd come to rehearsal, go to the control room and not talk to anyone."

"She surmised that Godfrey had a need for everyone on his show to be completely dependent on him. 'If he felt anybody was doing something on their own, he didn't like it.'"

"Schwartz remembered that Godfrey was quite demanding of perfection by his performers. 'He wanted things his way and he wasn't always diplomatic. He was the boss,' she said."

The article ended, "Still both Chordettes said they have fond memories of Godfrey and are saddened by his death. 'We had a very nice association, really and truly,' observed Schwartz. 'He was quite a special man.'"

Seven months later, another man important in the early success of the Chordettes, Milton Detjen passed away at the age of 75 in Manitowoc, Wisconsin. Detjen's obituary in the November 25, 1983 *Manitowoc-Two Rivers Herald-Times Reporter* reported on his music background. The obituary stated, Detjen "was employed with Manitowoc Ship Building Company as a timekeeper and also served as director of the Sub Mariner's Band which played for all submarine launchings at Manitowoc. Mr. Detjen was the first director of the Society For The Preservation of Barbershop Quartet Singing in America. For 42 years, Mr. Detjen had served as organist for Grace Evangelical Lutheran Church, where he also served as president of the congregation. Mr.

Detjen was a very active member of the Manitowoc Senior Citizens where he was the head of the Warblers singing group. Mr. Detjen also had his own printing company where he printed and published 31 organ music books for church use which is played in more than 2,000 churches in the United States and Canada. He was also a member of the Musicians Local Union."

In 1985, one of the most popular movies of the year was "Back to the Future" starring Michael J. Fox as Marty McFly. The movie was about a teenager in 1985, who accidentally gets sent back to his hometown of Hill Valley in November 1955. When Fox's character first arrives in Hill Valley of November 1955, "Mr. Sandman" is playing in the background. Many people think that it is the Chordettes singing the song, but it was actually another version sung by the Four Aces. Another reason that many people think it is the Chordettes is that McFly sees a record store and the first sign in the window is a Chordettes poster.

But, the poster is actually an error in writing for the movie. The poster in the window shows the Chordettes as pictured below. But, as mentioned previously, the movie was set in November 1955 and the poster in the record store window includes Nancy, who did not join the Chordettes until 1958!

This photo of the Chordettes was used on a poster in the record store window in the movie "Back to the Future" but was the wrong photo for the time. The movie was set in 1955. The above photo shows left to right, Jinny, Lynn, Carol, and Nancy. Nancy did not join the Chordettes until 1958, three years after the movie was set in. (From the author's collection)

Another sign of how the Chordettes stood as an icon of the 1950s was found in a set of music cards put out by a company from Canada. Between 1982 and 1988, this company issued six series of 45 cards each of rock stars. The Chordettes were card number 157 (fourth series) of the set, which was released in 1985. Each series of cards was sold mainly through ads in GOLDMINE, which is a music trade publication. The front of each card in the set contained a black and white photo, while the back contained information about the performer, including Group Members, Biggest Hit Record, and Other Hit Records. The information in the hit records section also included the record company name and the number of the record. In addition, the months and year that the record was on the charts was included.

For the Chordettes card, under Group Members, it listed six of the Chordettes, but left out three of the Chordettes. The card included as members, "Carol Buschman, Janet Ertel, Lynn Evans, Margie Needham, Jinny Osborn & Dorothy Schwartz. Notice some were identified by maiden names, others by married names. The three Chordettes' members that were left off, were, Alyce May Buschmann, Joyce Weston, and Nancy Overton. Nancy was not mentioned on the back, but she was pictured on the front of the card.

The Chordettes   157

Group Members:
Carol Bushman, Janet Ertel, Lynn Evans, Margie Needham, Jinny Osborn & Dorothy Schwartz

Originally From Sheboygan, Wisc.

Biggest Hit Record:
"Mr. Sandman" On The Cadence Label (#1247). A Big Hit From Oct. 1954-Mar. 1955.

Other Hit Records:
"Lollipop"—Cadence 1345 (Mar.-Jun. 1958)
"Born To Be With You"—Cadence 1291 (May-Oct. 1956)
"Just Between You & Me"—Cadence 1330 (Aug.-Dec. 1957)
"Never On Sunday"—Cadence 1402 (Jun.-Sep. 1961)
"Eddie My Love"—Cadence 1284 (Feb.-May 1956)
"Lay Down Your Arms"—Cadence 1299 (Sep. 1956-Jan. 1957)
"Zorro"—Cadence 1349 (May-Jun. 1958)
"No Other Arms, No Other Lips"—Cadence 1361 (Mar.-May 1959)

© 1985 Music Nostalgia

In 1985, a Canadian Company issued a set of Music Nostalgia cards. The Chordettes were number 157 in the set. The front and back of the Chordettes card is shown above. Pictured left to right are Jinny, Lynn, Carol, and Nancy. (From the author's collection)

On April 17, 1988, the *Sheboygan Press* ran an article, under the headline, "Trophy firm enters 20th year" and included a photo of former Chordette, Carol Buschmann and her daughter,

Janet.

The article reported, "Olympic athletes go for the gold every four years. When directors of athletic events in Sheboygan are looking for gold, they head to Toro Trophy Supplies at 514 North Eighth St."

"Toro Trophy has been supplying medals, plaques and trophies for area clubs and businesses since 1968. The trophy service was begun 20 years ago this month as part of Toro Sporting Goods. Robert Buschmann began the business with his son, Tory. The first two letters of the owners' names became the signature for the new enterprise."

"While the owners concentrated on the sporting goods end of the business, Carol, Robert's wife, managed the trophy service."

"Eventually Tory left the business. His father and mother continued, giving up most of the sporting goods lines and concentrating on ski supplies and trophies. While the ski business was sold, and Robert retired, Toro Trophy Supply continues under the management of Carol Buschmann and their daughter, Janet."

"Toro's has always had a downtown Sheboygan location. According to Buschmann, the business doesn't need to be downtown, but the owners are happy with the location. They do find it convenient to be centrally located, but could use better access for cars and vans which come to pick up large orders."

"Toro Trophy does more than just sell trophies and other awards. The products are actually manufactured right on the premises. The company runs a full woodworking shop to supply all of the trophy bases and 75 percent of the plaques it sells. Each trophy can be fully customized, with various choices of uprights, designs and figurines."

"Toro will also engrave anything it sells, and most things customers bring in. They have engraved everything from bedpans to boat bells and have recently purchased a computer engraver to go along with their two manual engravers."

"Buschmann said that when they first offered trophies, they never expected such a thriving business. Last year they had gross sales of approximately $100,000. This year they expect an increase in sales of approximately 5 percent."

"Business has changed quite a bit over the past twenty years. Originally, trophies were the mainstay of the trade. Currently, the firm provides more and more plaques, rather than free-standing awards. While the company still provides awards for athletic accomplishments, it is receiving more and more orders from business for employee and customer recognition awards."

"In addition to trophies and plaques, they offer pen sets, clocks, certificates and medals."

"Buschmann credits success to the service they offer their customers. "We do everything right here," she said. "Our prices are as good or better than anybody's, and the quality of work is excellent." She is also proud of the engraving work they do, citing their experience and "a good computer.""

On September 9, 1988, the *Sheboygan Press* announced that on Sunday, September 11, a Sheboygan Music Hall of Fame would be unveiled at the Fountain Park Bandshell with a ceremony that would honor 24 individuals and one group. The one group was the Chordettes.

The mention in the article for the Chordettes said, "The Chordettes, composed of Jinny Cole (Janis), Carol Hagedorn (Buschmann), Janet Buschmann (Ertel) and Dottie Hummitzsch (Schwartz) made a name for themselves and Sheboygan in both radio and television; began singing at barbershop shows and national conventions all over the country; made singing commercials and appeared on the Don McNeill Breakfast Club, Olson and Johnson show and with Fred Waring and the Pennsylvanians; won the Arthur Godfrey Talent Scout Show in September 1949, and henceforth his Wednesday night TV show and daily radio show, becoming famous as "Those lovely gals from Sheboygan, Wisconsin, The Chordettes," to millions all over the country, and making numerous records (including "Mr. Sandman") before disbanding.

Two other persons inducted that day included, Charles Faulhaber, high school music teacher of three of the Chordettes and Mel Hummitzsch, Dorothy's brother, famous for being the leader of Mel's Clown band.

Less than two weeks later, on September 23, 1988, the Chordettes were again the subject of a *Sheboygan Press* article, written by Rita Wigg. The article reviewed the early history of the Chordettes and also mentioned that Jinny had recently been in Sheboygan to visit with the other Chordettes.

The end of the article reported on what had happened to the Chordettes after the group quit performing. According to the article, "Eventually, all of the original Chordettes tired of life on the road and looked to settle down. Three of the original four eventually returned to Sheboygan. The pull of family and friends overpowered the attraction of the more popular places they had worked."

"Carol and her husband, Bob Buschmann, who is Janet's brother, decided to move back home. Jinny followed her family, too. Her mom and dad had retired to California, and she moved there to join them."

"Janet also eventually found her way home. After many years of living in New York and visiting exciting spots all around the world, she and her husband, Archie Bleyer, founder of Cadence Records, returned to Sheboygan in 1985. She, too, was pulled back by family ties."

"While today's royalty checks are nice, of much more value to the Chordettes are the wonderful memories of their days of stardom. All felt that the biggest thrills came during their very early barbershop days. Until they began seeing appreciative tears in the eyes of the audience, they didn't realize that the blend of voices they had achieved was so very unique. They claim much of their professional success came from being in the right place at the right time."

"Today, they get together only occasionally. Everyone's life has taken its own direction. Janet could not attend the most recent reunion due to illness. Dottie has raised her family and is helping out with the family business, William Schwartz & Associates, and enjoying her grandchildren. Carol is an active business woman running the family business, Toro Trophy in downtown Sheboygan, and Jinny lives in California, playing golf and helping with her son's business."

The final paragraph finished, "When they get together, they always sing a few songs for old times' sake. Their sound is still superb. There is no question as to why success found them. The perfect harmony and exquisite professionalism. Listening to the rich, full sound, there is no question why "Mr. Sandman" came through when asked by the Chordettes to "bring me a dream."

Two months after the *Sheboygan Press* ran the article mentioned above, Janet's obituary was published in the newspaper on Saturday November 25, 1988. It was a very short obituary, buried inside the paper, and went as follows, '**Janet H. Bleyer** Mrs. Janet (Archie) Bleyer, 75, of 5317 Evergreen Dr., died Wednesday, Nov. 22, 1988 at her home."

"The former Janet Buschmann was born September 21, 1913 in Sheboygan County, a daughter of the late Albert and Alice Janssen Buschmann. Janet was a member of the original singing "Chordettes" of Sheboygan.""

"On Nov. 12, 1954, she married Archie Bleyer. Mrs. Bleyer was a member of Ebenezer United Church of Christ."

"Janet is survived by her husband, Archie; one daughter, Jacquelyn Everly; one grandson, Jason Everly, both of Los Angeles, CA and one brother, Robert Buschmann, of Sheboygan. She was preceded in death by one sister."

"Graveside service for Mrs. Janet Bleyer will be held at 10:30 a.m. Saturday, November 26, 1988 at Wildwood Cemetery. The Rev. Robert Page, pastor of Ebenezer United Church of Christ, will be officiating. There will be no visitation at the NICKEL-LIPPERT FUNERAL HOME which is serving the family."

This was the only mention of Janet's passing in the *Sheboygan Press*. The Newsday newspaper from Long Island, New York also had a six-paragraph obituary about Janet's death in their November 30, 1988 edition. The headline was, "Janet Bleyer, Singer in "Chordettes" Quartet." Part of the article reported, "The Chordettes' run on Godrey's popular weekly program was from 1949, after their appearance on Godfrey's talent scout show, to 1953. They went on to produce hit records for the Cadence Record Co. and to make national and international tours before disbanding in 1964."

"Lynn Evans of the Chordettes, who also lives in Freeport, said of Mrs. Bleyer yesterday, "Never in the whole world could you find a bass like that. It was velvet, hearty, toney, a deep, throaty, warm sound you need." Their (Chordettes) last record before breaking up was "Never on Sunday.""

The following month, on December 11, 1988, the Milwaukee Journal ran an article on Janet. Their article contained 28 paragraphs and a photo of Janet. The Journal article also was on the front page of the local news section. The article written by Maurice Wozniak carried the headline, "She was a star from Sheboygan. Janet Bleyer's deep bass voice carried Chordettes to fame."

The *Journal* also picked up on the lack of space, Janet's passing brought in the *Sheboygan Press*. The *Journal* article started, "Although Janet Bleyer achieved fame and fortune as a member of Sheboygan's Chordettes, her death last month at age 75 was announced by only a small notice in the local paper. Bleyer, whose deep bass singing helped rocket the Chordettes to national stardom on the Arthur Godfrey show in the early days of television, died of cancer Nov. 22 at a home, she and her husband Archie, owned in Black River, south of Sheboygan."

"The Chordettes were formed in 1946. Bleyer was then Janet Ertel, 33, wife of (John Ertel Jr.) the furniture department manager at a Sheboygan department store. It was the first of two marriages for the former Janet Buschmann. The group's rise in popularity was stunning. Within months, they appeared on the "Breakfast Club" national radio show. The host was Don McNeill, another Sheboygan native."

"Bleyer's nephew, Tom Petkus, remembers her as a kind, generous woman with a deep, wonderful, sexy voice. "Every kid should be so lucky to have an Auntie Mame like my Aunt Janet," Petkus said last week in his office at an advertising agency in Mequon."

"When he was a teenager growing up in Sheboygan, Petkus said, he visited Bleyer in New York, hobnobbed with celebrities and used her "slinky black Jaguar convertible with beige hide upholstery" to drive to graduate school interviews at Eastern colleges."

"From the first time I knew her, she never changed that much," he said. "She was Janet at 20, and she was Janet at 75 in the year that she died." Bleyer's success with the group and in subsequent efforts in the business "wasn't just a fluke or a touch of a magic wand," he said. "She had a drive that never left her."

After talking about the beginning of the group, the article continued, "Before they left Sheboygan, Alice Buschmann, now dead, left the group. She was replaced by Carol Buschmann, a sister-in-law, who has kept track of the Chordettes through the years."

"I became a Buschmann when I married Bob, so in a sense, sisters were still singing together," Carol Buschmann said in a telephone interview from her Sheboygan home."

"After becoming Godfrey regulars, they all moved to New York, first to the city and then to Long Island. "When we moved back to Sheboygan [in 1968], our friends here couldn't imagine why," Carol Buschmann said. "But I think it's the kind of place you don't appreciate unless you've lived somewhere else."

"Dorothy Hummitzsch moved back to Sheboygan in 1953, leaving the group to start a family. She still lives there with her husband, Bill Schwartz."

"Lynn Evans, who remains in Freeport on Long Island, joined the group to replace Hummitzsch just in time for their recording days. Evans traveled to Sheboygan for Janet Bleyer's funeral as did Virginia Cole Janis, who has remarried and lives in Palm Springs, Calif."

"The Ertels were separated in 1951 and divorced in 1953, the year the Chordettes left the Godfrey show and struck out on their own. (John) Ertel, who never remarried, returned to Sheboygan, where he still lives." (Note: John Ertel Jr. died April 25, 1997.)

"In 1954, Janet married Archie Bleyer, the band leader for the Godfrey show. He had been fired in 1953, along with singer Julius LaRosa, in a breakup of the so-called "Little Godfreys" that caused a national stir."

"LaRosa sent flowers to Janet's funeral but wasn't able to attend, Carol Buschmann said. "However, we see him every other Christmas," she said. "His wife is from Manitowoc, and when they go there for Christmas every other year, they always drive down to see Archie." We were very close, the people from the Godfrey show, and, like family, we still like to see each other."

"Archie Bleyer formed Cadence, a record production company, and handled such performers as LaRosa, Andy Williams, the Everly Brothers, and Vaughn Meader, whose "First Family" spoof of the Kennedy White House was a record setter. The company made the couple millions." The article ended with the names of the people Janet was survived by.

A little over three months later, on Tuesday, March 21, 1989, the *Sheboygan Press* reported, "Archie Bleyer dies. Producer of Chordettes' hits in 50s." For Archie's death, unlike Janet's, the Press ran the article on the front page and a photo of Archie in a rowboat with the Chordettes.

Under the photo, was the headline, "Archie Bleyer Dies, Producer of Chordettes' hits in '50s." The obituary started with, "Archie Bleyer, a musical director and arranger whose Cadence Records helped launched the careers of Andy Williams, the Everly Brothers and the Chordettes, died here Monday at the age of 79."

"Bleyer, a former musical director of the popular "Arthur Godfrey and Friends" program in the early 1950s, was married to Sheboygan native Janet Buschmann."

"The pair met while she performed on the television program as a member of the Chordettes, a group of four Sheboyganites which wowed audiences with their pure four-part harmonies. They were married in 1954, and moved to the Black River area four years ago from Long Island, N.Y., to be closer to Janet Bleyer's relatives, said her daughter Jacquelie Everly."

Next in the obituary was a history of Archie's life in the field of music. The end of the obituary contained a comment from Carol Buschmann, who said, "All of the disc jockeys were always looking for his records. That's because he was a perfectionist, and he would not produce an arrangement until he was completely satisfied with it. They knew it would be good coming from him."

Janet Bleyer's gravestone in Sheboygan's Wildwood Cemetery (From the author's collection).

The above photo of Archie Bleyer and the Chordettes was on the front page of the Sheboygan Press on March 21, 1989, the day the newspaper reported on his death. The caption under the photo read, "ARCHIE BLEYER, musical arranger for the Arthur Godfrey Show and the Sheboygan based Chordettes singing group, posed with the Chordettes in New York's Central Park for a record album cover around 1960. Clockwise, from Bleyer, the members of the Chordettes are Bleyer's wife Janet Buschmann Bleyer, Jinny Cole, and Carol Hagedorn Buschmann, all of Sheboygan, and Lynn Evans." (Photo Courtesy of Carol Buschmann)

At the end of the obituary was a comment from Jacqueline Everly, who said, "that Bleyer, who was her step-father, was always willing to go out of his way for her and her son. There was nothing that was ever too much for him to do. He totally took care of us."

Four days later, in their March 25 edition, the *Sheboygan Press* again ran an article on the front page of their newspaper about Archie Bleyer. The article was written by Andy Rooney, who would still be working more than 20 years later on CBS's 60 Minutes. The headline was, "A Musician's Musician." Rooney had worked with Bleyer on the Arthur Godfrey show. It started out as a sad article detailing Archie's last days.

The beginning of the article stated, "Archie Bleyer died last week and the way he went wasn't too good. You'd have to be at least 50 to remember Archie. He was the musical director for the Arthur Godfrey radio and television shows in the 1940s and 1950s."

"Janet Buschmann Ertel, his wife was the familiar bass voice in that great hit song "Mr. Sandman," singing with a quartet known as The Chordettes. Four years ago, Janet decided that Archie, who was suffering from Parkinson's disease, would be more comfortable if they moved from Long Island back to Sheboygan, Wis., where she grew up and where the Chordettes came together. Janet knew Archie was dying and felt she could take care of him better in Sheboygan."

Archie Bleyer's gravestone in Sheboygan's Wildwood Cemetery is shown above. His wife Janet's gravestone is about one foot to the left of Archie's stone. (From the author's collection)

"But it was Janet who died first."

"Archie lived on without her for four months. During that time, he was alternately lucid and lost, often returning to consciousness to speak in vain to Jan, thinking she must still be nearby. In the other room, perhaps."

After reminding the readers about Bleyer's life at Columbia University, the article continued, "The first few years with Godfrey were good ones. Archie, always formally dressed in tailor made business suits, French cuffs and English shoes, was part of the show. The six men in the orchestra were fine musicians and distinguished themselves under Archie's meticulous direction. He was a musician's musician, an intellectual perfectionist as readily able to arrange a piece for Leslie Uggams as he was to work on complex music of the Hungarian composer Bela Bartok."

Rooney's article ended, "Andy Williams, the Everly Brothers, the McGuire Sisters and Pat Boone, all recorded hits for Cadence, but ironically, the biggest hit record that Archie Bleyer, the musician, ever had, wasn't a musical record. Comedian Vaughn Meader's takeoff on the Kennedy family called "The First Family" sold 100,000 copies a day at $5 each for weeks. It sold a total of 5 ½ million copies up until Nov. 22, 1963, the day John F. Kennedy was shot. All copies were withdrawn from store shelves. The joke was over."

"Archie Blyer became a multi-millionaire in his lifetime, but all he ever really wanted to be, was a musician."

The Press added at the end, "Graveside services for Archie Bleyer will be held at 11 a.m. today at Wildwood Cemetery."

Two years later, on May 27, 1990, the Newsday newspaper of Long Island, New York reported on the life of another former Chordette, Lynn Evans after the group stopped singing. The article under the headline, "At 66, Another Go at the Spotlight" started as follows, "Mr. Sandman, bring me a dream. . . After spending the last 25 years on Long Island in relative obscurity as a teacher, Lynn Evans is seeking the spotlight for the second time in her life."

"She did well the first time she tried her hand at show business: For nearly a decade in the 1950s and early 1960s, she was the lead singer of the Chordettes, a popular female quartet, whose hits included "Mr. Sandman" and "Lollipop.""

Now 66 and living in Freeport (New York), Evans has retired from teaching, her children are grown and she is working on a new dream: to break back into show business. She's teaming up with three other women in a new vocal group called the Swing Four, which hopes to make big band songs popular once more." The Swing Four also featured another former Chordette, Nancy Overton.

"After rehearsing for a year, the new group performed on stage for the first time last month (April 1990) at Don't Tell Mama, a Manhattan cabaret and piano bar. "They were delightful," said Sidney Meyer, owner of the club, a well-know show-business hangout on West 46th Street's Restaurant Row."

"It is the type of praise Evans received often in the 1950's"

"After appearing on Arthur Godfrey's show, the Chordettes gained international renown with a wide-ranging repertoire that included sentimental movie themes, tearful teen ballads and rhythmic rock and roll. They played before howling teenagers on "American Bandstand,' high rollers in Las Vegas nightclubs and royalty in European palaces."

"In addition to gaining fame and fortune, The Chordettes, all small-town girls of humble background, had gotten frequent chances to hobnob with the biggest stars of the entertainment world. "George Burns, Dean Martin, Jerry Lewis, Lucille Ball –we knew them all," Evans recalled. "It was wonderful, but it didn't seem that big a deal at the time. It sort of went with the territory."

"But the Chordettes ran out of such territory, known as Big Success, as times and musical tastes changed. After several years of meager record sales, the group disbanded in 1964. Its members left the business and scattered about the country. "It was a very tough and traumatic adjustment," recalled Evans, who had divorced after settling in Baldwin with her husband and two young children. "I had led a rather unreal existence, and now I was faced with things I had never really done before – like, shopping, cooking and housecleaning." She also faced a serious question: What should she do with the rest of her life?"

"Having earned a college degree in sociology, Evans, a native of Youngstown, Ohio, decided to stay on Long Island and start a teaching career. In 1966, after graduating from Hofstra University with a master's degree in special education, she was hired to tutor neurologically impaired children in the Brentwood school district – which she did, with great success, for the next 23 years."

"Although out of show business, Evans did not eliminate music from her new professional life. She used it as a teaching tool."

"I had a piano in the classroom," Evans said. "And I taught the kids by using music. I would write words on a chart, point to them and put them into song. It worked."

"It did more than that, according to Howard Brodsky, Brentwood's director of special services. "It was magic," he said. "Lynn was a superb teacher. She genuinely cared about the kids, and they knew it. Through her music and manner, she managed to reach them and get them to transcend their disabilities."

"Such achievements brought great satisfaction, but, deep down, singing remained Evan's first love. Evans retired last June with her colleague's gratitude and an ample pension. Her children are grown and its time, she feels, to try her first love again."

While a group of younger women calling themselves "The New Chordettes" is enjoying some success singing the original quartet's hits, Evans has teamed with three other former singers in their late 50s and 60s – Doris Pallatto, Jean Swain and Nancy Overton, who also was a Chordette – in the Swing Four." Jean Swain was Nancy Overton's sister.

"The Swing Four, whose repertoire includes "Mr. Sandman," presented three weekend shows at Don't Tell Mama. Each drew a near-capacity audience, most of them middle-aged, all of them unabashedly appreciative."

"There obviously is an audience out there for this type of music," Meyer said. "They are welcome back to my place any time."

"That judgment drew a broad grin from Evans. "We're not back in this business for money or fame," she said. "We love to sing and to share our pleasure with other people. If we can get a chance to do that, we'll be happy."

The original article also included two photos. One showed Lynn and Nancy, along with their fellow Chordettes, Carol Bushman and Jinny Osborn. The second photo showed Lynn holding her "Mr. Sandman" gold record.

In an email, Nancy Overton gave additional information about the Swing Four. Nancy said about the 1990s group, "I was putting a group together and took a chance on asking Lynn if she'd like to join us, even though we lived 95 miles apart. (She was in Freeport, Long Island and I lived in Blairstown NJ.) Her husband had just died (unbeknownst to me) and she was looking for a new direction in her life."

"I had already hooked up with a Barbershopper, Doris Pallotto as lead and my sister, Jean, who lived in NYC. It took a lot of juggling to get us all together, but we were gung-ho about it and had some great experiences. Lynn and Doris took turns singing the lead. And I must say that Lynn "fell into" the second voice with great ease, even though she'd previously only sung lead. Always so true and "right on."

"I guess our most memorable experience was rising up on that magical platform—just the four of us—at Radio City Music Hall at a Doo Wop concert. Not exactly our venue, but we were greeted with a standing ovation. Performing with the Eddy Arnold show was another biggie. He was a sweetheart of a guy and we loved dining with him between and after shows, and hearing all his interesting stories. We worked with him in both Laughlin and Branson, MO. Also in Hershey, PA. And then there was our performance on "Music City Tonight" which was quite an honor."

Nancy ended with, "My sister, Jean, died in 2000, and Doris in 2001. Lots of wonderful memories with those two—and the other who were so much a part of our lives." Nancy passed away on April 5, 2009.

Less than a year later, the Milwaukee Journal, in their March 23, 1991, ran an article about another performer with close ties to the Chordettes and the Arthur Godfrey show, Julius LaRosa. The article started out, "Forty years ago, fans were clamoring for his autograph. Nowadays, he still gets asked to sign his name to a picture. But, as the entertainer Julius LaRosa described it recently, "Times have changed."

"Sometimes when I'm doing a show, I like to tell the following story. When I was just coming onto the scene, I was pretty hot, and everybody wanted my autograph. Then, 20 or so years ago when someone would ask for my autograph, they would say, 'Thank you so much. My mother is crazy about you.' Nowadays they still ask for my autograph, but they say, 'Oh boy, wait until my grandmother sees this.'"

"At 61, the singer who began his show business career on Arthur Godfrey's radio and television shows is still entertaining audiences and singing. "Four decades and I'm still going strong," LaRosa said. "I guess you'd call that some kind of staying power."

"A resident of Irvington, N.Y., LaRosa performs in muscular dystrophy telethons in the United States and Canada, in nightclubs in New York, Las Vegas, and Atlantic City, in television commercials and at fairs and private parties. But, he said, one of his most special regular appearances, one for which he does not get paid, is for the Westchester County, N.Y., library system."

The article went on to talk about the publicity he does for the library system and his love of reading. LaRosa added how he loved reading because he had never gone to college. Instead he joined the United States Navy in 1947.

Included with the *Milwaukee Journal* article was this,
then current photo of Julius LaRosa. (From the author's collection)

The article continued, "He sang in a Navy choir, at the officers club and at bars to pay for his drinks, he said. When LaRosa was stationed at Pensacola, Fla., Godfrey heard him and offered the young seaman a job after his discharge. LaRosa said that his unpolished, untrained performance style was a "perfect foil" to Godfrey's high-profile personality."

"After a few months on Godfrey's daily radio and weekly television shows, LaRosa's popularity soared. Within a year, he said, he was receiving almost 7,000 fan letters a week."

"But by 1953, LaRosa said, the radio host had "fired the kid from Brooklyn," because, as Godfrey put it, "I had lost my humility.""

"I was 23 years old then and filled with myself," LaRosa said. "Who isn't at 23, especially if you're a celebrity? But, I still think of myself as just a kid from Brooklyn."

"Sure, I have an ego. You have to, to be in this business. But, my ego isn't all consuming. I know nobody comes to hear me sing to be knocked off their chair. I just want people to feel good after they've seen me."

Later the article reported, "Although his career has thrived and he is on the road much of the time, still performing, LaRosa said he missed the old days of TV."

"It's frustrating. They don't have the variety shows like they used to, the Ed Sullivan-type shows. And people lose sight of you when you're not doing television. You can only do Johnny Carson so much."

"Nevertheless, he said, the last three years have been the best financially. "I guess one could say I'm in an enviable place," LaRosa said, "I'm not a high-priced performer. But, those types price themselves out of the day-to-day jobs."

"I'm busy. I'm still working after all these years. And I'm still married to the woman I courted 36 years ago. His wife is the former Rosemary (Rory) Meyer of Rockville, Wis., a community in Manitowoc County." Manitowoc County borders Sheboygan County on the north.

The article ended, "I have my split-level in Irvington and I have two great kids." LaRosa said. "And yes, I've had my ups and downs, my disappointments. That's typical for show business. But for a kid from Brooklyn, I think I've done OK."

On July 6, 1990, the Boca Raton newspaper The News, about Joyce Creatore, the last member to join the Chordettes. The article gave some information about Joyce after the Chordettes stopped performing.

"When tenor Jinny Janis announced she was leaving the Chordettes in 1964, the group decided it was time to bow out gracefully."

"Creatore went to work for the noted New York songwriting and producing team of Hugo (Peretti) and Luigi (Creatore) in 1965. She also recorded a solo album for Reader's Digest Records in London. After 13 years of dating Luigi Creatore, she became his wife in August 1979 at age 47. The couple moved to an oceanfront condo in Boca Raton in May 1981."

"The Chordette story did not end in 1964. Their music has lived on in movies (Back to the Future), radio, television and theater ("The Tafftas"). Several years ago, a bogus group began performing under the name The Chordettes. Janis went to see the group and was so outraged at their theft of the Chordettes good name, she threatened to sue. The group is now called The New Chordettes."

"A year ago, Creatore was approached by the original members to reunite the group, but she declined. "Luigi was right in the middle of putting on his play, 'The Man Who Shot Lincoln,' off Broadway," she says. "I felt it was my duty to be with him. Besides I just couldn't see going back on the road."

"Creatore contents herself with an occasional imprompto performance at a piano bars."

"She's a fantastic singers" says Luigi, beaming with pride. "She's one of the best I've ever heard." "Luigi says he's going to buy me a piano player for Christmas," says Joyce.

In 1992, the *Sheboygan Press* ran a series of small articles about some of the business people of Sheboygan. One of the persons, selected as the subject of an article on March 15 was Carol Buschmann for the March 15 article, under the headline, "No Lost Chordette" and gave some information about what she had been doing since she left the Chordettes.

The short article said, "By the time Carol Buschmann's name was added to the Music Wall of Fame at the Fountain Park bandshell, she had left the world of bright lights as a Chordette and returned to her native Sheboygan to run her own business."

"Today the shine in her life comes not from her name in lights, but from the brass plaques she supplies to area sports teams and businesses through Toro Trophy in downtown Sheboygan."

"We lived in New York for 20 years, but wanted to get close to family. I didn't think we'd move all the way back, but Sheboygan is a great place to live," she said."

The February 9, 1994, Newsday newspaper of Long Island, New York featured an article about Chordette, Lynn Evans, under the headline, "The Rebirth of Harmony, Old Keys and New Stages For a Veteran Chordette." The article started, "When Lynn Evans of Freeport wants a reminder of the globe-hopping she did as lead singer of The Chordettes, she looks at her coffee table. There, arranged artfully under a custom-made glass top, are dozens of room keys from all the exotic - and noy-so-exotic - hotels she visited with The Chordettes, whose hits 'Mr. Sandman' (1954) and 'Lollipop' (1958) made them perhaps the most successful female barbershop quartet ever."

"Those scraps of metal and their brightly colored key tags reflect but a few of Evans' memories of her 13-year stint with the group: Like the command performance at an Aruba hotel for the princesses of the Netherlands, whose seemingly lukewarm response was just the result of the sovereign caveat against smiling with one's teeth showing. Or the White House performance after which a bald President Eisenhower remarked how much he loved 'Mr. Sandman' - except for the line that mentions 'lots of wavy hair like Liberace.' "We really went all over,' sighs the petite blond Evans, who gives her age as 'between 60 and death.' When the Chordettes disbanded in 1964, Evans embarked on a new career, which is also reflected in the décor of the Freeport apartment where she's lived for more than a quarter-century: In the foyer is a painting done by the special-needs children she taught until her retirement in 1989."

"Despite her challenging career in education, 'I never felt I was finished with The Chordettes,' explains Evans, who three years ago came up with a solution: She brought them back. 'A lot of older people still remember us and love the sounds,' says Evans, who has added senior condos to the group's list of performance venues. In fact, The Chordettes' music is so popular on the nostalgia circuit that it has inspired a younger rival group, the New Chordettes. Spurred by that unwelcome competition, the two other surviving Chordettes - Carol Buschmann and Jinny Cole Lockard, who originally formed the group in Sheboygan, Wis., gave Evans' new group their blessing, and the use of the Chordettes name. (The Chordettes' other founding member, Janet Bleyer, died several years ago.) Rounding out the re-energized Chordettes is Nancy Overton (who first joined the group in 1958), her sister Jean Swain (a former Heathertone) and Doris Alberti, all of whom live in the metropolitan area."

"Evans herself is not an original Chordettes: She joined in 1952, when the foursome performed in her hometown of Youngstown, Ohio. Evans had founded a local quartet of lady barbershoppers by memorizing the Chordettes songbook, and when The Chordettes' pregnant lead singer Dottie Schwartz didn't feel up to harmonizing in their hospitality suite, Evans stood in for her. By the end of the evening, she had a job offer."

"I said to my mother, 'I'm going to New York in the morning,' remembers Evans. That was in November 1952. A month later, Evans was performing with the Chordettes on the Wednesday night 'Arthur Godfrey and His Friends' TV show. She demurs when asked about the variety show host's reputedly tyrannical personality, except to say pointedly, 'He needed to be completely in control.' But her anecdotes are telling enough: After Godfrey canned singer Julius La Rosa on the air for "losing his humility" and dismissed Archie Bleyer, his orchestra conductor and Janet's husband-to-be, (Godfrey objected to the activities of a Bleyer owned company, Cadence Records), he turned his attention to the Chordettes."

"One night we sang 'River Seine,' and Godfrey told us, 'I've never heard you sing more beautifully,' Evans remembers. 'Then the next day, he called to say, 'I no longer want to interfere with your career."

"The Chordettes needn't have worried about their prospects: A year later, they hit it big with "Mr. Sandman," which Archie Bleyer discovered on the B-side of Vaughn Monroe's "Doin' the Mambo." The song topped "Your Hit Parade" for 32 weeks; one New York City disc jockey was fired for playing it too many times. After hits like "Eddie My Love" and "Born To Be With You" came chart-topping "Lollipop" in 1958. And even as their career was coming to a close, The Chordettes scored again in 1961 with "Never On Sunday," the title track of the movie of the same name. For all its glamour, their careers also provided its share of heartache for the four married Chordettes."

"It was very hard on our marriages," says Evans, who divorced before the Chordettes disbanded. "Sometimes we were gone for two weeks, sometimes a month, and even when we were home, working. Everything was infringing on our time, and the kids suffered. Maybe we weren't there for them, and for many years we felt guilty."

"But in the second dawning of the Chordettes, Evans sees an opportunity to fully enjoy the limelight. This go-around has even provided its share of firsts: In 1991, The Chordettes debuted at Radio City Music Hall as part of a nostalgia show, garnering a standing ovation for the bubbly "Lollipop."

The article ended, "And though The Chordettes are dressing a little more maturely these days - "no slinkies," laughs Evans - their autograph-seeking audiences are even more enthusiastic than when they first heard The Chordettes' barbershop harmonies. "People seemed a little more reserved back then," signs Evans. "Now they clap and cheer like crazy."

On April 27, 1997, the *Sheboygan Press* reported that John Ertel Jr. had died at the age of 85. His obit stated, "He was married to Janet Buschmann, of Sheboygan who preceded him in death in 1988." No mention was made that Janet and him had been divorced or that she was a member of the Chordettes.

Four years later, on Sunday, May 20, 2001, the Sheboygan Press ran an article titled, "Family passes business reins to new generation." Another title could have been, Carol Buschmann retires for the second time."

According to the article, "When Carol Buschmann, Janet Sly, and Donald Grunowo walked away from work at Toro Trophies & Awards Friday afternoon, it was for the last time. At least as employees."

"The trio has been running the business since about 1980 and while two of the three aren't quite retirement age, all three are ready to do something different."

"This is the 74-year-old Buschmann's second retirement. The first was publicized on a slightly larger scale, as she was one of the Chordettes, the female foursome began achieving national acclaim in the late 1940s and have stayed in America's memories with songs, such as "Mr. Sandman," "Never on a Sunday," and "Lollipop.""

"In September, the group will be inducted into the (Vocal) Group Hall of Fame in Sharon, Penn."

"After 20 years of performing, Carol had enough and retired. A few years later, she and husband Robert returned to Sheboygan. He opened a sporting goods store in 1968. By the early 1980s, it had evolved into strictly a trophy and awards shop, Buschmann said."

Toro's Trophies & Awards (center building) is shown in this photo from July 2005. After moving back to Sheboygan, Carol and her husband, Robert started this business, as a sporting goods store, then a trophy shop, which is now being run by three of their grandchildren. (From the author's collection)

"Sly remembers working in her father's store, primarily as ski-boot fitter. When her mother took over the trophy shop, Sly stayed involved. Now after about 30 years of working for and with her parents, Sly is ready for something different. She's just not sure what. "I want to be a vet," Sly said cautiously. "But that's a lot of school and I'm not sure I want to get $100,000 in debt.""

"Grunowo, Sly's ex-husband, is also ready for a change. He has a few irons in the fire but hasn't made up his mind."

"Buschmann didn't plan on becoming famous, it just sort of happened. She doesn't regret those years, but she doesn't miss them either. She didn't really plan on running a trophy business for 20 years either. But this time, walking away isn't so easy."

"We have a lot of wonderful customers." Buschmann said. "I can't begin to count how many customers we have – about 90 percent are repeat. We have one customer who's never even been in the store. They just call and say this is what we need, you know how to do what we want and that's it.""

"Walking away isn't any easier for Sly. "We're going to miss our customers," Sly said with tears in her eyes."

"When the store opens Monday, a new trio will be in charge; three of Buschmann's grandchildren purchased and will be running the business. Robert Buschmann and his wife Jelane and Kristine Buschmann Dewar. Three for three. Seems fitting."

In the last part of 2001, the Chordettes were inducted into the Vocal Music Hall of Fame in Sharon, PA. The ceremony was to have taken place the third weekend of September, but was cancelled due to the 9-11 attacks in New York and Washington D.C. earlier in the week. The induction ceremony was then moved to October. Other inductees in 2001 included, The Bee Gees, The Eagles, The Four Aces, The Four Freshmen, Gladys Knight & The Pips, The Lennon Sisters, Ben E. King & The Drifters, Mamas & the Papas, Three Dog Night, and The Bangles.

The write up about the Chordettes for the display and included in the induction program said, "The Chordettes. The Chordettes were one of the more popular white female groups of the '50s, but unlike most of their counterparts who needed record successes to get into TV and radio, they established themselves over the air and on the small screen years before ever cutting their first record. Formed in Sheboygan, Wisconsin, the quartet of Dorothy Schwartz (lead), Jinny Lockard (tenor), Carol Buschmann (baritone), and Janet Ertel (bass) practiced their barbershop-style harmony to perfection in the late '40s."

"They joined the Arthur Godfrey's "Talent Scouts" shows on radio in 1949 and soon graduated to his TV show as regulars. In 1953, both Dorothy and Jinny were replaced by Lynn Evans and Margie Needham, respectively. Early in that year Archie Bleyer, musical director for Godfrey, started his own record company called Cadence (it could have been dubbed Julius LaRosa Records since the first eight releases were all by the Brooklyn-born singer). The tenth single in April 1954, was by the Chordettes as Bleyer felt there was room on records for another Andrews or McGuire Sisters. The girls' first release, "It's You, It's You I Love,' went nowhere, but their second single, a lilting pop lullaby titled "Mister Sandman," took off (helped by TV exposure) and went all the way to number one in the U.S. and to number 11 in England. With seven weeks at the top and 20 weeks on Billboard's Best seller chart, "Mister Sandman" and The Chordettes were on top of the recording world. It was all the more embarrassing when their next two singles failed to chart at all; it wasn't until January 1956 that another Chordettes recording, "The Wedding," hit the top 100, though it quickly dropped from the list. It was during this drought that The Chordettes decided to take the route of other white pop artists of the early

'50s: when all else failed, cover a black artist's song and ride it up the chart. Thus The Teen Queens' "Eddie My Love" became The Chordettes first top 20 record in two years. (The Teen Queens' version fought it to a tie at number 14 Pop in the spring of 1957.) The girls' seventh single became one of their biggest yet, as "Born To Be With You" hit number five in the summer stateside and number eight in England."

Four of the Chordettes are shown in front of the Chordettes display in the Vocal Music Hall of Fame in Sharon, PA during the induction ceremony in October 2001. From left to right are Jinny, Lynn, Carol, and Joyce. (Photo Copyrighted by Chuck Miller, used with permission)

"The group's most remarkable quality seemed to be its survivability. Every time they were written off as another too-sweet-for-the-times female group, they would emerge with another hit, straddling the fence between the pop world and emerging rock and roll audience. After "Lay Down Your Arms" (#16, 1956 b/w "Teenage Goodnight" (#45) had a successful run, two more singles failed before the success of another two-sider, "Just Between You and Me (#8, 1957) b/w "Soft Sands" (#73). Then their next single failed to chart. In fact the only two back-back top 20 records in their career were "Born To Be With You" and "Lay Down Your Arms."

"In the spring of 1958 they burst onto the scene with a sound that both mature pop audiences and rock teens could like, embodied in "Lollipop." With its chime intro and verse like sing-along children's song, it was soon a number one hit from Malibu to Main (and number six on the United Kingdom charts). Four of their next five singles were charters, including the theme from the popular TV show, "Zorro" (#17, 1958) and the theme from the film "Never On Sunday" (#13, 1961). One that didn't make it, but should have, was the haunting Glenn Yarbrough folk song "All My Sorrows" in 1962"

"By then, however, the group had become passé - not hip enough for the emerging rock and roll set. But, The Chordettes accomplishments were enviable (14 chart records and four tops 10s in 22 releases) and their professionalism and attraction were undeniable. Archie Bleyer thought so. He even went as far as to marry one (Janet)."

In January 2013, Marjorie discovered that the Grammy Hall Of Fame had inducted the Chordettes' "Mr. Sandman" into their hall of fame in 2002, 11 years earlier. But, the Chordettes were never contacted about this honor, nor did any of them attend the ceremony.

The August 11, 2003 edition of the *Sheboygan Press* contained a photo of Carol and Robert Buschmann, in honor of their 50th wedding anniversary. The article, which was accompanied by a photo of the couple at the top of the article, stated:

"Robert and Carol Buschmann, Sheboygan, celebrated their 50th wedding anniversary on Aug. 17, 2002 at their daughter's house with a small reception. The event was hosted by the family."

"The couple was married Aug. 18, 1952 in Juarez, Mexico."

"The former Carol Hagedorn was born May 13, 1927 in Sheboygan. She was a professional singer with the Chordettes for 21 years, ending in 1965."

"Bob was born Oct. 23, 1918 in Sheboygan. He served in the Army during World War II."

"The couple owned and operated Toro Sporting Goods, and then Toro Trophies & Awards in downtown Sheboygan for 33 years. In 2001, they sold it to their grandchildren."

"The couple have three children: Jill Drews, Tory (Barbara) Buschmann, and Janet (David) Sly, all of Sheboygan. There are 13 grandchildren, 20 great-grandchildren and four great-great grandchildren."

On September 25, 2002, the New York Teacher magazine, the official publication of New York State Teachers, ran an article about a recently retired New York teacher, Lynn Evans Mand. The title of the article was, "Former Chordettes harmonized in the classroom. Brentwood retiree first achieved fame singing 'Mr. Sandman."

The article said, "A half-century ago, as she sang the sweet melody that goes with the words, "Mr. Sandman, bring me a dream," one of the Chordettes did not realize her dreams would move from the recording studio to the classroom."

"The two careers dovetailed. "Music reaches the soul," said Lynn Evans Mand. "It's important in any education because it builds intelligence."

"Mand was a member of the Chordettes, 1950s quartet that sang hits such as "Mr. Sandman" and "Lollipop." She also taught for 25 years on Long Island, using her musical ability in the classroom to capitalize on student's talents."

Mand joined the Chordettes in 1952, after graduating from college. The group disbanded in 1964. Soon after, Mand discovered an opening to teach at a BOCES (Board Of Cooperative Educational Services) school in Westbury. The school paid her to go to school for a master's degree, and then Mand took a job as a special education teacher in Brentwood."

"Lynn stayed the course for 25 years," noted Chris Veech in a profile of Mand in the newsletter of the Retirees of Brentwood Schools."

"The transition was tricky, Mand said, she de-emphasized her Chordettes career. "I insisted that they know me as a teacher. I was lovingly firm," Mand said.

"Mand used singing skill to help her students read. She would write lyrics on the blackboard, have students point to the words as she sang - over and over until they learned the words."

"Mand enjoyed unlocking the talents of her students. For instance, one student had no legs from the knees down and no facial muscles. But Mand taught him the song "These are a few of my favorite things" from the musical, "The Sound of Music" to sing at a school assembly.

"Everybody broke into applause, it was so melodic," Mand said."

"She retired from teaching in 1990. The Chordettes reunited and toured the country from 1990 to 1995 with Eddie Arnold. After that, Mand moved back to Elyria, Ohio, to be closer to her family. She still sings in the church choir."

The article ended, "As a teacher, I wanted to make a difference," Mand said. "And I think I did make a difference."

One thing not mentioned in the article, was that shortly before she retired, Mand was named New York State "Teacher of the Year."

With the internet making it easier to spread news, we can now keep updated on current news. On May 5, 2003, the following message was printed in a Barbershop Group on Yahoo. The message read as follows, "Friends, Here is the sad news about Jinny Cole Janis (Tenor of the Chordettes.) Would you get the news out about Jinny? Her last e-mail left everybody puzzled. She does have cancer of the lung, which has spread to the liver and lymph nodes, so it does not look good. She is at home with 24/7 caregivers, but is in too much pain to sit at the computer to send or receive e-mail. However, I talked to the caregiver today, and asked if she would please tell Kaye (Jinny's daughter) to see that any messages or e-mail be printed out and read to her, or given her to read if she is able."

Eight days later, on May 13, 2003, an update about Jinny was posted. The update reported, "Jinny's daughter (Kaye), and (granddaughter) Lisa, have moved into Jinny's home, and are caring for her. She is still planning to have some radiation in the hopes of easing her pain, which is still quite severe. Mentally, Lisa says, she (Jinny) is in good shape, and has accepted her fate, and is at peace with it. Lisa said depending on some of the tests, it will be determined whether she will be an inpatient at a hospice, or whether she can stay in her home and receive hospice. Of course, this means that she will be gone from us in less than six months. Kay says she has printed out her e-mails, and Jinny has read cards and letters, so please keep sending them. I'm sure just knowing that so many of us love and will miss her, has to be a help."

Less than one week later, on May 19, 2003, Jinny's daughter sent out the following email. "Dearest Friends and Family, This is Jinny's daughter, Kaye. I wanted to let you know that mom passed away early this morning after a short bout with lung cancer. She left this world as she lived it; never depressed, never afraid or regretful. She said that she viewed this as a diagnosis as a gift from God: much more preferable than dragging around an oxygen tank for another 10 years. She told me repeatedly over the past 25 days that she'd had a wonderful life, and she was so grateful to each of you for helping it be so. She was ready – even eager – to go and meet her Lord."

There was also one follow up e-mail that showed just how thoughtful and kind a person, Jinny was. This e-mail said, "Hello all: I just learned, with great sadness, that Jinny Janis, founder and original tenor of the Chordettes, passed away from lung cancer. Jinny's father was King Cole, once President of the SPEBSQSA. When Jinny left in June 1953 to have a baby, she allowed me to take her place, and let me have all the perks that went with it including recording with the Chordettes. I got to sing "Mr. Sandman" instead of her."

"When I retired in 1956, Jinny came back and sang with the gals until they retired in the early '60's. Jinny loved to sing and especially woodshed…as the Pioneers group will confirm. A little anecdote about our friendship: in 1992, when I broke my hip while playing tennis, and Walter was already handicapped with a stroke from the year before, we needed help. First Lynn, the lead of the Chordettes, came to take care of us (for two weeks), and when Jinny found out about it, she flew from Palm Springs to take over (in Florida). She stayed for 10 days and went back home on Christmas Day, and she wouldn't even let us pay for her airfare! Jinny was a beautiful gal with a beautiful voice and a dry sense of humor. We will miss her so much."

"Sincerely,

Marjorie Latzko"

Marjorie was a member of the Chordettes from 1953 to 1956 and again in 1959.

On May 21, 2003, the *Sheboygan Press* reported on Jinny's passing with an article on the front page of the newspaper, under the headline, "Chordettes member 'Jinny' Cole dies. The accompanying article written by Martha Shad, said "Virginia "Jinny" Cole Janus, one of the original Chordettes, died Monday in California. She was 76."

The rest of the article contained memories of Jinny by Carol. "She organized the group," Chordettes member and Sheboygan resident Carol Buschmann said of Jinny, whom she called her dearest friend. "I first met her when I started singing with the group in 1947. She was the soprano and had a clear, beautiful sound and she blended with the rest of us. I don't think I appreciated her voice until many years later when I listened to our records."

"Her father, the late O.H. Cole, was the international president of a barbershop singing association and helped the female quartet get started in Sheboygan in the mid-40s, said Buschmann, who was the group's baritone."

"The Chordettes achieved national status in 1949 when they won a spot on Arthur Godfrey's talent show. From 1949 to 1953, they were regulars on the show."

"Arthur Godfrey used to cry when we performed on his show. That was quite an honor," Buschmann said."

"The foursome stayed together until the mid-1960s. In 1982, they began getting together regularly again after they met at a barbershop convention in Salt Lake City, Buschmann said. Although they had many requests to perform, they sang only for themselves, Buschmann said."

"We were too spread out," Buschmann said. "One was in Florida, one was in New York, one was in Wisconsin and one was in Palm Springs (California). We got together once a year, and after we'd been together for a while we'd sing. It was amazing – after all those years, the sound was still there. She was the pretty one and she had a wonderful sense of humor."

Jinny's obituary found elsewhere in the paper added the following: "Jinny is survived by one son, Keith Osborn of San Francisco, Calif; one daughter, Kay (Terry) Hunt of Palm Springs; two grandchildren, Lisa Hunt and Daniel Hunt and two original Chordettes, Carol Buschmann and Dorothy Schwartz."

Jinny was also survived by ex-husband, Tom Lockard, who she had married while a member of the Chordettes. Lockard died three years later on September 3, 2006. A newspaper obituary from Eugene, Oregon on September 8, 2006, reported, "Thomas Blake "Tom" Lockard of Eugene died Sept. 3, of age-related causes at age 88."

"He was born March 17, 1918, in Baltimore to Blake and Mable Leech Lockard. He married Marilyn Filkins on Oct. 18, 1968, in Los Angeles."

"Lockard served in the U.S. Coast Guard during World War II. He sang in the U.S. Coast Guard Quartet. He later sang professionally in the Mariners quartet, including performances on the Arthur Godfrey Show."

"He served as a deputy clerk of the Superior Court of California in Los Angeles, retiring in 1978. He also was a restaurateur."

"Survivors include his wife; three daughters, Marlayna Christon and Paula Lockard, both of New York City, and Kathy Hunt of La Quinta, Calif.; a stepson, James Filkins of Covina, Calif.; and five grandchildren. A stepson, David Filkins, died previously."

With Jinny's passing, Bob Harker, executive director of the Sheboygan County Historical Society and Museum brought up the idea of doing something to honor the Chordettes and their special place in not only in Sheboygan's history, but also the world of music. By the spring of 2004, plans were being developed to have the Chordettes as the subject of one of the Historical Societies quarterly meeting programs. Among the members of the planning committee were former Chordettes, Carol Buschmann and Dorothy Schwartz and Dorothy's husband, Bill. The event was scheduled for Tuesday evening, September 14, 2004, in one of the halls inside the Blue Harbor Conference Center in Sheboygan. There were four halls inside the convention center, each with moveable walls. If needed, the walls could be opened for one huge hall or the walls could be closed creating four smaller halls.

At Sheboygan's Mead Public Library, just inside the main entrance is a large glass display area. In August 2004, to promote the Chordettes' program, this display case was filled with Chordettes items, including the gold record Carol received for Mr. Sandman. Items for the display were loaned by Carol and Dorothy of the Chordettes and Scott Lewandoske (author of this book). Items on display included a dress that Dorothy wore as a member of the Chordettes, records, photos, songbooks, and photos. The Sheboygan Beacon newspaper did a story on the Chordettes and the upcoming program and included a black & white photo of the library display with Carol and Dorothy standing by it. Not to be out done, the Sheboygan Press also did a story on the Chordettes and the upcoming program. The Press also included a photo of the library display, but their photo was in color and also included Dorothy and Carol standing next to it.

Carol and Dorothy also did live radio shows on Sheboygan's WHBL radio and on Sheboygan's cable TV station to promote the event and also talk about their memories being members of the Chordettes.

Celebrating Sheboygan's own

Chordettes

♪ Tuesday, Sept. 14, 2004

♪ Dinner, 6 p.m., program 7 p.m.

♪ Blue Harbor Conference Center

♪ $30 per reservation

A local history program co-sponsored by the Sheboygan County Historical Society, Sheboygan County Historical Research Center.

Shown here is the ticket that people received when they paid to attend the Chordettes program at Sheboygan's Blue Harbor on September 14, 2004. The same photo also appeared on the program booklet.
(From the author's collection)

Tickets went on sale at the beginning of August. The Historical Society was hoping to get at least 100 people for this event. The reason was that other quarterly meetings had a price of $12.00 or less, and this program honoring the Chordettes was priced at $30.00. Also, it was being held on a Tuesday night. The goal of 100 tickets was reached in less than a week. 200 total tickets were then quickly sold. Still ticket sales held strong and 300 tickets were sold, then 400, then 500. All together, 516 tickets were sold, making it the most successful history program, the Sheboygan County Historical Society ever held. Blue Harbor had to open the portable walls and use the entire hall for this event. Sheboygan showed that they still remembered and loved the Chordettes.

Carol and Dorothy both attended the event along with their families. Former Chordette Lynn Evans from Ohio also attended. Another former Chordette, Margie Latzko was there from New York with her husband, Walter. Walter had been the arranger for the Chordettes. This was Margie's first visit to Sheboygan. One touching moment occurred hours before the event, when Marjorie and Walter came into the hall. Dorothy saw Walter and bent over to give him a hug. It was the first time that these two good friends had seen each other in 51 years.

Two other former Chordettes, Nancy Overton and Joyce Creator were unable to make it. But, both sent messages thanking everybody for honoring the Chordettes. Also, sending a message of congratulations was Dick Clark.

The event included displays of Chordettes items to look at and Chordettes music over the radio before supper was served. Following supper, an audio tape of the Chordettes winning performance on the Arthur Godfrey Talent Scouts show of September 26, 1949 was played. This was followed by a video clip of an Arthur Godfrey show with the Chordettes, clips from four different Ed Sullivan, "Toast of the Town" shows, including one from December 1954, where the Chordettes performed, "Mr. Sandman." The last videos shown, were from the first ever music video of the Chordettes, performing, "A Girl's Work Is Never Done" followed by a video for "No Wheels" which also featured Janet's daughter Jaclyn.

Each of the Chordettes also had a chance to speak about their days as a member of the Chordettes. Letters were also read from the two Chordettes that could not attend, Nancy Overton and Joyce Weston. Also remembered were the three Chordettes who had passed away, Alyce Mae, Janet, and Jinny.

After the program ended, the four Chordettes were swamped with requests for autographs. People came with programs to be signed, photos, record albums, sheet music, and newspaper clippings. The four Chordettes signed until there was no one left and they had smiles on their faces the whole time.

This photo from the Blue Harbor event shows Margie (on the left) and Lynn, next to Margie, happily signing autographs. Notice the smiles on their faces. Carol and Dorothy were busy signing autographs at another table. (Photo courtesy of the Sheboygan County Museum)

A photo of the Chordettes, with the author, taken in Sheboygan, WI, September 14, 2004. From left to right, are Lynn, Margie, Scott Lewandoske (author), Carol, and Dorothy. (From the author's collection)

Shown here is the Chordettes' display at Sheboygan's Mead Public Library in August 2004. On the left is a green dress worn by Dorothy while a member of the Chordettes. On the far right is the gold record, Carol received for Mr. Sandman. (Photo courtesy of the Sheboygan County Museum)

Shown here is the front (right side) and back (left side) of the souvenir booklet that was handed out to people who attended the Chordettes program on September 14, 2004. This booklet was very popular after the program for autographs. (From the author's collection)

Following the Chordettes program at Blue Harbor, the Sheboygan County Historical Society newsletter from October 2004 ran a story about the Chordettes event, under the headline, "Wonderful! Great! Fabulous! Tremendous! Chordettes and Exclamations."

"Wonderful program!'

"Great evening!"

"Fabulous program."

"It was so wonderful!"

"I was hoping it wouldn't end!"

"Those were some of the exclamation marks voiced during and after the Historical Society's celebration of Sheboygan's Chordettes at the Blue Harbor Conference Center in Sheboygan on Tuesday, Sept. 14.

Dorothy (Hummitzsch) Schwartz and Carol (Hagedorn) Buschmann, the two hometown quartette members still living, expressed surprise and pleasure with the enthusiastic turnout of over 500 people for the nostalgic affair."

"It was awesome and humbling," Dorothy said. "There were so many people!"

Four members of the Chordettes at the head table, from left to right, Margie, Lynn, Carol, and Dorothy. (From the author's collection)

"Carol said the evening was "very nice" and that she was astounded by all of the people who wanted her to sign their program.

"It truly was a memorable evening which we shared with our friends and many barbershoppers when we got back home. I'll never forget it," Marjorie Latzko said."

"A marvelous evening, a wonderful affair, Mand echoed."

Part of the crowd that was on hand to honor the Chordettes at the Blue Harbor Resort on September 14, 2004.
(Photo courtesy of the Sheboygan County Museum)

"Bob Harker, Museum director, who co-chaired the event with LuLu Lubbers, a member of the Historical Society board of directors, called the tribute to the Chordettes a tremendous success."

"The 516 people made up the largest crowd we've ever had for one of our local history programs," Harker pointed out."

The newsletter article continued, "It enabled us to revisit a very special time in Sheboygan County History. Members of the planning committee stepped forward and created an event that delighted everybody. It was a celebration I am, personally, very proud of," he said."

"Ken Conger, president of the Historical Society, pointed out the wide spread popularity of the Chordettes. He said Los Angeles sportswriter Thomas Bonk, in a story about the PGA tournament in August wrote, "Sheboygan is the closest big town to Whistling Straits (Golf Course) and is famous for the Chordettes, who had a huge hit song in 1958 with 'Lollipop'.""

"Conger also noted that local historian Bill Wangemann appropriately said that the Chordettes were "Sheboygan's 'Fifth C', along with Churches, Cheese, Chairs and Children.""

At the end of the Sheboygan County Historical Society's year, they issued an annual report. This report also included a photo of the Chordettes and three letters. The first letter said, "Thanks to the committee and everyone involved for their efforts in connection with the Chordettes celebration. I was absolutely delighted with the whole evening. It was a classy affair. I never imagined the large elegant room filled with so many people and the huge viewing screens for the films and videos."

"The printed programs were great and a great souvenir for all the people who asked us to sign them. Friends, acquaintances and people I don't think I ever met before, stopped me in the super market days after the program to tell me what a wonderful program it was and how much they enjoyed it. The publicity about the event was fantastic. It was getting to the point where I thought about wearing my sun glasses whenever I was out in public." The letter was signed, "Carol (Hagedorn) Buschmann, a Sheboygan Chordettes quartette member (1947-63)"

The second letter added, "What a great evening!' That's what I hear when meeting people who went to the Chordettes testimonial. They enjoyed hearing the actual radio transcription of the winning Chordettes appearance on the Godfrey Talent Scout Show and seeing the film of some of the shows."

"It was an evening that our family will remember forever. All I can say is 'Thanks for the memories'."

The second letter was signed, "Dorothy (Hummitzsch) Schwartz, a Sheboygan Chordettes quartette member (1946-52)."

The third letter was also from a Chordette, Marjorie Latzko. Margie wrote, "My husband Walter and I were so grateful to be invited to the tribute for the Chordettes. We couldn't believe that over 500 people would attend the program. It was evident the very successful evening was the result of many hours of planning."

"The advance publicity, the displays, the showing of the videotapes of the Chordettes on the Arthur Godfrey and Ed Sullivan show were great. And thanks for giving Carol, Dottie, Lynn, and me a chance to see one another again."

"Walter, who was the Chordettes' arranger and coach on the Godfrey show, was especially thrilled to be reunited with Dottie who he hadn't seen in 51 years."

"Marjorie Latzko, Blooming Grove, N.Y., a member of the Chordettes (1953-56 and 1959)."

A few months later, on December 19, 2004, Dorothy, along with her husband Bill made the front page of the Sheboygan Press. The headline was, "Schwartz 'promoted' to trade Hall of Fame." The article reported that Bill Schwartz in January (2005) would become the 62nd member of the "Promotional Products Association International Hall of Fame."

One small section of the article stated, "After high school, Schwartz was a booking agent and promoted many successful show business acts, including Sheboygan's Chordettes, a women's barbershop group that reached national fame with hits and appearances on the "Arthur Godfrey Show.""

"We had a client who wanted us to come up with a girls' quartet to sing a commercial for a furniture store in Milwaukee," Schwartz said. He remembered meeting a woman from Sheboygan who told him about the Chordettes and he arranged for the group to sing the commercial."

"But while Schwartz was finding places for the Chordettes to perform, one member of the group found a place in his heart and has remained there since."

"Six months after they met, he and Dorothy were married. They celebrated 55 years together this month."

Carol's husband Robert Buschmann died on January 6, 2008. Robert was married to a Chordette and the brother of two other Chordettes. Part of his obituary said, "On August 18, 1952, Bob was united in marriage to Carol Hagedorn. They lived on Long Island where he owned and operated The White Rooster, a cocktail lounge and restaurant while Carol sang with the Chordettes." In 2013, Bob and Carol's daughter and son-in-law Janet and David Sly run Sly's Midtown Saloon on 8th Street in Sheboygan, a couple of doors down from the Toro's Trophy Shop, which Bob and Carol ran when they moved back to Sheboygan. On the sign for Sly's Midtown Saloon is a White Rooster in honor of the place that Bob had on Long Island.

On December 31, 2009, Bill and Dorothy Schwartz celebrated their 60th wedding anniversary. Bill passed away a few months later on September 19, 2010 at the age of 90.

Nine days before Bill Schwartz passed away, Walter Latzko, husband of Marjorie and arranger for the Chordettes, passed away at the age of 86.

In 2011, the Chordettes and their music was still remembered, as in that February's Super Bowl XLV, Carmax used the Chordettes' song, "Lonely Lips" from 1955 in a commercial. The following year during Super Bowl XLVI, Kia used the Chordettes' song, "Mr. Sandman" in another Super Bowl commercial. For both songs, it had been 55 years since they were first released, but they were still popular enough to be remembered.

On December 34, 2013, Janet Sly posted on Facebook, "Well , we have lost another wonderful, lovely lady, Joyce Weston Creatore, bass singer of the Chordettes has died. Our hearts go out to Luigi and family."

One example of how popular the Chordettes were. This record by the Chordettes was manufactured in the Philippines. Chordettes' records were also manufactured in Canada, England, Germany, Australia, and Japan,

(Photo from the author's collection)

CHORDETTES TIMELINE

AUG. 1946 The Chordettes are formed in Sheboygan, Wisconsin. Original members are Dorothy Hummitzsch, Virginia Cole Osborn, Janet Buschmann Ertel, and Alice May Buschmann Phelps.

SEPT. 1946 The Chordettes make their first public appearance as part of a Barbershop program at North High School in Sheboygan.

DEC. 1946 The Chordettes perform for the first time outside of Wisconsin. They perform at a barbershop program in Chicago.

FEB. 1947 The Chordettes perform for the first time on a nation wide radio show, the Fred Waring Show.

MAY 1947 Alice May Phelps marries Roy Spielvogel and leaves the group the following month.

JUNE 1947 Carol Hagedorn joins the group replacing Alice May Spielvogel.

SEPT. 1949 The Chordettes appear on the Arthur Godfrey Talent Scouts TV show in New York and win the contest. Later that same week, they are made regular members of the Arthur Godfrey's radio and TV shows.

DEC. 1949 Dorothy Hummitzsch becomes Dorothy Schwartz after marrying Bill Schwartz.

MAY 1950 The Chordettes first album is released by Columbia Records. It is titled "Harmony Time" and features barbershop songs.

SEPT. 1951 The Chordettes return to Sheboygan for "Chordettes Day" at the Sheboygan Armory where 3,800 people attend.

AUG. 1952 Virginia Osborn marries Tom Lockard of the Mariners, another singing group on the Arthur Godfrey shows.

AUG. 1952 Carol Hagedorn marries Bob Buschmann, brother of Chordettes' member, Janet and former Chordettes' member, Alice May.

DEC. 1952   Archie Bleyer, Music Director for Arthur Godfrey forms the Cadence Record Company.

DEC. 1952   Dorothy Schwartz leaves the group in order to have a baby. She is replaced by Lynn Evans of Youngstown, Ohio.

APR. 1953   The Chordettes are fired from the Arthur Godfrey show.

JUNE 1953   Virginia Lockard leaves the group in order to have a baby. She is replaced by Marjorie Needham of Chicago, Illinois.

AUG. 1953   The Chordettes sing at Chicago's Soldier Field in front of more than 75,000 people.

OCT. 1953   Archie Bleyer is fired from the Arthur Godfrey shows.

NOV. 1953   The Chordettes sign with Cadence Records.

DEC. 1953   Marjorie Needham marries Walter Latzko, music arranger for the Chordettes.

OCT. 1954   The Chordettes' second record for Cadence, "Mr. Sandman" reaches number one on the charts and would sell over two million copies.

NOV. 1954   Janet Ertel marries Archie Bleyer.

JUNE 1956   The Chordettes' record, "Born To Be With You" reaches number five on the charts.

NOV. 1956   Marjorie Latzko leaves the group. She is replaced by Virginia Lockard who returns to the group.

AUG. 1957   The Chordettes are the first performers on Dick Clark's first "American Bandstand" show.

MAR. 1958   The Chordettes' recording of "Lollipop" reaches number two on the charts and sells over a million copies.

APR. 1958	Nancy Overton joins the Chordettes replacing Janet on tours. Janet continues to record in the studio with the Chordettes.
JAN. 1959	Marjorie Latzko returns to the group for a few months while Carol Buschmann has a baby.
AUG. 1959	The Chordettes film a short video of them working in the kitchen while singing, "A Girl's Work Is Never Done." This is considered to be the first ever music video.
SEPT. 1961	The Chordettes' recording of "The Exodus Song" reaches number 90 on the charts. This would be the final Chordettes' song to chart.
MAR. 1962	Joyce Weston joins the Chordettes, replacing Nancy Overton.
1963	The Chordettes stop recording and touring.
1964	Archie Bleyer sells Cadence records to Andy Williams.
JAN. 1981	Alice Mae Spielvogel passes away in Little Rock, Arkansas.
NOV. 1988	Janet Bleyer passes away in Sheboygan, Wisconsin. Her husband, Archie passes away four months later.
OCT. 2001	The Chordettes are inducted in the Vocal Music Group Hall of Fame in Sharon, PA.
MAY 2003	Virginia Lockard, now Janus, passes away in Palm Springs, CA.
SEPT. 2004	The Chordettes are honored in their hometown of Sheboygan.
SEPT. 2010	William Schwartz, husband of Dorothy Hummitzsch Schwartz passes away.
DEC. 2013	Joyce Creatore passes away.
APR. 2016	Dorothy "Dottie" (Hummitzsch) Schwartz passes away in Sheboygan.

Here is another example of how popular the Chordettes still are. This envelope was sold in Australia around 2009. (From the author's collection)

Schwartz, William W.

Bill, age 90, of Sheboygan died unexpectedly Sunday, September 19, 2010, at St. Nicholas Hospital.

Bill was born May 19, 1920, in Omaha, Nebraska, to Samuel and Jane (Hohenberg) Schwartz. At an early age, his family moved to Green Bay, WI, where Bill graduated from Green Bay West High School, Class of 1938. While a senior in high school, he formed a company, Badger Sound Service with his neighbor. Using rented audio equipment, they served as master of ceremonies for dances, county fairs, and social events. Soon, the business expanded into several states. Thus began Bill's long career in promotional advertising. He soon formed the Bill Schwartz Agency that booked orchestras for proms and events throughout Wisconsin, Illinois, and upper Michigan.

WWII interrupted Bill's career when he enlisted in the US Army/Air Corps right after the Pearl Harbor attack in 1941. Because of his business activities, he was asked to serve in the Special Services Unit where part of his responsibilities were to book bands and performers to entertain the troops. He was also the public relations officer while serving in the Supreme Headquarters Expeditionary Command in Norway, becoming the American voice on a weekly radio show.

Following his honorable discharge, Bill resumed his successful booking agency. He booked the Chordettes, a ladies barbershop quartet, and immediately fell in love with Dorothy Hummitzsch, the lead vocalist.

On December 31, 1949, they were united in marriage in Milwaukee. The couple celebrated sixty years of wedded bliss this past New Year's Eve. In 1952, Bill and Dorothy settled in Sheboygan and formed William W. Schwartz Associates. In the course of selling promotional advertising, they began selling and producing several unique products such as the Weatherama, the Bow Maker, and the Stumpf Fiddle.

In 1975, their son Jeff joined his father in the family business and it continues on today, expanding into fulfillment and distribution of radio and television personalities online stores. Bill's many accomplishments include induction into the Promotional Product Association International Hall of Fame in 2005 for his 54 years of creativity and exceptional contributions to PPAI and the industry, plus his tireless involvement in community activities.

In the early 1960's he was elected to serve on the Guild's Board of Directors and later as its chairman. He was instrumental in merging the Guild and Advertising Specialty National Association. Over the years, Bill served as a Director of Citizens North Side Bank and First Interstate Bank as well as past president of the Sheboygan County Shrine Club and the Sheboygan County Chamber of Commerce.

He was an active member of Congregation Beth El and Congregation B'nai Zion in Key West, Florida. In addition to his loving wife, Dorothy, he is survived by his son, Jeff (Wendy) Schwartz of Milwaukee; his daughter, Sandi (Duke) Long of West Bend; grandchildren, Emily (Kevin) Klug of Grafton, David Schwartz of Milwaukee, Sam Long, Ben Long, and Emma

Long, all of West Bend; two sisters, Virginia Graff of Madison and Susan (Tony) Blinstrub of Pulaski.

Bill will be sadly missed by his family, friends, and his cat, Buddy. In addition to his parents, he was preceded in death by a brother, David Schwartz. Funeral services will be held at 11:30 AM Wednesday, September 22, 2010, at Ballhorn Chapels, 1201 N. 8th St., Sheboygan, WI. 53081. Allen Stessmann of Congregation Beth El, will officiate. Burial will follow at Sheboygan Hebrew Cemetery with Rabbi Menachem Rapoport officiating. A time of visitation and support will be held at Ballhorn Chapels from 10:30 AM until the time of service.

In lieu of flowers, a memorial fund has established in his name for Congregation Beth El, 1007 North Ave., Sheboygan, WI 53083, Congregation B'nai Zion, 750 United St., Key West, FL, 33040, and Tripoli Shrine, 3000 W. Wisconsin Ave., Milwaukee, WI 53208. Bill will always be remembered for his smile, his great sense of humor, and his gentle and kind ways.

Schwartz, Dorothy

Dorothy "Dottie" (Hummitzsch) Schwartz, age 89, of Sheboygan, died Monday afternoon, April 4, 2016.

She was born on February 18, 1927 in Sheboygan to Arthur and Emma (Kuhnert) Hummitzsch. She graduated from Jefferson Elementary School and was a graduate of Sheboygan Central High School, Class of 1945.

Dorothy's love of music began with piano lessons at the age of 5 and continued throughout her life. At age 12, she was singing solos in her brother Melvin's Minstrel Shows and also sang in the church choir. While in high school, she sang in the a cappella choir and formed and sang in 2 trios.

She was also very athletic, playing tennis and playing 3rd base on a girls fast-pitch softball team which won 2 city championships. She was rated as the "best all round performer in the circuit".

Upon graduation, she was employed in the business office of the Telephone Co. for 2 ½ years.

Dorothy was an original "Chordette", a girls barbershop quartette, making appearances across the United States. They were in New York and made an appearance on the Arthur Godfrey Talent Scout Show. They won the contest and Arthur Godfrey was so impressed with their talent that he asked them to become permanent members of the "Little Godfreys", appearing on his morning radio show 5 days a week and his Wednesday night television show.

On December 31, 1949 Dorothy married the love of her life, Bill Schwartz. After 7 years with the Chordettes, she left the group and a promising career to return with Bill to Sheboygan and wait the birth of their son, Jeffrey, and four years later, a daughter, Sandra. She and Bill were able to take the family overseas to England, Greece, Italy, Hong Kong, Switzerland and Yugoslavia. She loved spending the summer months with Bill and the family at their summer home at Crystal Lake. She and Bill wintered at their condo in Key West, Florida. After 60 years of marriage, Bill preceded her in death on September 19, 2010.

Dorothy was the secretary-treasurer in her husband's business, Wm. W. Schwartz Assoc., an advertising and Promotional business, which their son, Jeff and his wife, Wendy are now running.

Dorothy was an active member of Congregation Beth El. She was involved in her community, being a den mother, on the board and president of Beth El Sisterhood, Sheboygan Women's Club and working with the Red Cross Blood Bank.

Dorothy is survived by her son, Jeffrey (Wendy) Schwartz of Milwaukee; her daughter, Sandra (Duke) Long of West Bend; grandchildren, Emily (Richard) Fuchs of Tennessee, David (Beth) Schwartz of Milwaukee, Samuel (Haley) Long, Benjamin Long and Emma Long, all of West Bend; great-grandchildren, Maxen Long and Alison Fuchs; nieces, nephews, and other relatives and friends.

She was preceded in death by her parents, her husband, Bill, and two brothers and sisters-in-law, Melvin (Loretta) Hummitzsch and Harold (Doris) Hummitzsch.

Funeral services will be held on Friday, April 8th, 2016 at 11:00 a.m. at Ballhorn Funeral Chapels. Rabbi Menachem Rapoport will officiate. Burial will follow at Sheboygan Hebrew Cemetery in Kohler, WI. A time of visitation and support will be held at the funeral home from 10:00 a.m. until the time of service.

In lieu of flowers, contributions may be made to Congregation Beth El or the Sheboygan Humane Society.

The Schwartz family wishes to thank Dr. Coulis, Dr. Pawlak, Dr. Matthews, Dr. Wolfert, Rosa Siguenva and Val Tutas, and the St. Nicholas Hospice team for their dedication, support and excellent care of Dorothy.

Dorothy was a devoted, loving wife, mother, grandmother, and great-grandmother. She never regretted leaving show business and returning to Sheboygan with Bill to start a new chapter in her life. Her legacy of love lives on.

Published in Sheboygan Press on Apr. 6, 2016

Made in the
USA
Columbia, SC